Sacred Quantum Metaphysics

Easy-to-Understand Scientific Shortcuts to Ancient Wisdom

Rich Haas, BA, CHT, CHT, CLBLT, CHI.

Foreword written by Prof. Gary Schwartz, PhD²

Sacred Quantum Metaphysics

by: Rich Haas, BA, CHT, CH$_T$, CLBLT, CHI.

Copyright © 2016 by Rich Haas, BA, CHT, CH$_T$, CLBLT, CHI.

All rights reserved.

This book or part thereof may not be reproduced in any form, stored in a retrieval system, or transmitted in any form by any means-electronic, mechanical, photocopy, recording or otherwise-without prior written permission of the publisher, except as provided by United States of America copyright law.

Published by

Insight Publishing

P.O. Box 1195

Morrison, CO 80465

ISBN: 978-1539351856

Printed in the United States of America

Testimonials

I am very grateful to these supportive people—especially the various editors—who added their thoughts and opinions below:

- "After decades of study, research, and reflection, Rich Haas has been able to coalesce time-honored principles of ancient wisdom with current scientific fact. In his work, he has given us easily understood guidance for achieving harmony within ourselves and our universe. A must read!" — Eileen Berling, editor.

- "This could be one of the more insightful and enlightening books you will read in your lifetime." — From the Foreword by Gary E. Schwartz, PhD[2], Professor of Psychology, Medicine, Neurology, Psychiatry and Surgery, and Director of the Laboratory for Advances in Consciousness and Health at the University of Arizona. Author of *The Afterlife Experiments, The G.O.D. Experiments, The Sacred Promise, Synchronicity and the One Mind,* and other books.

- "Delightful presentation. Very inspiring and hopeful for our planet. You are a true gift, thank you for being a spiritual ambassador in creating the book!" — Susan Pegram — unsolicited comment after attending a *Sacred Quantum Metaphysics* PowerPoint presentation.

- "When I got a chance to read the draft of *Sacred Quantum Metaphysics,* I was impressed of how Rich was able to make the comparisons and connections between ancient writings and modern science so easy to understand!" — Anne Haas, reviewer.

- "A fascinating book, with much to think about and discuss." — Betty Alexander, editor

Acknowledgments

I would like to thank Katy, who allowed me to change without pressure, and in any direction I knew I needed to go at the time.

I am forever grateful for the various editors who unselfishly gave their time to make this book the very best possible, including Anthony, Katy, Eileen, Betty, Mary, Kate, Valerie, as well as the experts who gave opinions needed to make sure the facts are as concise and complete as possible.

I would also like to thank all the participators in the Friday night group meditations, including Reverend Dee, one of the most spiritual women I have met in this lifetime.

I want to acknowledge Carole who was instrumental in making the 501(c)(3) charity an astounding success.

I'm grateful to the website Pixabay for access to an incredibly broad range of public domain pictures.

Table of Contents

FOREWORD *The Emerging Post-Materialist Metaphysics* Gary E. Schwartz, PhD*..i

Unlimited Potential 1
   Why Sacred Quantum Metaphysics? 5
   Knowledge for You 7
   Real Dreams 13
   Sacred Quantum Metaphysics Examples 15
   Your Better World Awaits 19

Metaphysical Principles 21
   Spiritual versus Religious 25
   Enjoying Life—Precious Moments 27
   Distracting Bliss—The Past 31
   Your Precious Gift—Forgiveness 39
   More Tragedy—Anticipation 43
   Inevitability—Change 55
   You Have It Already—Inner Power 59
   True Sight—Inner Knowledge 63
   What's to Know?—The Akashic Records. 69
   Metaphysical Immortality—Consciousness Never Dies 73
   You Are an Enlightened Master (Someday)—Your Path 77
   Lotus Blooming—The Observer 83

Quelling Monkey Mind—Meditation 91
Love Is All You Need—Not Really 99
Ultimate Freedom—Free Will... 105
Your Heart's Desire—Karma... 111
Do-Overs—Non-Religious Reincarnation... 117
Creating Reality—The Law of Attraction... 121
Supernatural Understanding—Metaphysical "Magic" 129
Unlimited Possibilities—The Golden Chains 133
True Healing—Mind-Body Connections.. 137
Your Thoughts—Changing Reality 139
Select Your Frequency—The Vibrational Universe............................... 143
Beyond the Veil—The Astral Planes... 147

Our Divided Science... 151
The Veil of Ignorance—Materialism 155
Piercing the Veil—Emerging True Science 161

The New Sciences 165
Store Me Some Energy Please—Space-Time Continuum 167
What Lies Beyond—The Hidden Universe 171
Your Quantum Leap—Quantum Physics Simplified 175
The Essence—String Theory Simplified 181
The Brane New World— 11-Dimensional Space 183
The "God Particle"—The Higgs Boson... 187
New Medicine—Healing with the Mind 189
Over and Back—Near-Death Experiences 199
Altered States of Consciousness 209
Mesmerizing Possibilities—Hypnotic Journeys................................... 223

Trips Down Memory Lane—Past-Life Evidence 231
"Going Home"—Remembering the "Afterlife" 241

Mysticism Explained—Applied Metaphysics 247
Unlimited Potentia—Supernatural Abilities 249
Cease Suffering—Precious Moment Example..................................253
Give Me A . . .—Manifesting Material Objects 261
Pick Your Reality—Transforming Physical Objects..........................265
Changing Reality—Applied Quantum Physics 267
Gravity Pushes—Levitation 271
Future Medicine—Real Healing...275
The Wow Factor—Paranormal Abilities...283
Meaning of Life—Practical Karma 287

Choose Your World—Manifesting Miracles 297
Co-Creators of the Universe—Your Birthright.................................299
Applied Sacred Quantum Metaphysics...305
Practical Applications—Creating Your Changes..............................317
Your Glorious Future 325

Appendix A—What Is a "Dimension"? 329
Appendix B—Healing Modalities 335
Appendix C—The Emperor's New Clothes 341
Historical Reincarnation...341
Appendix D—What This Book Is and Is Not...................345
Appendix E—Vital Further Reading 349
About the Author..351

FOREWORD
The Emerging Post-Materialist Metaphysics

Gary E. Schwartz, PhD[*]

> *Metaphysics: The study of the true nature of reality*
> *—the "unseen" part of the universe.*
> **—Rich Haas**

When I read Rich Haas' definition of metaphysics (quoted above), and connected it to a book I had written titled *The Sacred Promise: How Science is Discovering Spirits Collaboration with Us in Our Daily Lives,* I knew I had to accept Rich's invitation to write a Foreword for *Sacred Quantum Metaphysics.* Applying Rich's simple yet profound definition to my professional life (especially as it has unfolded over the past fifteen years), one could say that I am functioning as an "experimental metaphysicist." Whether our research is documenting how hypothesized spirits can influence "unseen" photonic and electromagnetic signals, or how "unseen" quantum synchronicity fields can produce complex and high meaningful serial patterns of synchronicities in daily life, the common denominator is the power of contemporary science to "make the invisible visible"—at least in terms of its effects in what we experience as the physical world.

Sacred Quantum Metaphysics essentially gives us a fresh look at ancient wisdom, which has recently been verified by scientific breakthroughs. While

i

FOREWORD

Einstein, Quantum theory, M-theory's multidimensional physics, String theory, the Higgs boson, etc., all appear to support evidence of a nonphysical-based universe, there are important connections that all of us should evaluate for ourselves.

Written in everyday language that even novice enquirers can grasp, it makes even the most difficult scientific subjects like Quantum theory understandable. There is also an Appendix A to the book explaining what a "dimension" is, allowing readers to finally comprehend the significance of Einstein's four-dimensional Space-Time Continuum. This is artfully explained without formulas or mathematics.

I found Rich's definition of a dimension especially interesting, since my colleagues and I had just published a chapter on "Dimensions of an Enlightening Understanding System" (D.E.U.S., in Black and Spencer, Editors, *The Beacon of Mind*). D.E.U.S. outlines twelve fundamental dimensions for understanding nature and the cosmos. The twelve dimensions of understanding in D.E.U.S. curiously compliments the beautiful exposition provided in *Sacred Quantum Metaphysics* (including its featuring the number twelve as well, see below ☺).

Instead of taking a single phenomenon and trying to prove its truthfulness, author Rich Haas expertly interweaves twelve recent scientific breakthroughs with twenty-four historical insights to present a complete picture of our previously misunderstood universe. After intertwining the science and the ancient wisdom together, there is a section called "Applied Metaphysics" that explains the probable scientific insights behind many misinterpreted metaphysical phenomena. Next, he shows how advances in our understanding can be used to improve the everyday lives of the readers. Then there are "19 very concrete steps" you can use to improve your own life—and the futures of your loved ones.

Since this book addresses a multitude of scientific and metaphysical instances, it is going to be almost impossible for the skeptics to continue to deny the existence of non-materialistic phenomena. Cynics can no longer pick apart a single piece of evidence, a book written about a particular topic, or a solitary study to create doubt. They will ultimately have to refute the advances made by Albert Einstein, Werner Heisenberg, Max Planck, String Theory, Membrane-theory, astrophysics' Dark Energy, the Higgs boson, plus many other scientific breakthroughs revealed recently. My colleagues and I explain this emerging revolution in science and understanding as the shift from materialist to post-materialist science (see www.opensciences.org).

One topic that I extensively researched is the possible continued existence of consciousness after the body dies. Rich interweaves modern scientific investigations and ancient principles to verify that this is not only possible, but entirely plausible. This is just a single chapter out of the jam-packed book full of profound insights and connections.

When many pieces of evidence are examined within the context of solid scientific principles, it leaves little doubt that our society needs to reevaluate a lot of the basic assumptions. One of those is the materialistic dualism that has dominated our intellectual and scientific pursuits since being established in 1641 by René Descartes. Obviously, since this outdated philosophy didn't have the benefit of recent scientific discoveries, it needs to be modernized immediately. Perhaps it is time that all of us open our minds to some new possibilities.

After reading *Sacred Quantum Metaphysics*, you may not be convinced that science has verified every one of the listed twenty-four historical principles, but it will certainly give you abundant implications and associations to ponder. This could be one of the more insightful and enlightening books you will read in your lifetime. Only after evaluating all the evidence will you be able to decide for yourself if this is true.

---

* Gary E. Schwartz, PhD[2], Professor of Psychology, Medicine, Neurology, Psychiatry and Surgery, and Director of the Laboratory for Advances in Consciousness and Health, at the University of Arizona. Author of *The Afterlife Experiments, The G.O.D. Experiments, The Sacred Promise, Synchronicity and the One Mind,* and other books.

Unlimited Potential

"Every journey begins with a single step."
—Ancient Wisdom

You are about to embark on the first step of the most wondrous journey you will undertake in this lifetime!

You alone will decide where this journey will take you because you will choose what kind of world you would like to create for yourself and your loved ones. The only obstacle that will stop you is yourself—if you cannot open your mind to the possibilities.

Sacred Quantum Metaphysics can make your life something many people only dream of; a most creative and fascinating place, as it is meant to be. My fervent desire is, as you put this practice into use, you will transform your life into one absolutely fascinating and blissful.

This book is a blueprint for learning Sacred Quantum Metaphysics techniques, then using them to transform your life and your world.

- First, you will be given an outline of the pertinent metaphysical principles you will need to understand in order to make those changes.

- Next, you will get a glimpse into the causation of why our society has evolved into the dysfunctional chaos we have today.

- Details of amazing, recent scientific advances, which will empower you to utilize these relevant metaphysical principles, will be revealed.

- Showing you how to combine both the ancient Metaphysics and the new sciences will allow you to create supernatural feats that only Enlightened Masters have been able to accomplish previously.

- Since you will have concrete steps to put all these parts together, you will be able to create the future you desire.

Are you ready to make these changes? The important thing is you don't have to spend decades in cloistered isolation anymore to accomplish extraordinary achievements. This is because you will have the benefit of stunning scientific discoveries intertwined with some powerful ancient wisdom.

You can make any size changes you need, because nothing is too big or too small for these principles. This is the incredible opportunity you find yourself in today! You will discover everything you need in this book to make the changes you desire in the world, including:

- Concrete examples of how these techniques have worked in the past, and how you will adapt or duplicate them.

- Insights into the greatest intellectual battle in history, discussed in future chapters, which is raging around you right now. Discover how each one of you can be a big part of resolving this conflict.

- How and why our society is desperately resisting change right now, and what you can do to hasten this transition.

- A detailed overview of 5,000 years of ancient metaphysical wisdom, so that you can be knowledgeable and confident about the mysterious marvels achieved by sages throughout history. You will be able to accomplish equally amazing feats by understanding these secrets of nature.

- Understanding exactly how scientific advances since Einstein interrelate perfectly with ancient wisdom, which allow you to see the connections between the two. You will be astounded at how simply these can be combined to produce true changes to your real world.

- Learning 19 specific step-by-step applied metaphysical techniques, combining all of the principles in this book, will allow you to make every change to your life you desire.

Without further delay, let's just jump right in and learn about what you can accomplish.

Why Sacred Quantum Metaphysics?

Metaphysics: The study of the true nature of reality—the "unseen" part of the universe.

Welcome to a world where all things are possible!

Just for a moment, imagine something amazing. Picture in your mind's eye that you understand secrets of nature, can combine them with recent scientific advances, and utilize both to create a new and better world for yourself. Now imagine, it's not just you or a few friends doing this, but thousands of people putting these techniques into practice. What kind of future can *you* envision?

- Would it be a world of peace, without international conflict and war?
- How about the end to hunger and poverty?
- Could you create a new energy source, which would neither degrade the earth nor leave it polluted?

All of these are possible if you and your friends can open your mind to *Sacred Quantum Metaphysics.*

You will also be able to change the smaller things in your everyday life, which will make your time on this planet much more enjoyable. This is the beauty of Sacred Quantum Metaphysics. Nothing is too big or too small to transform. Suppose, for a moment, you would like to have more money and abundance in your life.

You can have this! Suppose you would like to see your annoying boss or neighbor become more agreeable. The good news is, as you make small changes in your life, your actions ripple out into the world and universe, creating ever-bigger changes.

Think about someone who seems to have a very easy life. They undoubtedly found a way to use these techniques, even if they had no idea this was what they were actually doing. Since they can do it accidentally, you can do it also, but you will be able to do it with conscious intention whenever you want. Nothing is impossible when you know how to make your desires a reality—and you will very soon!

Here are some examples of what has been accomplished with Sacred Quantum Metaphysics techniques:

- One person halted being so anxious and fearful.

- Another stopped procrastinating and utilized time more effectively.

- Still another person formed a successful charity to correct an injustice and thus altered our society for the better.

- A friend utilized these techniques to help counter years of abuse and neglect to his body in order to find a pain-free healthy future.

- Someone else was able to get along with disagreeable coworkers.

These will be detailed later, but this is only the beginning to what you can accomplish when you open your mind to the possibilities!

Knowledge for You

"The first step to knowledge is to know that we are ignorant."
—Lord David Cecil

Who hasn't heard the stories of great Metaphysical Masters who are able to do astonishing things that appear to be impossible to the rest of us? They are reportedly able to:

- Heal people instantly and inexplicably.
- Anticipate or manipulate the future.
- Alter the physical world around them at will.
- Levitate, disappear, and then reappear.
- Access a reservoir of knowledge instantly, without education or study.

To the rest of us, when we see or hear of these Metaphysical Masters performing extraordinary feats, seemingly at will, we could call them "supernatural." With the multitude of reports recording the awe-inspiring actions of Sages and their disciples over thousands of years, a rational person would conclude that there must be some truth behind these documented occurrences. There are detailed discussions of these phenomena in later chapters, but have you ever wondered if these ostensibly impossible marvels could be possible?

Once you wonder if these things might be possible, the next question is, "How are these Metaphysical Masters able to perform such incredible and marvelous skills?" Once you understand how these things are possible, would you like to accomplish similar life-changing feats yourself?

Previously, these Metaphysical Masters, who have often spent decades in meditation or other spiritual practices, were among the select few to be documented as having achieved these almost impossible accomplishments. While many of us would like to accomplish miraculous feats, very few of us have the time or inclination to put forth this much effort, even for a few hours, much less decades. In the end, we may fail to produce any extraordinary feats whatsoever. After all, not every person who studies a spiritual path reaches the abilities of a Master.

Conceivably, you have heard the following legendary story of how a student is left to uncover spiritual truths by trial and error:

> A student went to see his spiritual teacher and said, "My meditation is terrible! I feel so inattentive most of the time, my feet hurt, or I fall asleep. It's horrible." Without emotion his teacher said, "It will pass." A few days later, the apprentice returned to his teacher and reported, "My contemplation is perfect! I feel alive, serene, and connected!" The teacher replied matter-of-factly, "It will pass."

It becomes even more problematic to realize, when you're in the middle of these studies, that there is no concerted effort to reach the goals of manifesting paranormal abilities. The stated goals of most spiritual practices are not to be able to perform supernatural activities at all. The only declared goal is the attainment of some elusive "enlightenment" or a nebulous expanded state-of-consciousness. No wonder these spiritual practices don't have massive numbers of followers.

What if you understand that these otherworldly phenomena are really just perfectly logical adaptations of our newly revealed scientific discoveries? Is it possible to learn the sciences behind these seemingly impossible wonders, and then easily put them into practice? This is what the principles of *Sacred Quantum Metaphysics* will show you. The process can be fun, and the results astounding.

What would you like to accomplish if you could control powers that only Ascended Masters previously harnessed? Would you . . .

- Imagine a world where people are intrinsically valued and empowered, and thus do not become addicted to drugs and alcohol?
- Create a world where people do not rob, rape, or murder each other?
- Discover a way for mankind to manipulate gravitational forces to allow safe exploration of interstellar space?
- Envision an honest government with ethical politicians who won't deceive us, when we all work together to create it?

Do not assume these things are impossible. Instead, continue to learn how our current understanding of science and the principles of ancient Metaphysics perfectly mesh together to provide the tools necessary to make achievements like this very feasible. Really, the only danger is not thinking big enough.

Since something like this is actually possible, why hasn't it become common knowledge for all of humanity before now? The short answer is that humankind was not ready to hear it until now. Another reason is our science has finally evolved to the point where we can comprehend the principles behind the feats we used to label as "magic" or "miracles." Once you understand the basic ideas of Metaphysics and the new scientific advances, all of you can easily put them together, accomplishing what was previously considered a "magical" transforming of our universe.

Society is just emerging from a period of 400 years of cultural and scientific blindness. We now know much of what we thought was true about our world has been proven little more than wishful thinking. Daily, new scientific discoveries reveal truths previously deemed impossible.

ALBERT EINSTEIN

Albert Einstein's incredible revelations launched a shake-up in the world of science, physics, and our understanding of consciousness. Each newly revealed insight since then propels us towards a wider understanding of the true nature of our universe. Happily, you can understand these rich new insights without having to understand mathematics, formulas, or equations.

New scientific insights including Quantum Mechanics, String Theory, and Multidimensional Physics—explained in future chapters—revitalize the validity of metaphysics. I will explain the metaphysical and scientific relationships so anybody, regardless of level of education, will be able to understand the interconnections, and then put them to use in real-life practice. If you're interested in other details of how this book is structured, please go to "Appendix D—What This Book Is And Is Not," for more information.

I believe you are smart enough to Google something when you encounter a term here and there that you are unfamiliar with. This way we can dispense with glossaries, technical footnotes, citations, etc. This is not meant to be a scientific treatise. This is imparting wisdom so each reader will have the knowledge and skills to be a practiced Metaphysician.

Details of how to mesh together the Metaphysics with the new scientific discoveries are in the "Mysticism Explained—Applied

Sacred Quantum Metaphysics

Metaphysics" section of this book. You will then have facts explaining how these supernatural occurrences are possible. The step-by-step techniques, given later, will allow you to duplicate them—and eventually surpass these wonders. This book will provide you a very efficient shortcut to make delightful changes in your life and the world!

It is important for you to understand that there is not one idea presented here that you *must* believe in order to understand and accept the rest of the ideas. Remember, this is just information. What you do with it is up to you. In the end, if you still don't want to agree with some of it, or any of it, it is your choice.

One of the basic principles of the Spiritual Universe is you have the total right to have your own thoughts and beliefs. You are encouraged to make your own decisions based on what is right for you. Nothing will or should be forced upon you, because this is inconsistent with Spiritual principles.

You also have the Free Will (future chapter) to take or leave any part of these techniques. Give the ideas presented in this book a fair chance, at least until you've had an opportunity to evaluate the related science and its connections with the Metaphysical.

There are three major categories of people who will benefit from the insights contained in this book:

The first group is people who are already fascinated with metaphysical principles. You will find a captivating wealth of updated information. Not only will you understand the deeper connections between metaphysics and the new scientific discoveries, but you can also use all this knowledge to create a better life for yourself.

The second category is people who are not sure what to believe. If this describes you, you will finally have all the information compiled in one place that will help you to decide for yourself what is true. You will be exposed, as impartially as possible, to an enthralling array of recent breakthroughs from modern science, plus major insights into 5,000 years of ancient wisdom. This will allow you to comprehend the full nature of this glorious universe much better than you could before.

The last type is the cynics who earnestly wish that these connections between metaphysics and science were not true. Major recent discoveries from Albert Einstein, Werner Heisenberg, String Theorists, Quantum researchers, Multidimensional physicists, Prof. Higgs, Dr. Michael Newton, etc., have all revealed fascinating insights into the true nature of the cosmos, which cannot be limited by classical physics. In order to prove that there is not a connection between science and metaphysics, these critics will have the daunting task of refuting these discoveries, but I suppose it is theoretically possible.

These detractors will need to keep an open mind. If they are to be successful in poking holes in our new understanding of the vastly expanded universe, they must comprehend the complete overall interrelationships between ancient wisdom and today's scientific discoveries. If they cannot find fault with these modern insights, they will need to reevaluate their basic assumptions, which is not easy for humans to do. The good news is that everyone will begin to understand the real nature of the universe, rather than relying on the outdated theories of the last four centuries.

Once you have the knowledge of how *Sacred Quantum Metaphysics* works, and what techniques you can use to actually affect the changes, you can then decide when you want to make them a reality. If this process intrigues you, you should at least practice the principles to create some changes you want to see in your personal life, and then you can verify how effectively they work.

Real Dreams

"Whether you believe you can do a thing or not, you are right."
—Henry Ford

How did I get so fortunate to uncover these discoveries? As I educated myself about the new scientific discoveries, I was astounded to realize that our modern sciences were verifying ancient wisdom. The more I studied these revelations into the true nature of the universe, the more connections I made to metaphysical truth.

My background allowed me to understand how the language of these cosmological insights were simply similar words used by Spiritual Masters and modern scientists. I have lectured on many different metaphysical topics over the years, have taught meditation to various groups, and I am a science as well as a metaphysics enthusiast—as you may be.

In 1975 I attained a psychology degree at San Jose State University, California. I became a Certified Hypnotherapist and Certified Hypnotherapy Instructor—as well as other certifications—making me accredited to supervise clients' spiritual journeys. I used hypnosis to help ease individuals' pain and suffering, which then allowed them to open up to their own greater potentials for health and happiness. Decades  spent helping others attain deep-seated relief from their problems gave me insight into what is holding back many other people from realizing their own hopes and dreams. Some of these insights include:

Unlimited Potential

- Clients allowing their fears, real or imagined, to paralyze them from taking any action, can easily find relief to make their lives better.

- People who have difficulties with internal negative "chatter" have been unable to find the courage and confidence to accomplish even their simplest goals until they reverse their thinking.

- No matter how much good is in their lives, people who cannot be happy—because they are haunted by guilt, resentments, and regrets—can find almost instantaneous relief.

- Understanding the true nature of family dysfunction or interpersonal conflicts can provide an on-the-spot sense of healing and empowerment, not only for the client, but also for their loved ones.

- Instant changes often happen when people discover the "source" of their difficulties, then they can resolve those difficulties quickly and easily once the cause is known.

Inspired by witnessing my clients' amazing empowerment during their spiritual journey sessions, I began practicing various meditation traditions. This gave me insights into various altered states of consciousness and their tremendous benefits. Being able to quietly meditate on the connections between metaphysics and the new sciences prompted me to conclude that both are really describing the same reality, but with slightly different terminology and suppositions. It also helped me realize how simple it will be for anyone to make positive changes in their life.

Sacred Quantum Metaphysics Examples

"The day science begins to study nonphysical phenomenon, it will make more progress in one decade then in all the previous centuries of its existence."
—**Nikola Tesla**

Here is a personal example of what has been done with Sacred Quantum Metaphysics:

Since I began meditating, I craved having a serene place in nature to meditate where I would become "one" with nature. My current property was a home and office combination in a nondescript subdivision with no natural water features. Naturally I assumed that the way to have this serene place would be to purchase one with the characteristics I desired.

This is when I decided to put Sacred Quantum Metaphysics into practice. It started with a clear vision of what I wanted my life to look like. I decided my best plan was to manifest my dream utilizing modern Quantum theory to help me create my vision on the property where I was already living.

Combining metaphysics and science, I used my vision for the future to create a sloping raised area to allow for a waterfall. I then cut a stream into the landscape to meander around my back deck. I dug out a pond area large enough to have lilies, lotuses,

fish, frogs, and various other water plants. Next, I installed a re-circulating pump to create the waterfall, little stream, and the pond.

Hurrah! Here was my vision made manifest, right out my back door, with very little money needed to create it. What a blessing!

I can't tell you how much joy the waterfall, pond, lotuses and fish have brought to my life, and to many others. Our local newspaper, the Denver Post, selected my backyard for an article with photographs of my gardens, waterfall, stream, and the pond. If you'd like to see these fabulous color pictures, see the link to the article below.[1]

Do you want to know the real miracle of all this? The garden reporter, who has surveyed the vast metropolitan area looking at the best gardens, later told me, "When I meditate, I mentally go into your garden."

How is it possible that just a simple desire for having a serene place to meditate can turn into one of the most impressive ponds and gardens in the area? It is really simple. I just put my "mind" to it—which is just combining science and metaphysics.

Another example of using Sacred Quantum Metaphysics:

I was merrily living my life when I recognized there was a huge injustice in our society. I was dismayed to see that a vast majority of the general public held very specific, destructive attitudes and assumptions about teenagers, which were reinforced by our culture. Political and media leaders were

---

[1] http://www.denverpost.com/homegarden/ci_26070344/pond-garden-lakewood-creates-outdoor-meditation-space

inadvertently discouraging people from attaining their hopes and dreams by creating a "self-fulfilling prophecy." I just knew I had to do something to reverse this injustice.

I started with a clear vision of what the future should look like. I then utilized the step-by-step methodology of what is now known as Sacred Quantum Metaphysics to literally change society.

I created a 501(C)(3) non-profit organization to facilitate these changes. Since this was a radical change in our existing society, I had to create everything "out of thin air." New obstacles inevitably cropped up. With no template to follow, I relied on the metaphysical principles of Inner Power and Inner Knowledge (future chapters) to find the best solutions as I went along.

The exact details are not important for you to understand *Sacred Quantum Metaphysics*, so suffice it to say the successes changed society's attitudes for the better. A United States President honored this society-altering non-profit organization as one of this nation's "Thousand Points of Light."

Are you beginning to believe in "magic"? Such amazing high-level recognition can be considered miraculous in and of itself. It may seem like magic, but it is just science combined with ancient insights—which is now called Sacred Quantum Metaphysics.

I can give you many more examples, but I don't want this book to be about me or about what has been done in the past. This is really about YOU and how you can use these principles to improve your life in the future. Thankfully you don't need to be a master of metaphysics anymore to accomplish astonishing results.

Once you practice these principles, you will become confident in your abilities, especially when you realize how much intrinsic power you really have (see the "You Already Have It—Inner Power" chapter). If I can put these principles into practice, you can do it too. Once you do understand this, you will also believe in marvelous outcomes, because you will be accomplishing them!

Your Better World Awaits

"Things do change. The only question is that since things are deteriorating so quickly, will society and man's habits change quickly enough?"
—Isaac Asimov

Everyone wants to know, "How can we help create a better world?" There is an old adage: If you change your outlook, you can change the world. Metaphysicians have known since the beginning of recorded history that if you always see the world from the same viewpoint, you will likely stay in a rut. As you integrate *Sacred Quantum Metaphysics* into your life, you will be able to maneuver among the many opportunities for change around you. You can co-create a new reality—a better world.

If you desire to help mankind achieve great and miraculous things, you will also benefit because obviously you are part of all of "mankind." There is a saying, "A rising tide raises all boats." If this is your true heart's desire, you will be able to accomplish it.

It isn't difficult to alter your future, but it will take a bit of discipline. It entails a basic discernment of the metaphysical principles outlined in the next section. We will then add some scientific discoveries made in the last century. Afterward, you will implement some basic step-by-step techniques to empower and enhance your skills and performance. This will result in amazing heartfelt accomplishments based on new scientific understanding of how our vast universe operates.

Now that you have had a chance to envision what is possible, it is important for you to understand how 5,000 years of trial and error experience have evolved into metaphysical principles, which are now being verified.

Metaphysical Principles

"We are drowning in information, while starving for wisdom."
—E. O. Wilson

What exactly is "Metaphysics"? Metaphysics is the study of the true nature of reality—the nonmaterial portion of our universe. As you will soon understand when you get to "The New Sciences" section, astrophysicists have determined that what we thought was important—the material world of molecules, atoms, etc.—is only 4% of our known universe. The other 96% is the important metaphysical/spiritual, "unseen" elements.

Most of the metaphysical principles listed in the following chapters have been around since ancient times. Science today is verifying many metaphysical truths—starting when Einstein proposed his groundbreaking revelations. You will be fascinated to learn how ancient wisdom perfectly meshes with these new scientific discoveries and how modern science is confirming them.

Some of you might ask, "Why is it important to go back and revisit these metaphysical principles?" It is obvious that some of the metaphysical accomplishments, described in earlier chapters, have not been duplicated by our modern society. Why not?

Since scientists were ignoring 96% of the known universe, the metaphysical/spiritual part, they could never completely understand the true nature of science. A vast part of our scientific knowledge, history, and culture is incomplete and inadequate, which means it is imperative to revisit the significant metaphysical evidence.

Metaphysical Principles

In order to understand the science behind Sacred Quantum Metaphysics, we need to start with the same basic foundations and common terminology. Then when all of us are putting these principles into practice we will be able to work together.

Metaphysical details vary, but they still have common basic elements, which are consistent within different cultures, geographic areas and various religious traditions. You need to ask yourself, "If there were not a common thread of truth in these principles, why is it so many cultures, in separate parts of the world, independently arrive at similar conclusions?" It strains credibility to think that so many different societies came up with similar conclusions entirely accidentally. Obviously, there must be an underlying truth within these metaphysical principles, and this is why it is vital to reexamine these insights, especially since recent scientific research is validating many of them.

It is also important to remember thousands of years of trial and error have gone into these metaphysical principles. Any time during those thousands of years, when a metaphysical principle failed to be successful, it would have been discarded. For example:

> Let's assume somebody tried a particular technique, herb or potion to cure a disease, and discovered that it worked. He or she would then teach this technique to other people, who would determine for themselves whether or not it was effective. Those successful healers would then teach these validated techniques to future generations, who in turn would have the opportunity to decide whether or not it was a valuable cure. Anywhere along the line if a technique, herb, or potion failed to cure the disease, it would have been rejected and would have been discarded by future generations. This is a very efficient, self-correcting system over centuries of time.

Sacred Quantum Metaphysics

Another important reason to reexamine metaphysical reports is, if you think it is impossible to change the physical world, it *will* be impossible for you! Those who refuse to believe these observations are real will also deny they should be studied, documented, and verified. This is what has kept mankind ignorant for centuries. It is important to keep an open mind for the benefit of all humanity.

If you think you already know about a certain topic, please don't skip over it. There have undoubtedly been many fascinating updates from new research since you looked into it. Also, many of these particulars interrelate perfectly with recent scientific discoveries (detailed later in "The New Sciences" section) so you might miss the interconnections. Without understanding the connection between the two, you may miss a detail needed to successfully make the changes you want to see in the world.

This is not meant to be a complete list of all metaphysical principles. To try to list all the nuances of each metaphysical topic from the last 5,000 years would take many encyclopedia-sized tomes just to scratch the surface. I will include relevant metaphysical principles that are now being confirmed and verified by the new modern sciences. This does not mean to imply that there is anything wrong with other metaphysical principles; they are just not pertinent here. It is very possible that science will verify those principles in the future. Until then, I must give you the prerequisites you need to understand *Sacred Quantum Metaphysics*.

I believe you are smart enough to look up something when you encounter a term here and there that you are unfamiliar with. This way you don't need glossaries, technical footnotes, references, etc. The best approach is to learn about each principle generally and save any questions about the details when you can research them more fully. Besides, when you get ready to create the specific changes, it is always best to have the most up-to-date information.

By the time you finish with the following chapters, you should understand the history, remarkable reports, and the wondrous alterations

Metaphysical Masters have made over thousands of years. It will give you insight into what is available to you when you are ready to create your new world.

Since you now have a broad concept of how to approach the following metaphysical principles, it is time to comprehend the differences between spiritual and religious viewpoints.

Spiritual versus Religious

"Revere those things beyond science which really matter and about which it is so difficult to speak."
—**Werner Heisenberg, Creator of Quantum Mechanics**

What is the difference between "spiritual" and "religious"? These terms have become intertwined in the minds of many people, but they shouldn't be. The difference is simple to understand.

"Religious" has to do with following the beliefs of a particular religion—hence the word "religious." If you follow the doctrines of a particular religion, you would be considered religious, because you accept as true most of what is taught in this religion.

"Spiritual" means you are interested in ideas about consciousness and metaphysical phenomena, which do not necessarily follow a specific religious doctrine. Metaphysicians usually take bits of wisdom from a variety of spiritual thinkers, who may or may not be considered religious leaders. People who are spiritual and interested in metaphysics may find concepts in one philosophy or religion that are plausible, and integrate those findings with other beliefs.

When people read the word "spiritual," they often assume a religious dogma will be promoted. This won't happen here. Our discussion will be entirely scientific, spiritual, metaphysical, and with practical, nonreligious applications presented. It will answer the age-old questions: "Where did we come from?" "Who am I truly?" "Why am I here?" "What is the purpose of life?" "Where are we going after this?" Those questions won't be answered

Metaphysical Principles

from a religious viewpoint, but rather from a scientific/metaphysical approach.

I may draw on relevant illustrations from various religious teachings, or from sages who are not affiliated with any religion whatsoever. One example might be taken from the teachings of Jesus, the next one a quote from Buddha, and another illustration from the writings of a completely independent spiritual master. The important part is the wisdom within, not necessarily who said it.

One overriding metaphysical principal is that no one should tell you exactly what you should believe. It is perfectly acceptable to hold some basic religious beliefs and still be able to integrate the metaphysical principles presented here. I believe all spiritual philosophies likely share a deep metaphysical connection and a common source of wisdom, but no religion will ever encompass the full majesty of the infinite Spiritual Realm. This is because as soon as you begin to name, describe, or explain something, you have had to condense the information to make it understandable, and many of the details get lost.

I also think that whatever is behind the metaphysical/spiritual universe is big enough that it can be called many names and does not care what we call it. Some people may call the spiritual power "Cosmic Consciousness," others could call it "God," and still others might call it "Higher Power" or "nature." Feel free to substitute any terminology that helps you understand the principles a little more easily. When one word seems to resonate with you, by all means, use it. If another brings up uncomfortable images or disconcerting memories, feel free to substitute another in its place.

Now that you have a better understanding of what some of the differences are between spiritual and religious, it is time to examine why life appears to have so much disappointment attached to it.

Enjoying Life—Precious Moments

"Happiness is impossible except when you are experiencing the present moment."
—**Buddha**

Would you like to enjoy more of your life today than you did yesterday? How about being more content and less stressful throughout the rest of your life? When you become tired of the agony and distress in your life, pay close attention, because there are some very easy solutions. By the time you finish the next few chapters, you will more clearly understand how easily you produce your own frustration—without even trying.

Metaphysicians say that you can find true happiness simply by enjoying the "here and now"—by appreciating what is truly happening to you at this very instant. You might ask, "How does being in the present moment allow us to be happy?"

There is a powerful ancient principle, "There are two tragic ways to waste a lifetime: The first is agonizing over the past. The other is obsessing over the future." The reason these are a waste of a lifetime is because it distracts you away from the only thing which will ultimately make you happy—the here and now. You are lucky because you will soon be one of the few people who will understand this powerful principle, and be able to use it to find true happiness.

When you waste your lifetime being distracted away from what is really important, what have you missed? You missed out on your "precious moments." I call them "precious" because they really are what make life worth living, and normally most of us get so very few of them.

Metaphysical Principles

When you don't enjoy a moment when it is available, what happens to it? Unfortunately, it is gone forever! Why? There is no way to rewind and re-experience a moment that has gone by, which is now part of your past. Like any lost opportunity, if you don't seize it while it is here, it just slips away. You will never know what pleasure you might have found had you transformed the moment into one of happiness.

Creating Suffering

There is another very insightful metaphysical principle—"You create your own misery." Not everyone reading this will generate his or her own suffering, but most do. Those who do not produce their own misery have almost certainly learned this principle—and then changed their life to avoid it. If you are like the vast majority of us who have not learned about this concept yet, you are in for one of the biggest insights in your lifetime! First a caveat:

It is a natural human tendency to read about how we can sabotage ourselves and then instantly think of someone else that it is describing—*certainly not ourselves!* The immediate response is, "This is exactly what _____ does all the time!"—fill in the blank: your spouse, brother, aunt, colleague, or best friend. "He/She can really use this book to make his/her life better!"—

Remember, it is not your spouse, brother, aunt, colleague or good friend who will change your life by understanding these hazards—it is you! You are the only one who can remove your own self-imposed misery and find true joy. When you seek true serenity and contentment for your life, you must examine if you are sabotaging your own happiness. *The only one who can do this is you!*

Certainly you can tell your spouse, brother, aunt, colleague, or friend to read this book, and hope they pay attention to the part you think pertains to them. Most likely they will read this book, and their normal human inclination, similar to yours, will be to focus on the part they think applies to you! They are almost certainly thinking to themselves, "This is exactly what (you) do all the time" instead of trying to discover how it pertains to their thinking.

Many of us are so accustomed to life being unhappy and unfulfilled we think it is normal. When we observe others enjoying their lives while we continue to be miserable, we then assume there must be something "wrong" with us. We look to doctors to give us a pill to uplift our "moods," or we seek out a therapist so we can feel "normal" like other people we see around us.

Converting Suffering into Joy

For those who don't like suffering, there is also the flipside principle: "You create your own happiness." You really do have the opportunity to choose either joy or pain. You can also choose which of those you would like to increase in your life.

When you get to the "Applied Metaphysics" section, the "Precious Moments Example" chapter will give you a very easy example of how to turn any moment of distress into moments of happiness. For now, just understand that today is the beginning of the rest of your life, so resolve you will not waste the time you have left by creating your own suffering!

Now you have a basic understanding of how you create your own misery or happiness; now is the time to examine why agonizing over the past is so destructive.

Distracting Bliss—The Past

"To be wronged is nothing, unless you continue to remember it."
—Confucius

Whether you're talking about resentment, regret, guilt, sadness, bitterness, grievances, or revenge—all negative mental constructs from your past—they certainly cause a great amount of suffering. We will closely examine each one of these so that you can end much of your self-created misery.

First, I have to ask you, have you ever been able to rewind and change one second of the past?" No, of course not. As Agathon said, in approximately 400 BC, "Even God cannot change the past." Wanting this will only create your own suffering. This doesn't stop us from remembering, and then reliving, something that happened in the past, over and over again.

Why agonizing over the past is considered one of the "two tragic wastes of a lifetime" is because, while you are recalling something you can't change, you are missing out on the beautiful moments that should be making you happy. You certainly can't be enjoying your priceless moment while you are ruminating over something that happened before—especially since it is impossible to change now anyhow.

You will also be happy to know that there is a very effective solution presented later that will help you remove this pain. Let's examine how regretting the past wastes your time and energy and keeps you from enjoying the present moment.

Regret

We usually "regret" something when we believe we should have done something better or differently. Usually it's because we made a wrong decision that didn't work out, or we have hurt someone—even if it was not our intention.

We want to learn from our mistakes so we don't keep making the same error over and over again. The misfortune is we continue to replay the memory long after we have learned from our mistake. Plus, when we are reliving a past event, we can't be enjoying the moments of happiness that could be possible.

There is an important solution given later for resolving lingering emotions like regret, but for now, remember none of us are perfect. Each and every one of us is an imperfect human, and all of us will eventually make many mistakes. Sooner or later we will all have done something we regret. Remorse is always about the past—which can never be changed—so agonizing about it just wastes our present moment. This ultimately self-creates more suffering.

Guilt and Shame

Guilt and shame are related to the emotion of regret, but are even more insidious. When you internalize regret and make it part of who you are as a person, it becomes "guilt or shame." Obviously, you don't feel guilt and shame for the good things you did, so you start to define yourself by focusing on a few of your most negative past memories. An example might help you to understand how many people ruminate:

> Humans sometimes feel like we should be perfect, which none of us are, and think we should never make a mistake. If we do make a mistake, especially a moral one, some religions

tell us we risk eternal torment—certainly a heavy consequence for being flawed. If we should never make a mistake, but eventually do make one, we feel guilty for being so imperfect. Since we are obviously less than perfect, we might be ashamed of who we are.

This is a destructive, unnecessary, self-perpetuating cycle, because every human will make mistakes sooner or later, and none of us will ever be perfect.

Not only does guilt and shame hurt you emotionally, mentally, and spiritually, but you also just wasted your moments focusing on something from the past, which you know is impossible to change anyway.

Resentment

If someone did something to hurt you or make you angry, and you are not able to let go of the anger or pain, we call this lingering emotion "resentment." The word "resent" literally translates from Latin into "re-feel." You are literally re-feeling the emotions—if you cannot let go of the memory.

Something might suddenly remind you of a past event when you were wronged or angered. As you remember it, you will recall the details, likely re-feeling your disappointment and pain—resenting it. When you are re-feeling the emotions, you are actually creating your own misery. How? Unless you can use the great metaphysical tool (presented later) to end this re-feeling, you may resent (re-feel) it forever. Not only is this perpetuating your negative emotions, you are again missing out on your valuable moments. This is why it is so destructive.

Metaphysical Principles

Have you ever heard the saying, "Holding a resentment is like taking a poison pill . . . hoping the other person dies"? Metaphysicians know it is the person who cannot release resentment who is eventually destroyed from the "poison pill." The resentment eats away at us, while the person who harmed us probably couldn't care less, and may not even know that it bothers us.

Let me explain this by comparing the differences between human resentfulness and the animal world:

Have you ever watched dogs interact at the dog park? Most of them are content to be free of leashes and running joyfully around, interacting with other dogs and humans. A few more aggressive dogs are driven by instinct and are intent to exert dominance over other dogs. 99% of the time they will resolve the dominance issues, shake off what just happened, and quickly get back to enjoying "the moment" of running around, chasing balls, playing with the other dogs, humans, etc.

If a dog thought like a human, the likely reaction would be for the intimidated dog to keep ruminating about what just happened. As a human, he would say to himself, "Who does that Doberman think he is? He is so arrogant he acts like he owns the whole damn dog park. Didn't his owner ever teach him any manners? Why did this inconsiderate jerk pick on me? Is there something about me that makes me a good target for aggressive Dobermans? I must have a big target sign painted on my back. I should have lifted my leg on him when he wasn't looking."

Do dogs really think like this? No, but some humans do. Most of us can relate to how hard it is to put conflicts out of our thinking entirely. This is the point. Dogs would never let something like this interfere with their enjoying a nice day at the dog park. Humans, however, may allow perceived slights to fester, sometimes forever.

When you are fixating over a perceived past hurt, you cannot benefit from being in the here and now. By obsessing over something from your past, which you can't change anyway, you miss out on enjoying the priceless moments. How can we humans rid ourselves of this self-created misery? It is easier than you think.

A great metaphysical solution is outlined later, which allows any of us to resolve this self-inflicted suffering for many past memories. For now, understand how it can consume your thoughts and actions when you do nothing to stop it. You *can* decide that you will not allow the actions of others to keep you from enjoying your precious moments.

Bitterness

Bitterness is actually the result of the chronic feeling of resentment. You might have so many unresolved resentments that they begin to define a major part of your personality. It is no longer a single person, or a single event, creating your suffering, but a whole series of previously unresolved hurts and resentments causing you to become "bitter."

Few of us call ourselves "bitter." This term usually comes from others, who observe our chronic complaining—usually about repeated or long-term resentments. Others see it in us first, even though we are not able to see it in ourselves. When we hang on to so many resentments that others think we are "bitter," we are obviously not very happy. Unfortunately, this will not change until we do something to correct it.

METAPHYSICAL PRINCIPLES

We rid ourselves of bitterness the same way we get rid of individual resentments—by using the same great metaphysical tool presented later.

Anger

Anger is the emotion you feel when you are reacting to something you do not like. If you are reacting, by definition it has already happened. You might get instantly angry when something happens, but it is still a reaction to something that has already occurred, even if it was just a second ago. You can only get angry over something that has already occurred.

You might anticipate getting angry over something that *may* take place, but you can't experience actual anger until the event has in fact happened—which means it's already in the past.

Let me give you an example of how this creates suffering, by describing something that makes most of us angry from time to time—traffic:

> Partially because we are bored and do not have much else to think about, other drivers can be very annoying. If someone is driving erratically, and he or she suddenly startles us out of our comfort zone, we might get instantly angry.
>
> The problem is that there usually isn't any long-term danger, so the angry response is really self-created. When we pause to realize this happened in the past, even though it was just a few seconds ago and now everything is safe, we can let go of the temporary anger and get back to enjoying the moment.

We create more suffering for ourselves when we falsely assume we know all the motives of another driver. We might presume an erratic driver is simply an inconsiderate jerk, but there might be many other reasons for this behavior. It could be he or she was panicked and hurrying home for a family crisis or a critical medical emergency. Suppose the driver is late for a vital appointment, which might have major consequences for this person or the person's family. Simply making the decision to assume every driver has a good reason for his or her behavior allows us to avoid some of our self-created anger.

If anything *ever* makes you angry, realize that it must have happened in the past. Remember, nothing you do today will ever change the past—so let it go. Now you can get back to enjoying the moment.

Revenge

We contemplate revenge when something so egregious has happened that we feel as if we have to repay the grievance in kind. Implicit with the idea of retribution is that we need to correct some injustice, or someone will have "gotten away with it." The desire for revenge is the result of extreme anger. We cannot take revenge on something that has yet to happen. Like anger, revenge must be about the past—which we can't change.

When contemplating revenge, you may believe you are certain of the other person's guilt, motivations, or participation. You might be completely mistaken, deceived, manipulated, or even be deluding yourself. Even when you are right, you will still have to accept the spiritual consequences of your actions. You may be just trading your rage for regret, guilt, shame, etc. Metaphysicians advise that when we do exact vengeance, we are just perpetuating the injustice.

We have examined the extent of the suffering we create by agonizing over the past, now it is time to get the metaphysical solution to your self-imposed suffering.

Your Precious Gift— Forgiveness

"Without forgiveness life is governed by . . . an endless cycle of resentment and retaliation."
—Roberto Assagioli

Sometimes people shut down their minds when they hear the word "forgiveness," because they think they have already heard too much about it. Due to misinformation, perpetrated over thousands of years, much of what is taught today is really a distortion of this powerful metaphysical principle. If you can keep your mind open for just a few minutes to what forgiveness really is, your effort will be greatly rewarded.

In our Western culture, you have likely been told you *must* forgive someone who has harmed or offended you or others. You do this as part of your obligation to fulfill a higher standard of morality. Forgiveness, from this obligatory standpoint, is benefiting the person who has already harmed you. He or she may not realize they hurt you and may not be asking for forgiveness. Not only is compulsory forgiveness very difficult for most people to do, it also misses the long-term point the gift of forgiveness holds for all of us.

I call it the "gift" of forgiveness because this is an awesome tool for allowing us to end our self-created misery when we allow ourselves to understand it completely, and then put it into practice. Forgiveness is a very powerful Spiritual principle when used correctly, but it is far from a simple moral obligation. I wouldn't have mentioned all the problems arising from agonizing about the past: resentments, bitterness, anger, revenge, etc., if metaphysicians didn't have a potent solution to remove them!

Forgiveness has always been one of the major principles in classical metaphysics, as well as Eastern philosophies and the Judeo-Christian teachings. Why would so many differing beliefs consider this vitally important? Once you understand the solution, you will finally understand why so many different beliefs from all over the world consider it so vital.

The real magical part of forgiveness is not to benefit the person who might have harmed you, but it ultimately heals yourself. You don't forgive the other person to relieve them of their guilt; you use the gift of forgiveness to relieve yourself of your self-created suffering.

Do you remember the earlier discussion of resentment, which showed that when you hold a resentment you constantly re-feel the hurt and pain? While the person who hurt you is likely oblivious to your suffering, you are still remembering and re-experiencing the emotions from the original incident. The gift of forgiveness is the tool you have that will end your self-created pain from re-feeling those emotions over and over.

This is really simple. Since forgiving is not to benefit the inconsiderate other person, you never have to approve or condone their actions or decisions whatsoever. You can still detest what he or she did to you, but you can make the decision that you're not going to allow it to interfere with your happiness and serenity. When you forgive, it relieves you of the "eating away" at your emotional core, and allows you to put it aside and release any negative emotions still lingering from the long-gone event. When you do this for yourself—not the other person—it frees you from the burden of reliving those terrible emotions.

All you do is simply make the decision to forgive, then you vow you will let go of the feelings of resentment, anger, bitterness, revenge, etc. The promise to forgive allows you to get back to what is important in life—enjoying the moment. For anyone still having problems releasing these emotions, in the "Mysticism Explained—Applied Metaphysics" section there is help. In the "Cease Suffering—Precious Moment Example" chapter, you will find a fabulous tool allowing anyone to cease these compulsive thoughts, and get back to enjoying the here and now.

The Gift of Self-Forgiveness

Sometimes forgiving another person is much easier than forgiving yourself for something you have done. You might assume other people will be less than perfect in their decisions or actions, but somehow you expect yourself to be perfect and to never make a mistake. When you inevitably do make a mistake, you might agonize over it—until you learn to forgive yourself.

Forgiving yourself can be one of the hardest, though arguably, one of the most important and powerful metaphysical tools for liberating yourself from self-created agony. There are wise spiritual sages who teach, "Before you can reach enlightenment, you must learn the art of forgiving yourself."

Again, this is simply a decision. When you make the commitment to forgive yourself for your past mistakes, you automatically remove any regret, guilt, and shame. This is why it is also a "Gift." Forgiving yourself allows you to realize you are just human, and humans will always slip up.

Permit yourself to compassionately consent to forgive yourself when you make an error, just as you might for another human being who has made a similar mistake. It may take some time and practice, but the joy and relief of self-forgiveness is worth the work.

While you are consumed by regret, guilt, or shame, you are certainly not enjoying the here and now. When you have mastered the art of self-forgiveness, it allows you to release your obsessive and negative thinking and get back to enjoying being in the moment. No longer will you needlessly create your own suffering by replaying the details of a past error. I simply suggest that you give this powerful metaphysical principle a try, and experience for yourself the incredible benefits this Gift has in store for you.

You now have some understanding why diverse spiritual philosophies consider Forgiveness vitally important. You are now ready to examine why obsessing about the future can also be a waste of a lifetime.

More Tragedy—Anticipation

"You cannot plan the future by the past."
—Edmund Burke

Take a moment to think about how productive it is to try and predict the future. Is there any way to calculate all the variables that might change between now and a future event? Not likely. You would need an array of supercomputers, plus infinite time to input the data from all those variables, just to make an educated guess on what the future *might* be like. As physicist Niels Bohr was fond of saying, "Prediction is very difficult, especially when it is about the future."

Since trying to predict the future is pretty much a wasted endeavor, why do we spend a lot of mental and physical resources trying to anticipate it? The future is not promised. It is only a series of possibilities. Trying to control the future is simply more of our self-induced anguish.

It is important to understand that fear, expectations, and worry always involve thinking about the future (each of these are examined later). Metaphysicians realize these fixations are a major source of your stress and will likely continue until you are aware of the reasons you do them. Next, you need to find some tools to alleviate this self-created misery. What makes this even worse, of course, is it prevents you from experiencing the joy from your missed moments.

Setting Goals

You might ask, "Shouldn't I at least plan for the future?" It is important here to differentiate between setting goals versus obsessing over the future. It is perfectly reasonable and prudent to set goals for yourself and then work to accomplish those goals. What causes your own suffering is when you project an expectation into the future about what will happen after accomplishing your goal. An example will help you to understand:

>Let's say you think a prudent and reasonable goal would be completing a college education. There is nothing wrong with setting this goal and taking steps to accomplish it.
>
>Problems arise when you attempt to predict what will happen after you accomplish your goal. If you imagine that once you finish college your income is going to be over $100,000 a year, you'll get a sexy sports car, and you will marry a super-model. You've just created suffering for yourself. How? Because unless you get these things, you will be dissatisfied.
>
>Suppose after graduation your job is close to home with little commuting, paying $80,000 a year, you can only afford a Honda, and your kind and loving spouse is less than your physical ideal. In reality, you have a very good job, a reliable car, and a loving partner, but you will ultimately be discontented. Why? Since you created overly enthusiastic expectations about your future lifestyle, you will become dissatisfied, because it does not meet your self-created fantasy. This self-induced disappointment was a natural consequence of that first unrealistic hopefulness anticipating the future.

The real tragedy is you missed out on enjoying the good things you had. While you were disappointed about not having the Mercedes, you missed the great qualities your Honda had, including many miles of reliable transportation. As you were obsessing over the $20,000 per year you didn't get, you failed to appreciate all the extra time you had to enjoy life's current moments instead of spending endless hours commuting with all the other stressed-out commuters. When you were being disenchanted about your non-supermodel spouse, you missed out on the beautiful moments you could have spent with this kind and loving person, who loves and cherishes you enough to marry you.

Can you see now why this was all self-inflicted misery? All the distress might have been avoided if you hadn't first attempted to predict the future. It is perfectly okay to set goals; just don't set expectations for what the future will be like once you accomplish your goal. Now that you have an understanding of the difference between goal setting and obsessing over the future, let us begin by examining what we call fear.

Fear

Fear is a very natural human reaction to imminent danger and is a healthy response when there is something occurring in the present moment. It keeps you from walking over a cliff or attempting needless high-risk behaviors. When you rationally examine your fears, you realize only a minuscule amount comes from something happening in the present moment—the rest has to do with the future.

Metaphysical Principles

You can't be afraid of the present unless there is something like a mountain lion leaping towards your body at this exact moment. You also cannot be afraid of the past. You may be afraid of the *consequences* from something occurring in the past, but this is still the future. Fixating over the ramifications of a past event is like needlessly trying to anticipate the future and just creates your own misery.

So what actually happens when you fear something? Whether you're talking about anxiety, worry, stress, tension, or unease, all of these can be considered different forms of fear. It is clear that any of these will cause you a great amount of stress. Are they necessary? No, most are simply self-created. If they are self-created, then obviously they can be *not* created, if you know how.

Since fear is largely self-created, then obviously you can create less of it. Pay attention so that you don't create more of it than necessary. The purpose of examining fear is to show you how much of it can be controlled, after you understand how you invent most of it. Once you realize that when you are fearful, you are always anticipating the future—and the future cannot be accurately predicted or changed. Comprehending this eventually gives you a simple way to end your self-inflicted anguish.

If you would diligently record each and every fear you have all day long, you would realize that 99.99% of the time there is actually nothing to fear. All your obsessing over the future is totally useless, because fear rarely translates into reality. The real problem arises because those distractions add up to a great deal of wasted time each day and simply creates stress in your life—even though there is little or no reason for it. You have heard about how incredibly stressful our modern life is, but much of this stress is actually self-created.

Since you are unable to change even one second of the future, why do humans spend so much time agonizing over something that cannot be predicted or controlled? 100,000 years ago, the human brain was constantly on the lookout for dangers ahead that could end up injuring the body and possibly resulting in death.

In modern life you don't need your mind constantly watching out for predators, but it is still relentlessly anticipating things which might go wrong, even though you are rarely exposed to dangerous situations. When you are safe and secure in your own home, especially when you go from your living room to the bathroom, you don't need your brain watching out for dangers.

The reality is your brain has a hard time not being vigilant. You would think the brain would eventually learn from all the thousands of false alarms it has put you through over the years, but it just keeps on alerting you to the slightest distraction. It really can't help itself because this is what it was programmed to do. When you realize this is just the natural way your brain responds to the environment, it gives you a way to resist being caught up in the cycle of fear.

The human brain is primarily concerned with protecting the human body. It cares little about whether you are happy or not. The problem is, while you are allowing your brain to fixate on potential problems, you are missing out on your beautiful moments, which allows you to be truly happy and content.

Can you focus on being in the moment while your brain keeps you fearful about something that might happen someday? No, of course not. This is one of the biggest ways you create your own suffering. As you have learned earlier, since you are instrumental in creating your own misery, you can obviously create less of it.

You are beginning to understand your fears; perhaps now is a good time to understand your expectations.

Expectations

Metaphysicians tell us expectations are the flipside of fear. Both expectations and fear always have to do with the future. Expectation is imagining something good, while fear is anticipating something bad. We can easily understand why we fear bad things, but it is harder to comprehend how we create our own pain and suffering by imagining good outcomes—our expectations.

Previously we looked at the difference between goal setting and expectations, but think about how often we expect things "should" be this or that way. When they don't happen the way we expect them to, even when they are better than we imagined, we can get disappointed. Suffering almost always results when things don't go the way we expect them to.

You have likely heard the complaint, "Life is unfair." Is life supposed to be fair? When you expect life to be fair, you will almost always be disappointed.

> Let me tell you the story of a Rabbi in Moscow at the height of the Jewish persecution. Every day the Rabbi would pass by one of the Russian guards as he headed off to the synagogue. The guard would make small talk and ask him, "Where are you going Rabbi?" The Rabbi would respond, "Only God knows."
>
> Each time the Rabbi said this to the guard, the guard got madder and madder, because he knew the Rabbi was heading over to the synagogue. This happened regularly, until one day

the guard got so angry he arrested the Rabbi. He handcuffed him and threw him into a jail cell. After the cell door slammed shut, the Rabbi said, "You see? Only God knows."

The point of this example is this spiritual person knew better than to have expectations about where he would be later that day. This way when "life happened" and things changed, he would not be disappointed, because he did not have a certain belief about the way things "should" end up.

Often what people consider to be unfair is when they don't get everything they would like. If one person gets everything they want, everyone else will consider life to be unfair. This cycle can only cause misery for everyone.

Relationships

Some of the expectations that cause the most stress have to do with human relationships. We think our friends and loved ones *should* psychically anticipate our wants and needs, and *should* instinctively meet those needs. When these "shoulds" don't happen, we get frustrated, angry, and disappointed—more self-inflicted suffering.

Many of us go into a relationship with the expectation that the other person should behave a certain way, and he or she almost never does. At the same time, they expect us to conform to their preconceptions. This is what causes so much conflict in our relationships. It all starts with expecting the future will be a certain way.

For example, look at parent-child relationships: Parents get a mental picture of what a child should or should not be and get disappointed when they don't conform to this imagined ideal. Children sometimes get expectations of what their parents should be like, and when the parent does not live up to what the child thinks is the perfect parent, it causes them to become disillusioned. Few children or parents are perfect, so when we create unrealistic expectations similar to these, self-created misery is almost always the result.

You might get angry because someone has done something you feel is unfair. For instance, "After all I've done for you, you turn around and do this to me?" Think about it—you *expect* someone to behave a certain way because you acted a certain way towards them? Unless there was a clear agreement, the other person is under no obligation to behave in a particular manner. People rarely realize their disappointment started when they created the expectation that someone else "should" behave as you hoped they would.

Expecting someone to be like you is another way to create more difficulties for yourself. For example, perhaps you are a very considerate person; you will likely get frustrated and disappointed when someone else is inconsiderate toward you. Just because you believe being considerate is the proper way of acting doesn't mean others will treat you this way. If you suppose humans will be considerate of other humans, you are creating unrealistic expectations, and thus more self-inflicted disappointment for yourself.

Worry

What is worry? Metaphysicians tell us worry is just a self-created projection into the future of bad things that have not yet happened. Perhaps you have heard people say, "Worrying is like praying for something bad to happen." Worrying is so ingrained in our experience and culture we hardly ever look at what really happens when we do it. When someone tells you, "Be careful," what they are really saying is, "Be fearful." They have just taught you to worry.

First of all, worry has to be about the future—which you know cannot be changed. You cannot worry about the past because it has already happened. You might worry about the consequences of something that happened in the past, but those consequences haven't happened yet, so they are by definition in the future.

You may not completely understand exactly what happens when you worry, but you certainly know it is extremely uncomfortable and leaves you stressed out. Since you know it leaves you anxious and tense, why do you do it in the first place?

Most of us feel that when we anticipate the bad things, we will be better prepared for them, making it easier when they do happen. The trouble is 99% of the things you worry about never become a reality, so all this agony and stress was for nothing. Think back to how many times you have worried that something awful might happen. When you are realistic, you comprehend the imagined catastrophe almost never happens. Maybe one in 100 times, something resembling what you feared actually materialized into a problem that you needed to address.

Not only are you worrying about something which will almost certainly never happen, often you invent some negative consequences of this imagined future event, and then worry about those made-up consequences! Remember, nothing bad has happened up to this point, it is all in your mind's imagination—but it has already created a huge amount of needless mental and emotional stress in your life.

You may say, "What about the 'one in 100' when something actually does happen? Doesn't this remote chance mean I am justified in preparing for the worst?" Think back to a time when something bad did happen:

- Did you see it coming or were you blindsided? Most often it is something you didn't anticipate at all.

- If you actually did predict this negative event, did it happen exactly as you mentioned? Of course not! You can never foresee all the details, so you were still unprepared for it.

- There are always options that would make a better outcome, such as friends or family who step forward to help.

- Generally, most of the imagined consequences you worried about also never materialize.

After all the time and energy you wasted worrying, you are beginning to comprehend it rarely softens the impact when something bad does happen. When something does arise, your worrying, in all probability, didn't help your situation. Why spend a lot of time obsessing over something that did not help your situation in the end?

In order to rid yourself of this needless misery, you first need to comprehend what takes place in your thoughts when you worry. Let's examine a hypothetical example to show you how imagination can run rampant when worrying. Remember, the actual thoughts will vary from person to person. No one will have exactly the same thinking, but all of us will have needlessly worried at one time or another.

Worry Example

Suppose you are on your way to an important dinner at a restaurant with your spouse and business associates. You promised you would be there on time, but decided you had a few extra minutes for one more errand. After you finish this extra errand, you then encounter stop-and-go traffic to the restaurant.

You immediately start thinking how embarrassed you will be for being late and making everyone wait. You feel ashamed for only considering your own selfish needs by running the extra errand. You hate it when you are inconsiderate.

You start planning your excuses, testing several plausible reasons why you couldn't possibly avoid being tardy: car problems, road construction, etc. You anticipate the other people's snide remarks about your tardiness, and then you construct several witty comebacks just in case they are needed. You know your spouse will likely complain later about your inconsiderate lateness, so you create several imaginary conversations, back and forth, about how to quell this anger. Once you start worrying, this mental chatter will likely continue without mercy until you arrive at the restaurant.

When you finally do arrive at the restaurant, you realize others also got caught in the heavy traffic, and you are not the last one to arrive.

Most of us have allowed our mind to run wild like this, even though the details might be entirely different. It is a common human trait to worry about future events, even creating imaginary scenarios anticipating what might occur. What is sad is these self-imagined complications, which are not certain to occur, waste our mental energy over nothing.

What actually happened in this example? You squandered many moments of peace and joy by imagining negative scenarios. In the process, you needlessly made yourself feel embarrassed, unworthy, deceptive, and inconsiderate. What did it accomplish? You produced a great amount of unwanted stress and ugly emotions—all self-created!

How many beautiful moments were lost while your mind created those imaginary conflicts? You may have ignored a beautiful sunset. Instead of worrying about the make-believe consequences of being late, you could have

METAPHYSICAL PRINCIPLES

done a mini-meditation at a red light, releasing calmness and joy, instead of the self-created angst and stress. Maybe you missed a powerful insight, which would have added meaning to a conversation when you reached the restaurant.

Are you beginning to understand why worrying about the future is one of the tragic wastes of a lifetime and why it is so destructive? While you are jumping through all these hoops—creating these imaginary scenarios with make-believe consequences—you are missing out on your moments, which can never be recaptured.

You must realize you're the only one who can remove this self-created distress and find your own happiness. It is up to you to choose a better way and not let suffering control your life. Do not despair; you will be given a magnificent tool in the "Mysticism Explained—Applied Metaphysics" section to stop needless worry and allow more happiness into your life.

Don't worry be happy

Since you are now beginning to understand how agonizing over the past or anticipating the future can be a waste of a lifetime; next you need to understand the metaphysical principle of Impermanence.

Inevitability—Change

"The only thing that is constant is change."
—I Ching

Often when people think about change, they remember a time when life was going great—then something went wrong. They immediately associate change with bad things because it is associated with the unknown. Many of us fear the unknown, because it is in the future. As you know from the previous chapters, the future can never be controlled, which automatically creates anxiety.

The good news is change is inevitable. You might ask in bewilderment, "That's the good news? If this is the good news, I would hate to see the bad news when it comes!" There is an incredible benefit to change, when you will give yourself a chance to really embrace it.

Change does not mean everything inevitably needs to get worse. Since change is unavoidable, why not make it your ally? If things are absolutely wonderful for you today, why can't you make it even more incredible tomorrow? You can always make things better along the way, with the right thinking and perseverance.

There is a metaphysical principle stating, "We are not the same person we were just a second ago." During this second, cells in our body have died and others were formed. Blood has circulated, carrying nutrition and oxygen to parts of the body, which were depleted just a second ago. At the same time, the cell's waste products were carried away. Our muscles were strengthened slightly, or atrophied a little, depending on our level of activity. We might have had a new thought, which strengthened or bypassed certain neuro-pathways in the brain—all of which made us different from whom we were before we had the thought. People learn, grow and evolve constantly.

It is entirely possible, with recent scientific advances into mind-body connections, to end sickness and disease in your lifetime. How would it be possible for you to accomplish a better tomorrow like this without change? We could be entering a time when, unless people abuse their bodies in some way, it is possible to stay perfectly healthy into old age.

Would you rather stick with the old system where old age necessarily meant deterioration and sickness? Why not create a better world where you can take the pain, sickness, and misery out of getting old? This is the good side of change.

There is a parallel metaphysical concept called "Impermanence," which says everything will change eventually. When you fight against inevitable change, you only create more of your own suffering. There is a huge difference between fighting to keep things the same and using inevitable changes to create a better tomorrow. With recent discoveries you will soon understand why things necessarily must change over time. Since this is true, it is almost impossible to try and keep things static and unaltered in the long-term.

An old adage in psychological circles states: "A man will marry a woman hoping she will never change. The woman will marry the man hoping she can change him."

The reason this gives psychotherapists such a chuckle is because there is more than a grain of truth in these statements. Attempts to control others rarely succeed and usually just produces disappointment and resentment.

Sacred Quantum Metaphysics

What are the chances this wife will *not* evolve over any length of time? Expecting she will never change certainly is self-created despair for the husband. Likewise, when a woman intends to marry a man because she hopes she can alter him, it is almost certain she is only creating her own disappointment and unhappiness. Any spouse will change eventually, but he/she may or may not transform in the ways their partner would like.

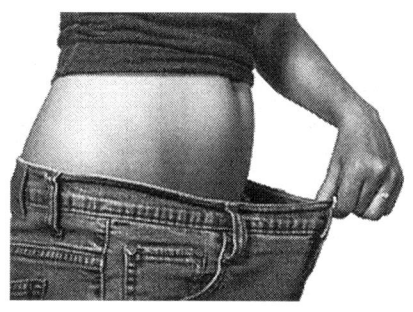

Think back to how hard it was to do something as simple as varying your eating habits in order to lose a few pounds. You may be highly motivated, but you find it is very difficult to avoid falling back into old eating habits. If changing yourself is this difficult, after you resolved to go on a diet, what makes you think you could ever transform another person—who probably doesn't want to change? Usually the only time changes are possible is when each person has internal motivation to modify their own behavior. Since transforming another person is almost impossible, why would anybody be deluded enough to think this is a reasonable goal?

Now you are beginning to understand change is not only possible, but inevitable. Next, you need to understand how much metaphysical power you have at your disposal to modify your world.

You Have It Already—Inner Power

"There is a science and there are ideas that are so wonderful that suggest that you have enormous power locked within us. What we're suggesting is that you have divinity inside you, that it's leaking out all the time and you have the power to change."
—Mark Vincente

Many thousands of years ago, metaphysicians discovered an energy source that humans can tap into at will. New scientific advances have recently verified this power. Before you are able to change the world to your liking, you need to understand the enormous amount of power you already have at your disposal. All of us have the ability to access this power source, which when utilized correctly produces amazing changes.

Physical Manifestations

Most of us have heard reports about how a mother will suddenly acquire superhuman strength to lift a car to pull her child out from under it. There are many reports of average people in immediate danger suddenly obtaining supernatural powers, like the ability to slow down time. These are well known and not unusual.

> There is a well-documented report about an elderly martial arts master who was being harassed by a young bully. In front of many onlookers, the master focused his energy, and without ever physically touching the young man, he knocked

the bully down. He explained this was done by channeling a universal energy source he called "Chi,"—sometimes referred to as "Kundalini."

Since this master can utilize this powerful energy source, you also have this power available to you. Conceivably you have never been able to do these things because you haven't tried. Maybe you didn't try because you didn't realize you had this power available!

Spiritual masters or sages have reported for centuries that they are able to manifest a huge amount of power at will, in order to manipulate the physical world around them. Scriptures tell us if we had enough "faith," we would have the power to move mountains. How would you move a mountain without access to some immense source of power?

We know from archaeology that ancient Egyptians were able to move 50-plus ton stones to build the great pyramids. Similar huge blocks were moved great distances at Machu Picchu and Cuzco in Peru—without using a wheel. In Jerusalem, one block of stone, called the Western Stone, is estimated to weigh 1.4 million pounds. There is another massive stone in Balbeek, Lebanon, likely weighing 4.8 million pounds!

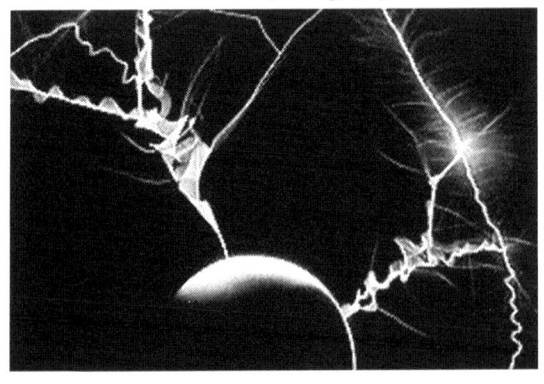

These are examples to show you that even primitive cultures had access to huge amounts of power. Was this simply mind over matter? Were they able to master gravity or antigravity? Some reports say they were able to use sound or other means to overcome gravity. Others speculate certain octaves resonate and magnify the earth's vibrations, giving the ability to move these massive stones. Whatever the source, you too have this power available for you to use.

Your Power

So far, I've only mentioned physical forces needed to effortlessly lift stone blocks, pick up a car, or projecting Chi. Metaphysicians know that, when this energy source is used properly, it can be utilized for miraculous healings, altering the material world, and bringing more wealth and abundance into our lives.

When you can accept that you have a huge power source available to you, as metaphysicians have told us for thousands of years, you will begin to understand how powerful you really are inside. When you get to "The New Sciences" section, you will have a much more detailed explanation of how those recent discoveries have verified this power.

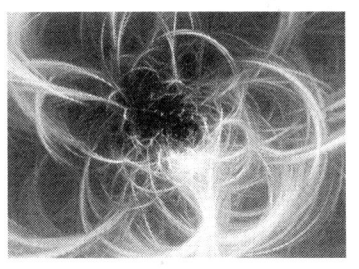

Are you ready to experience the power within you? When you practice the techniques of Sacred Quantum Metaphysics, you will experience much more power than you ever thought possible. Without getting too far ahead of ourselves, you will later be given details of the scientific principles behind this power, plus the knowledge you need to harness it. You will then be able to use these secrets of nature that Ascended Masters previously accessed.

So far, you are beginning to understand how much power you really have. You next need to know how to tap into an unlimited source of knowledge to be able to utilize your incredible power.

True Sight—Inner Knowledge

"Man Know Thyself"
—Inscription on Temple door

One of the main principles of metaphysics, which separates it from 17th century worldview, is how you can obtain information. We have been taught for some 400 years that you are incapable of finding knowledge yourself, and you need to be told what to think. Our misguided science of the day told us we are unable to find information from any direct source, even with much evidence to the contrary.

Metaphysicians have long told us, "Remove the veil of ignorance." They say it is like a curtain that has been placed over humanity's eyes, so that we can only perceive what we are told to believe. The veil of ignorance is really just people not believing in themselves and being told they cannot access true knowledge directly. Now is the time in history when science is taking the veil off our eyes, so we can finally recognize our true personal and scientific insights.

Where did Einstein get the knowledge for his amazing theories? He certainly was not taught those things. He transcended traditional education by participating in his own "thought experiments," which allowed him to produce some of the most profound insights mankind has ever encountered.

Nikola Tesla, the famous inventor and visionary, told people he got his inspirations from a source beyond his education and training. He reported he would picture a new invention in his mind, spin this image looking at it from any direction, disassemble it to locate any flaws, and reassemble it in

Metaphysical Principles

his imagination. He believed there was a knowledge base located somewhere in the universe which all of mankind can tap into:

> *"My brain is only a receiver, in the universe there is a core from which we obtain knowledge, strength and inspiration. . . . I know that it exists."*
> **—Nikola Tesla**

If he can access this knowledge base, so can you.

Srinivasa Ramanujani, who had no formal mathematical training, wrote down an extensive list of mathematical equations and formulas from a vision. He had no idea what these formulas meant, but as physicists and mathematicians analyzed them, they were consistent modular equations. Physicists speculate these equations will someday allow mankind to travel through time.

Many people have received information from a purely transcendental source. For example:

- Fredrich August Kekule received information on the Benzene molecule from a "dream."

- Dimitri Mendeleev was shown a vision of the periodic table of elements in its entirety.

- Metaphysical Masters consistently report they can access a vast resource of knowledge called the Akashic Records (future chapter).

If these people can tap into this knowledge, you can also!

Coincidences

Have you ever had the feeling that you just know something was true, but you discounted it because you didn't know where the insight came from? People who pay attention to these hunches realize they have access to some form of inner knowledge, even though they don't know exactly where this information originates. Too often they pass it off as "just a coincidence." New scientific discoveries have verified that many of these "coincidences" are not random at all and should not be ignored.

The biggest mistake you can make is to ignore these experiences, as cynics tell you to do. Usually what happens is you ignore something until you realize later you should have paid attention to it. You vow to pay attention to it next time, but when it happens again, you tell yourself to ignore it once more. Eventually, however, most people start paying attention to their "coincidences," which are really inner knowledge.

Intuition

When you first meet somebody, have you ever had an instant like or dislike for this person? Did you get a gut feeling this person is a bit creepy and should be avoided? You might explain events like this by saying your "intuition" gave you this insight.

What exactly is intuition? We generally think of intuition as information we receive from a source outside of ourselves and our normal three-dimensional human brain.

For example, you might get a feeling you know what is going to happen soon. When it does happen, you explain that your insight came from your intuition. Now you have to question how you received these insights in the first place, since our culture tells you it's impossible. You have no other reasonable explanation for how you were able to access this information, but you definitely got it from somewhere.

Unscientific Deniers

Today's culture tells us there is no way we can access instant information—like Tesla and others have. Obviously, this was before science discovered

Quantum Entanglement (future chapter). Just because materialists could not explain where this information came from doesn't mean it isn't real. Since some cynics could not explain how it is possible, they simply closed their minds to the possibility and denied phenomenon like this existed.

If skeptics want to ignore any information from their intuition or inner knowledge, they are free to do so. The problem arises when they arrogantly tell you what you should believe, what you are feeling, or what is true for you. No one ought to tell someone what he or she is experiencing isn't real, especially when this someone has seen intuition work many times before. The assumption should be that the facts are true until proven wrong, not assuming they are false without any evidence.

A denier can always say "there is nothing to it" without ever having to prove his assertion is correct. Asserting there is "nothing to it" is a bogus argument, because it does not use any evidence to back up the position, whereas the people with intuition have enough personal evidence to prove to themselves that it does work. A true scientific critic would have to prove that *every* case of intuition is false, which is clearly impossible, because intuition has been proven true in many cases.

You will soon learn that there are recent discoveries scientifically verifying how this knowledge is obtained. Yet even when faced with overwhelming scientific evidence, some people still refuse to examine the facts.

Scientific Preview

Modern scientific discoveries have revealed that information from intuition is very real. In order to receive this information, of course you need to be open to it and believe this resource is available to you.

There is often a logical, consistent pattern to your intuition. These patterns eventually verify you have access to a vast inner wisdom. Not only can you tap into it consistently, you can begin to access it any time you wish (see the next chapter on the Akashic Records).

If you will only look inside yourself for knowledge, and then trust what you find, you can access a vast array of scientific and spiritual truths. "Truth" is not something to be found outside of you, but is something waiting to be discovered—or remembered—inside of you. You can begin to experience this inner knowledge, which has been there all along, but you haven't allowed it into your awareness until now.

You are able to use this internal knowledge today, tomorrow, and forever, now that you know for certain that it exists. First you need to understand an easy way you can find this vast reservoir of knowledge.

What's to Know?—The Akashic Records.

"What we observe is not nature itself, but nature exposed to our method of questioning."
—**Werner Heisenberg, Creator of Quantum Mechanics**

In the previous chapter you learned about the vast reservoir of knowledge available to you. Now you need to know what it is. For many millennia, metaphysical investigators have repeatedly found a spiritual place where all knowledge is stored, often called the "Akashic Records." It contains every thought, action, emotion or experience since the beginning of time.

In ancient times this vast base of knowledge was only available to adept sages and yogis, but now we know it is available to all of us. In "The New Sciences" section, you will be given practical details about how to easily access this wisdom, but for now just understand that it exists.

Is it real? Absolutely! How about an example:

> You can access the Akashic Records and repeat word for word what your parents were saying to each other as they brought you home from the hospital as a baby! This is even more astounding considering that this was supposedly before you had developed any communication skills. You can recall the entire conversation, and now that you are an adult,

you understand the meaning of the words. These memories have been repeatedly verified by parents who confirmed they had these conversations right after their babies were born.

Edgar Cayce

Edgar Cayce, the "Sleeping Prophet," made the term Akashic Records commonplace in the US in the early part of the 20th century. He found unorthodox, but effective, cures for medical maladies suffered by people he had never met while in a self-induced trance—hence the word "sleeping." Some of these medical remedies made no sense at all, based on our mainstream medicine, but he had an almost 100% cure rate from his nontraditional healings. When they asked him, a devout Christian, where he got this extraordinary information, he said that it was from the "Akashic Records."

Unless he was accessing true knowledge, how could he recommend very intimate cures for a person he has never met, who was often thousands of miles away? He did this with literally thousands of strangers! Obviously, there was profound wisdom he accessed somehow.

Uncovering Lost Knowledge

It isn't just personal cures that are available through the Akashic Records. Edgar Cayce, by accessing this knowledge base, reported that there was a library of ancient knowledge buried under one of the paws of the Egyptian Sphinx.

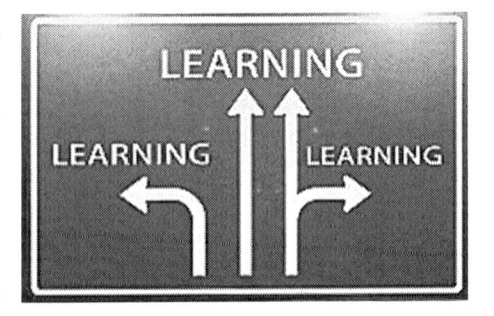

Do you suppose the current political and religious leaders in Egypt would allow an excavation that might contradict their beliefs? Not likely. Does this mean you can't access this wisdom? Absolutely not. The real power you are learning about today is you don't need to excavate this library; all you need to do is open the Akashic Records to access the information!

What other wisdom would you like to be able to find? Have you heard about the lost "Emerald Tablets," purportedly containing Wisdom of the Ages? When you have an interest in uncovering hidden knowledge similar to this, you may find it by going to the Akashic Records.

Throughout history many people, who have been called geniuses, have described accessing their insights through a supernatural source of wisdom and knowledge. Do you suppose that what we call genius is simply the ability of a few very fortunate people to stumble upon the Akashic Records, perhaps through an altered state like meditation? Once people learn to open these Records, anyone can make similar contributions to humanity. Mankind certainly needs this kind of help right now.

Finding Proof

These Records are readily available to everyone, requiring very little training. I have witnessed many people over the decades access physical, emotional, and spiritual insights and healing by tapping into these Records. My hope is that all of you will soon be able to open the Akashic Records and learn truths about yourself—and the rest of the universe.

Imagine what you can do with this reservoir of knowledge once you have mastered Sacred Quantum Metaphysics! The world will be at your fingertips. In "The New Sciences" section, you will be given practical steps to access this fascinating reservoir of knowledge.

You have just gained an inkling of understanding about the incredible knowledge you have available. Now you need to comprehend how much time you will be around to use this understanding.

Metaphysical Immortality— Consciousness Never Dies

"A man has only one way of being immortal. . . . He has to forget he is mortal."
—**Jean Giraudoux**

One of the major metaphysical principles is that there is some part of you that will continue to exist long after your body and brain cease. Exactly what this part is can be debated, but most spiritual masters say it is your consciousness that never dies. It is all your memories, thoughts, attitudes, and experiences that carry forward into the future, regardless of what might happen to your human body.

This makes perfect sense scientifically. Consciousness must be some form of energy, since it is obviously not made of molecules. We know from classical physics that energy cannot be created or destroyed; it can only change forms. If energy cannot be destroyed, then the energy of your consciousness must continue someplace after your body ceases to exist.

If you knew for certain that your consciousness continued to exist after your body dies, would you live the rest of your life differently? Suppose you learned you were going to die tomorrow, but you were absolutely certain you would experience an incredibly beautiful "afterlife" beyond this one. Would you still be afraid? Could you relax a little more and not take things quite as seriously if you were convinced your current lifetime is not all there is to "life"?

Scientific Proof

Many current researchers are investigating the newly discovered scientific advances proving there is so much more to you than just the material body and brain. The incredibly good news is we no longer have to rely on someone else's opinion about what happens after the body dies.

What the research is showing is the "real you"—the consciousness which makes you who you truly are—is something quite separate from the materialistic human body. The body and brain eventually die, but the essential "you" never ceases. It is the undying eternal part of you that escapes the prison of the human body, when it gets broken or worn out.

If, like me, you've asked yourself, "Since our consciousness doesn't die, why hasn't science proven it?" Science has verified this—but I bet you haven't heard about it!

For example, one of the most important pieces of research is from the University of Arizona by Professor Gary Schwartz who wrote the book, *The Afterlife Experiments,* which definitively proves that consciousness continues after the body dies. The scientific results of his study were 2.5 billion to one that it was not the result of random chance.[2] And if this isn't good enough for you, there is another part where the results were hundreds of trillions to one.[3] The threshold for acceptance and scientific journal publications is usually only hundreds to one. This is by far the highest statistical result I have ever seen in any scientific study!

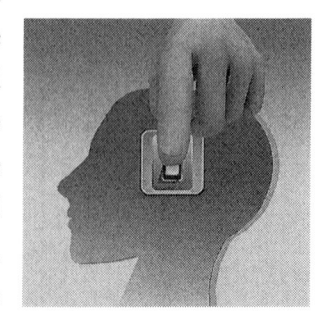

Here is a respected academic, doing thorough scientific research, and arriving at conclusions far surpassing the statistical threshold for

---

[2] Page 115 of *The Afterlife Experiments.*
[3] Page 222 of *The Afterlife Experiments.*

significance. Do you think it was well received? Certainly you can guess this answer by now.

The skeptics could not refute the amazing statistics or the methodology, so they just ignored his research! These cynical people know that unless someone like me brings this scientific proof to your attention, you will probably never hear about it. The details of his research are not important to understanding Sacred Quantum Metaphysics, but is very fascinating if you are interested.

When you do read his book, I believe you will find proof that it is the skeptics who must use deceit and deception to convince you *not* to believe that the new scientific implications are real. For some reason they are intellectually invested in preventing mankind from progressing to its highest potential. Dr. Schwartz asks the perfect questions:

> "What does it mean when a person concludes that an event 'must be due to fraud' no matter how strong the data are? At what point does the instinct to dismiss data reflect a bias so strong that it begins to border on the pathological?"[4]

There are many more details delineated in later chapters, but suffice it to say he is just one of many researchers who have proven consciousness exists long after "death."

Conceivably you are beginning to accept the eternal nature of your consciousness. Would you like to get a glimpse into the true meaning of life?

---

[4] Page 216 of *The Afterlife Experiments*.

You Are an Enlightened Master (Someday)—Your Path

"All of us, one day will reach their level of avatars, who you have read about in history, the Buddhas, the Jesus."
—**William Tiller**

Once you realize consciousness never dies, the next question is, "What is the purpose of this consciousness, which never ceases?" Metaphysicians have told us for millennia that we are on a path to enlightenment, and the journey along this path is the true purpose of life. What exactly is Enlightenment? A working definition is:

> **Enlightenment is a heightened level of spiritual illumination, which permanently transforms a person's worldview into a deep connection to all other living beings, and the surrounding world.**

In the West, we call this transcendent awareness "enlightenment," but there are many other names from different cultures from around the world: Satori, Bodhi, Prajna, Buddhahood, Haskalah, Illumination, or Shamanism, to name a few. Sages have also called it "Liberation," which is defined as "freedom from all negativity."

All these accounts of a common spiritual transformation beg the question, "How could so many diverse cultures, from so many different parts of the world, experience a similar 'advanced state of awareness' unless it was real and something very attainable?" Are they all reporting a phenomenon that does not exist? This is highly unlikely. More likely it is very tangible and profoundly significant.

Many metaphysicians believe that the great teachers and sages throughout history have achieved some form of enlightenment. Is it possible some of our most revered past Masters and thinkers were able to reach this elusive Enlightenment, and then use their new understanding to teach the rest of the world profound spiritual truths? Certainly it is possible. Since they can attain this advanced state of awareness, which transcends the normal everyday human mind, there is no reason why you can't do it also!

Progress to Enlightenment

Since the purpose of all of our lives is to evolve towards illumination, how do we get there? Metaphysicians tell us we all begin as a brand-new consciousness, eventually progressing into enlightenment. Each of us is an awakened sage in the making and will eventually perfect our character, attaining the attributes of an enlightened being. Since all of us are potential awakened masters, it certainly must be very hard to do, because so few of us on this earth seem to have attained it.

In spiritual circles they tell us that we simply haven't yet uncovered, or remembered, our true nature. If we would only shed our delusions, and rid ourselves of "attachments" to this material three-dimensional world, we would allow our true inner enlightened master to emerge. In other words, metaphysicians advise us that we have the inner wisdom to become an ascended master, but we haven't yet evolved to our full potential.

The idea that we are enlightened beings in the making is a hard concept for most of us to envision, considering the lack of spiritual evolution for most of humanity. But remember, today's society was created before mankind had the advantage of combining recent scientific discoveries with these metaphysical truths. This is about to change because of Sacred Quantum Metaphysics.

Perhaps all we need to become an enlightened being is to accept that we can achieve this, and then make purposeful decisions and strides to develop it.

Enlightenment Attributes

Once someone reaches Enlightenment, his or her permanent viewpoint changes markedly. There is a new awareness and understanding of positive connections, which are generally believed to include: enhanced love, wisdom, tolerance, altruism, compassion, and comprehension.

A first-hand description from someone who reached enlightenment might help clarify it:

"All at once I understood the nature of creation; the Way of a Warrior is to manifest Divine Love, the spirit that embraces and nurtures all things . . . I saw the entire earth is my home, and the sun, moon, and stars are my intimate friends. All attachment to material things vanished."
—Ueshiba, founder of Aikido—Japanese martial arts

Upon reaching enlightenment, many Masters have displayed profound metaphysical "miracles" of one kind or another. Think about the many ancient Scriptures reporting how Masters were able to perform astonishing feats. Metaphysicians tell us those abilities are also available to each of us.

Many of those apparent supernatural deeds are explained in the "Mysticism Explained—Applied Metaphysics" section of this book, and will give you possible ways you can also achieve those wonders. Where would you be today, if since birth, you understood it was your birthright to become a future enlightened being? Where would mankind be today if our misguided science and education system hadn't ignored the spiritual essence of the universe for so many centuries? We can't go back and change the past, but we can all make a fresh beginning starting today.

Evolution or Illumination

Envision the immense vastness of our visible universe. There are hundreds of billions of galaxies, each containing hundreds of billions of stars, probably each having several planets with moons circling them, and perhaps having their own life forms. Now comprehend how minuscule our earth is in the grand scheme of this immense universe. On this tiny planet Earth, there is a life form called "humans," which is so tiny 7 billion of them roam this planet with room to spare. We are pretty insignificant in the broad scheme of things, aren't we?

important

The amazing thing is most of us have an innate sense of our own importance. How is this possible? We know that we must be more than the insignificant molecules that make up the body and brain. Somehow we realize our consciousness is precious and unique. We understand that we are connected to a consciousness that never dies.

What is it that makes mankind's consciousness so unique? Humans have been on this planet for about 200,000 years, and at the top of the food chain for 50,000 years. During this time, we have acquired a basic understanding of science and have begun to explore outer space! If you think this is an accident, you just don't understand how slowly evolution creates advanced consciousness.

For example, if consciousness was just a matter of evolution, don't you think dinosaurs would have evolved an advanced consciousness during the 165 million years they dominated the planet? They had all this time at the top of the food chain, and they didn't create even one university. They didn't even construct a simple shack! All they did was eat, sleep, procreate, and die with little progress shown for their time on this planet. Where do you think mankind will be in our evolutionary path after we evolve for another 165 million years?

If the advances in mankind's consciousness were not due to random evolutionary mutations, then where did they come from? The intelligence in humans is innately different from all the other animals on this earth. Once we understand how radically different our consciousness is, we will begin to explore the exact nature of it.

When you put Sacred Quantum Metaphysics principles into practice, mankind's "quantum leap" will be finally at hand for all of us. How fortunate you are to be born and alive at a time when science and metaphysics allows you to take control of your future.

You have just learned about enlightenment; now it is time for you to comprehend how you can get one step closer to it—by comprehending which part of you actually reaches enlightenment.

Lotus Blooming—The Observer

"Maybe we are just poor observers. Maybe you haven't mastered the skill of observation, and maybe it is a skill."
—**Joe Dispenza, D.C.**

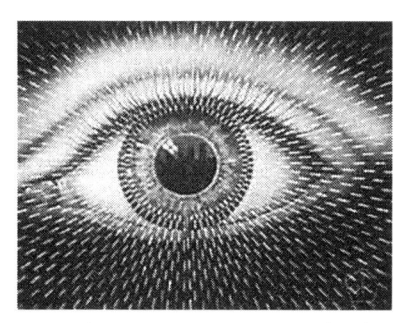

Metaphysics has told us for many thousands of years that we have a deeper "self," existing alongside our human ego, brain, and body. This consciousness is very different from the "chatter" going on endlessly in our human mind. Metaphysicians call this secondary consciousness, which is watching you from somewhere outside your normal brain and mind, the "Observer." Others have called it your "Higher Self" or "Essence-Mind" to differentiate it from the normal human stream of consciousness.

Understanding this Observer is critical to implementing the concrete steps detailed in the last section of this book, so carefully pay attention to these concepts. When you are connected to the Observer is when you are most easily able to manipulate the physical universe. When you get to the chapter on Quantum Theory in "The New Sciences" section, you will understand how important this Observer really is.

We mentioned "chatter" when describing the Worry Example earlier in the "More Tragedy—Anticipation" chapter, but some people have a hard time recognizing what chatter actually is. It is the "voice" in your head that is active every waking moment, which constantly interrupts your awareness.

Some people call it, "the incessant stream of thinking," which interferes with your concentration. When you are in a meeting or lecture and suddenly you're thinking about what you need to pick up at the store, or remembering the details of a conflict you had previously, this background thinking is what is called your chatter.

If you have ever tried meditating, a thought will suddenly appear out of nowhere. Those thoughts have many forms, but they are always inconsistent with being calm and relaxed. They usually involve remembering something from the past, or planning something in the future—the "two tragic wastes of a lifetime" mentioned earlier. These thoughts are almost always a wasteful distraction, interrupting your awareness with meaningless sidetracks. This is why chatter is called "monkey mind" in some spiritual and meditation traditions.

Our monkey minds are so cluttered with "to do lists," fear, worrying about the future, agonizing over the past, watching TV, talking on the phone, checking emails, saving money, planning, daydreaming, getting angry, creating expectations, etc., that we miss out on what is really important. Observing this random prattle, which interrupts our attempts at being quiet and still, is the first step to perceiving your Observer, which leads to understanding the true nature of our real consciousness.

Simply realizing that you do have an almost constant babble going on behind your awareness is a very big step, so do not minimize your achievement. Why is this so significant? As long as you are caught up in these insignificant thoughts and distractions, you don't have the mental focus or energy to live mindfully or to concentrate on creating your own happiness.

SACRED QUANTUM METAPHYSICS

Finding Your Observer

Ask yourself, "What is it that is observing my chatter?" If you believe that your mind *is* your thinking, then what is watching your awareness in action? There must be some other consciousness, which is able to observe your thoughts, as they enter and exit your mind. The voice in your head (chatter) is not the real consciousness; what is genuine is your Essence-Mind, which is observing your thoughts come and go.

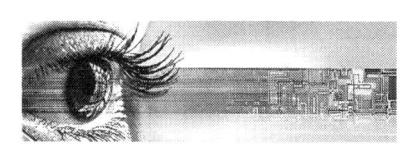

What is certain from a metaphysical standpoint is if you don't believe a part of your awareness exists independent from your ego, body, brain, etc., you will not be looking for it. You can't tap into something you don't believe in. If you are having a hard time believing your Observer is real, just keep an open mind that your Essence-Mind probably exists.

The purpose of many spiritual traditions is to dampen down the ego and chatter to get in touch with your Observer. Certainly you can spend many decades in a cave or monastery practicing meditation and other spiritual techniques to get rid of the ego and tap into your Higher-Self. New scientific advances have thankfully provided simple shortcuts to connect to your Observer—without decades of asceticism or seclusion from the world.

It is the Observer that gives us unlimited wisdom, fantastic powers, peace, and joy when our egos get out of the way. This is the gift of Sacred Quantum Metaphysics. You are uncovering the essence of what Masters and sages have experienced over the millennia. You will find many

85

Metaphysical Principles

techniques here to help you take those shortcuts in the following pages, and your efforts will be joyfully rewarded.

Ego versus Observer

A simple way to look at the difference between ego and Observer is to realize that your chatter originates from the ego and brain, while the Observer exists independent of your body and brain. Once you realize there is an awareness outside of your usual babbling thinking, you can begin to connect to your Higher-Self.

What is it that you need to do to find your Observer? One of the easiest ways to begin is to realize who you really are. Remembering that you are an eternal spirit, temporarily inhabiting a physical human body, gives you a timeless perspective.

Anything not terminating, like consciousness, awareness, thinking, mindfulness, etc., is part of your infinite-self. Anything temporary or changing rapidly cannot be your eternal-self. Attributes like profession, status, race, gender, nationality, etc., are transient. The ego creates a false division between a fabricated "you" and the rest of humanity. As you recognize these made-up separations are only mental constructs, you get closer to the true infinite-consciousness, which is your Observer.

Spontaneous Connections

Sometimes people can experience this Observer almost by accident. Let me give you a few examples:

> A good friend was making a very high income in the financial industry when a major market crash occurred. Like many people, his whole sense of ego and identity were tied up in the status of his high income and his profession. As the

financial collapse happened, he watched the fear and panic of his colleagues. He described seeing himself in the midst of this turmoil, but from a viewpoint "outside" of himself.

His next profound insight was understanding that there was another part of his consciousness "observing" all this turmoil; he subsequently learned this was his Observer. More importantly, he understood the absurdity of thinking his status and ego were his true self. For the first time he had questions like: "What is really important in life?" "What is my purpose?" "Is there anything I still need to do?" These questions started his spiritual journey.

Another example will give you a further perspective:

A woman who had just lost her mother to cancer was struggling with her own mortality. She started experiencing intense pain on the right side of her stomach. The hospital discovered it was a ruptured appendix.

She had a profound brush with death, which she later learned was called a Near-Death Experience (future chapter). As she floated above her body on the operating table, she was "observing" herself from above. Somehow she was comforted knowing her consciousness, with all her current memories, etc., existed independently from her body. After this experience, she no longer feared death.

She came away from this incident with a renewed sense of importance in her life, and she vowed to make the most of every moment while she was here. When people ask her how she is today, she usually answers, "Life is beautiful."

There is a vast body of scientific evidence supporting these experiences (discussed later in "The New Sciences" section), but my hope is you can connect to your Observer without almost dying or going through a crisis, similar to the examples above.

Conscious Observing

Another way of connecting to your Essence-Mind is to avoid the negative emotions of everyday experience. When you allow yourself to engage in feelings of anger, fear, resentment, anxiety, etc., you are connecting with your ego. When you can begin to step back and watch your reactions objectively, you can separate from the emotions and feelings consuming your thinking. As you watch these thoughts come and go, you are observing them, thus you are connecting with your Observer.

For example, when you start getting angry over a situation, pause and step back and see yourself as a human being who is allowing something from the past to distract you from the here and now. View this human being (you) with love and compassion, rather than judgment.

Remember, you are nothing more than a spirit in a human body that is programmed to overreact. Forgive yourself for being angry, and then let it go.

Eventually you will see how you are at "One" with other spirits also trapped in their human body. Do you see how this perspective lets you get one layer closer to enlightenment? The more you practice this, the easier it becomes, and the deeper connection you can find to your Observer.

Once you have glimpsed this Essence-Mind, it often becomes a lifelong goal to tap into it again and again. You will realize how incredibly profound it is, once you begin to look for it. Now that you have an insight into what the Observer is, are you ready to understand how to train your mind to get in touch with it?

Quelling Monkey Mind— Meditation

"Your mind just slows down, you see a tremendous expanse in the moment and you can see so much more than you could see before."
—Steve Jobs discussing meditation

For thousands of years, metaphysicians have advised that meditation should become a part of each person's life. Why? There is an old saying, "Prayer is when you talk to your Higher Power . . . meditation is when you listen." The ultimate goal of the science of meditation—yes, there is a science to it—is to link the mind and spirit together, ultimately allowing us to find the Observer.

There is a wonderful apocryphal story about the Buddha; he was asked, "What did you gain from meditation?" He replied, "Absolutely nothing. Let me tell you what I lost: sickness, anger, depression, insecurity, the burden of old age, the fear of death. That is the good of meditation, which leads to Enlightenment."

Remember the chapters on Inner Knowledge and Akashic Records? This vast reservoir of knowledge is difficult to access from the ego-centered mind. Meditation allows you to put aside your ego, allowing access to your everlasting true consciousness, which is how to obtain this spiritual knowledge.

Scientific Benefits to Meditation

Instead of waiting until "The New Sciences" section, it is important to convince everyone that meditation provides far more benefits than simple mental and emotional enjoyment. There are so many benefits, it is impossible to list them all in just a short chapter, but a few examples should inspire you. Science has proven meditation can cure diseases, change genetics, enhance mental capacity, etc. There are no known side effects to meditation—except perhaps some added ecstasy and joy! It has been proven to also slow the aging process, actually keeping the body younger longer. Why don't people take advantage of this free, proven process? Do you suppose people just want to get older faster? Not likely.

Many of us think it takes a decade or more of consistent meditation practice to achieve any beneficial results. This might have been true 100 years ago, but it is not at all true today. Science has recently discovered phenomenal shortcuts available to anyone.

Here are a few more examples of the benefits of meditation:

> A column by Doctors Oz and Roizen, on Tuesday, March 17, 2015, referenced a study concluding "... long-term (meditation) practice protects the brain's gray matter from age-related atrophy."

If this one study doesn't convince you, forty years of consistent study will wake you up to the miraculous benefits:

> Dr. Herbert Benson, a Harvard Medical School professor, spent four decades studying the power of meditation. He has written many books and articles, including *The Relaxation Response* and *The Relaxation Revolution*. Being part of a medical university, he was required to prove meditation cured diseases or relieved symptoms scientifically, beyond random chance.

He proved his type of meditation can cure many diseases or maladies, including hypertension, stress, headaches, angina, anxiety, depression, insomnia, pain relief, PTSD, PMS, etc. Most diseases or conditions that he studied were mitigated or cured by his meditation techniques. He even proved meditation alters a person's genetics! It does not change a person's DNA, but it can switch on good genes and switch off bad genes—for example, a cancer gene.

Dr. Benson was able to prove his meditation technique was often more effective than pharmaceuticals in curing patients for certain conditions or diseases such as depression. This is especially astounding considering that drugs often have significant side effects, while meditation does not.

Meditation was also studied using novice and seasoned meditators to see what degree of improvement can be made in emotional outlook. The findings were reported by the Proceedings of the National Academy of Sciences (paraphrased):

"These findings indicate that mental training to increase compassion and loving kindness has profound effects on brain function.

The results further suggest that these qualities are not fixed characteristics of people, but rather can be improved through practice and training."

You now have scientific proof that this simple mind-body exercise, called meditation, can actually make enormous strides in curing yourself of many diseases—with just your consciousness. Can you think of a better reason to meditate? The good news is that this is really just the beginning of

Personal Insights

I tell people there really is no right or wrong way to meditate. Whatever you can do to calm your mind is the right way for you. Some meditation teachers will wholeheartedly disagree and insist there is a "right" way to practice meditation. For these people, adherence to a specific tradition is the right way. Remember, whatever technique this person is teaching is the one that worked for them. Just because it is right for them does not mean it has to be right for you. Your personality and body might need something totally different. Try several different traditions and different techniques and never give up entirely, until you find the one that works best for you.

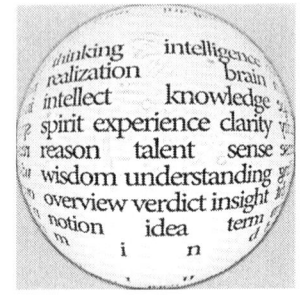

> A great meditation teacher advises that there are two styles of meditation. The first is what he calls "passive" meditation. This is the Westernized "Zen" version where you sit on a pillow and attempt to shut down your thoughts completely. This quote will give you insights into this tradition:
>
> One Buddhist monk leaned over to another and quietly asked, "Are you not thinking what I'm not thinking?"

"Not thinking" is extremely challenging. I have a friend who spent 20 years in a monastery practicing meditation. He told me people never get rid of the "chatter"—the "monkey mind"—entirely, all we can do is dampen it down.

Sacred Quantum Metaphysics

I believe many students give up because they have tried meditation once or twice and decided that they weren't doing it correctly. Sometimes it's because they can't seem to "quiet the mind" like they are told to do, and then they feel like a failure. Since none of us is ever going to be completely successful in getting rid of our chatter, we should not consider ourselves failures when we are not able to quell the monkey mind during meditation. The most important practice is to be kind to yourself, and when a thought inevitably does come, just tell yourself, "Oh well . . ." and then get back to enjoying the peace and calm.

The second meditation style is what this famous teacher calls "active" meditation. You still shut out the world, turn off the TV and cell phone, removing any distractions as you would in any other meditation. You then use this quiet time to completely ponder a spiritual concept, or use the time to contemplate something completely, from beginning to end.

This way you don't have to stop somewhere in the middle, and then later rejoin your thought process, perhaps forgetting where you left off, or what decisions you had already made.

People often ask me how I meditate. I hesitate to describe my methods, because I don't want anyone to think this is the best technique. Try it—if it works for you, great! If not, find something that does work.

When I have something I want to empower in my life—for example, *wisdom*—I would use this word as part of a mantra during meditation. A mantra is a single word or phrase repeated over and over during meditation to help focus the mind.

As I breathe in, I would mentally pull wisdom into my lungs, allowing it to permeate my mind, body, and soul. As I exhale, I would "breathe out" anything that is the opposite of wisdom. So when I exhale, I would mentally push out ignorance, close-mindedness, judgment, biases, or anything else interfering with wisdom.

If instead, I wanted more love in my life, I would breathe in "true love" into my consciousness and lungs—visualizing it permeating my entire body and spirit. As I exhale, I would expel indifference or apathy—whatever I felt was contrary to experiencing love.

It's a very easy process, the possibilities are endless, and the results are *extraordinary*.

After many years of fairly consistent group meditations, I found that when I meditate with others the benefits are magnified exponentially. There is something magical about being in close proximity with other spiritual people while meditating. In "The New Sciences" section you will be given scientific principles that confirm this. Until then, suffice it to say that I believe the insights gained are vastly more powerful than when I meditate alone.

You can probably find group meditations in your area. There are always Meetups, churches, spiritual groups, etc. If you are unable to find other people with whom to meditate, do not despair, because you will find a way to connect with other spiritual people in the last chapter of this book. Until then, you can find fabulous benefits even when you are meditating alone.

Are you ready to start on your path to become a future enlightened master? Your meditation practice will help you get there. Next you need to understand how our culture has entirely distorted the idea of Love.

Love Is All You Need—Not Really

"The energy frequency of pure love will heal anything."
—Alexander Loyd

Most of us think we know what love is, but society has distorted the real meaning. Metaphysicians tell us that love is one of the most potent powers you have at your disposal in our universe. At any moment, you can tap into this powerful force to positively direct your thoughts and actions. Similarly, when you want to transform the world, you can also harness this amazing power to help create those changes.

There is a very pervasive cliché, "Love conquers all." I hate to be the bearer of bad news, but, no, it doesn't.

- Anyone who has watched a marriage fall apart has seen one or both spouses still loving the other, but they cannot resolve the conflicts.

- Sometimes we can love our children unconditionally, and still watch them self-destruct as they make terrible decisions.

- You can love someone with all your heart and mind, and they will still get old, sick, and die someday.

So you now know love isn't completely all-powerful, but the Power of Love can be incredibly potent.

METAPHYSICAL PRINCIPLES

Romantic Love

Before we examine the significant reasons love is advanced as a potent metaphysical principle for society as a whole, let's look at how distorted the idea of romantic love has become in our culture.

We often talk about how we "fall in love" with our partners—as if it is something happening to us by accident for no good reason. This treats romantic love as if it is something occurring to us when we are out of control. It is almost as though we are calmly living our lives, then we stumble and fall into some sort of quagmire, and when we get up, we are magically "in love." This is not at all what happens in real life, but many people patiently wait for love to magically appear.

Think back to whatever attracted you to a partner, and you will find it was something very real and concrete. Generally, he or she fits a certain number of attributes that you wanted in your future mate or spouse, usually starting with attractiveness, sex appeal, or "chemistry." After these desires are fulfilled, you may then appreciate other aspects of this person, including intellect, accomplishments, or potential. Once this person meets certain criteria, the decision is made to see if it develops further. This certainly isn't something that happens accidentally.

The flipside is society tells us we can "fall out of love"—again, it is as if it happens when we are not looking. Most of us have had a relationship fall apart. This is not something that is just happening to us. It is a decision we make acknowledging the relationship is no longer working for us or is no longer meeting our needs. Telling ourselves and others that we have "fallen out of love" is a good way to avoid taking responsibility. This certainly doesn't describe what is actually going on.

Marriage counselors know before a relationship ends, there is a long period when one or both spouses start creating a separate lifestyle. Perhaps the decision has yet to be made to end the relationship completely, but there have been many decisions preparing for the possibility.

Another misconception is that love can be an equal exchange of activities. You exchange your love for another person's actions. "I love this person so much, because he or she does this or that for me. In return, I do this and that for the other person's love." This is a very distorted view of what love actually is. You cannot buy somebody's love with your actions. You can certainly manipulate their feelings by ingratiating yourself by your actions, but this isn't love.

Worse yet, this mutual trade of "love" for specific actions often leads to a blackmail situation, where one person says, "If you love me you would _____ (fill in the blank)." The other person decides what is an acceptable behavior that you must perform in order to "prove" your love. The trouble is, the proof of what "love" is changes daily. Tomorrow it might be a totally different requirement to prove your love.

For example, an addict might say, "If you love me, you will give me all the money I want." The next day it might be, "If you love me, you will give me a ride to my drug dealer's house." In reality, if you really loved this person spiritually, you will do neither. But this is a hard argument to make, especially to someone who is not thinking clearly. Some people, fearful of losing someone's "love," will allow the blackmail to work, thereby keeping that person addicted and dependent.

Metaphysical Principles

Love Is a Decision

What metaphysicians understand is that love is a decision—actually a series of many decisions—rather than an accidental falling in or out of love. Once we know that we can choose to love, or choose not to love, another person, we can make this decision much more often.

- You can choose to love the difficult coworker who often makes your workday miserable.

- You always have the opportunity to love the people who vote for the opposite political party than you do.

- You can also send love towards the government or corporations who seem to be so impersonal and apparently have little regard for the feelings of others.

Nobody said this would be easy, but it is entirely possible. It all starts with you *deciding* to love or not to love others.

Societal Love

When we think of "love" we naturally think of romance, but societal love can be more powerful than romantic love. Since love is a decision, then you can decide to "love one another," or you can choose not to. You can decide to "love your neighbor as yourself," or not. We certainly don't have to do these things, but it is clear that good things happen when we do choose love.

Consider, for example, we are told to "love your enemy." Why? Similar to the metaphysical principle of Forgiveness, you don't love your enemy in order to help him or her; you decide to love them because it ultimately helps you. If you chose to fear or hate your enemy, it erodes away at your own serenity and happiness. When you choose to love them, it makes you a happier person. Rather than wallowing in negative emotions of hate, fear, and revenge, you can bask in the positive feelings of tolerance, understanding, and forgiveness.

Is it possible to love the terrorists who are trying to kill us and impose their religious dogma on anyone who survives? To answer this question, it is important to separate government policy from what you, as a future awakened master, need. What collective society needs to do, to prevent or deter future attacks, is one thing, and your personal path to enlightenment is entirely another.

Certainly you have the personal choice to either love or fear your enemy. The difference is what it does to us personally. The terrorists don't care what you are feeling, except they want you to be "terrorized." Are you going to allow them to control what you feel? Since the terrorists are going to act the same way no matter what you do, why not choose what is best for you? The greatest benefit to loving your "enemy" is the immediate reward of switching away from negative emotions of fear and hate, into positive, compassionate, loving ones.

Putting the Power of Love into Action

Start with simply noticing a stranger who is having a bad day and needs a kind word. Take a moment out of your day to generate some love and compassion, then project them toward this person saying something nice about the clothes, jewelry, or anything else you think might make the stranger feel good.

What was their reaction when you complimented them? Was the happiness the recipient felt worth a second or two out of your day? Now pay attention to how it made you feel! Did it make you feel more joyful, compassionate and loving? Next, try it on someone you really care for, for example, a family member or a fond acquaintance. Watch the reaction then pay attention to how it made you feel.

If you really want to challenge yourself, try it on someone you really dislike. Watch the reactions again. Sometimes this simple act will reset the hostile environment you two have created. Even if it doesn't change things permanently, what have you lost? Nothing except a second or two out of your day.

What you will experience, when you start doing this, is that the more you give out this love, the more you will feel it in return. This is undoubtedly why so many sages told us to love our neighbors. Not only does it send loving energy to people who may not be receiving it from anyone else, but it will enhance your life as well. The more loving energy sent out, the more loving energy returns to everyone. This is the real Power of Love, if you will allow yourself to find it.

Now you are starting to understand how important the Power of Love is, and how you can use it to enhance your life. Next you need to understand how important your free choices are.

Ultimate Freedom—Free Will

"When you introduce the word choice. . . . For the first time, science encounters free will."
—Amit Goswami, Ph.D.

Central to understanding metaphysical principles is you have the "Free Will" to decide your actions—but you also must accept the consequences of those choices.

Metaphysicians who have studied the Spiritual Realm know it is not guided by fear, force, judgment, or condemnation, but love. All of us are tenderly and compassionately supported by the principle of Free Will, because the spiritual universe realizes you will ultimately learn to make the best decisions. Since you will find your true spiritual path to becoming an enlightened master eventually, there is no reason to force you to do something you do not agree with today.

Your Choices

Metaphysicians also tell us that you either agreed to your major challenges before you were born, or you make decisions in a lifetime creating natural consequences from those decisions. Either way, you have chosen the life you are living. I know this is very hard to accept if you have had a difficult life—especially a very difficult childhood (see my personal example given later). How does this work in real life?

> Something like juvenile diabetes had to have been chosen prior to incarnating into a body. This is something affecting a person for their whole life, and they have done nothing to create it after they were born. There is no evidence at all in

metaphysical literature that a higher power would force a spirit to take on a challenge like this; therefore, it must have been agreed to before incarnation.

Here is a personal example to show you how this works:

> I almost died at five years old of carbon monoxide poisoning from a faulty furnace. It left all of us who were in this house with permanent nerve damage, manifesting in everyone having tremors (similar to the symptoms of Parkinson's disease) for the rest of our lives. Thank God for computers, or none of you would be able to read my handwriting! I did nothing as a child to create the faulty furnace, so it is clear I chose this challenge before I was born.

When we get to later chapters you will have a better understanding of why we would choose or agree to challenges like this, but there are good reasons for doing so. Understanding this was my Free Will choice allowed me to never think of myself as a victim and gave me the determination to make the best of my situation. What a gift!

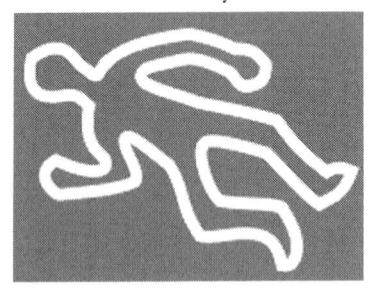

Much of our modern society is invested in convincing you that you are a victim, and whatever you are struggling with is not your fault. Once you learn it is all free choice, there is a comfort in knowing there is a purpose to your challenges, and there is no reason to blame others.

The other way you "choose" something is by creating it once you are here. An easy to understand example is:

Imagine a hypothetical scenario where you desperately need money, so you decide to rob a bank. You will certainly intimidate the terrified clerks; perhaps somebody will get hurt or not, but either way you set up a lot of naturally occurring consequences.

One of the worst consequences is you might get away with it. Once you get away with it one time, you will be tempted to do it again and again until somebody gets hurt or you finally get caught. Perhaps you go to jail, and your children grow up without you. Maybe you get divorced, file for bankruptcy, and have your life changed forever. All these are natural consequences of your original decision to rob the bank. Part of the responsibility of making your own choices is you have to accept the consequences.

As you have seen by these examples, everything happening to you either will be agreed upon prior to coming into this lifetime, or you have made decisions while you were here that created natural consequences from these decisions. Either way, it is free choice.

Human Free Will

Since Free Will is one of the basic principles of the spiritual cosmos, it should be essential to how we treat other humans.

If you force your *will* on others, either by manipulation or intimidation, you are not living spiritually. Someone who treats you well at the moment, but cheats, robs, manipulates, or hurts other people, should not be part of your life. When someone is hateful and vindictive toward other people, it is only a matter of time until they turn the venom and anger towards you.

If you are an adult, and someone forces you to do things you don't want to, you should run away as quickly as possible. If someone is incessantly texting, calling, and checking up on you, do not mistake this for love. This person does not care what you want or need; they care only about what *they* want.

While not every controlling person is a domestic abuser, psychopath, or serial killer, almost all domestic abusers, psychopaths, and serial killers are controlling! If someone attempts to dictate what you should do with your life, this is a huge red flag.

Sometimes people say to themselves, "Look how much he/she loves me" when their lover says, "If I can't have you, nobody can." Threatening to kill or hurt you because you do not submit to their demands is not love—in fact, it is pure selfishness. True love is wanting the very best for your loved ones, even when this means they would be happier living life without you.

Periodically, you hear horror stories about a cult abusing people. A truly spiritual leader would never force another adult to do anything against their will. If someone forces you to marry a specific person, go live in a certain place, or relinquish your wages, they are not treating you spiritually. Love is allowing every soul the freedom to make his or her own choices, regardless of what the other person thinks is best.

There is an important caveat here: If you are entrusted with the spiritual growth of children, you need to balance their safety with their ability to learn from their mistakes. While learning to learn and evolve, children should never be allowed to wander aimlessly in the street, have no structure or discipline, or to hurt themselves and others.

Changing Others

There is another important point to consider by way of a perfect example:

> When using *Sacred Quantum Metaphysics*, you might decide to create a world without addictions. Can you force another person to give up addictive behaviors? Spiritually you cannot change anyone without their Free Will consent. Unless they make the decision to accept your help, your efforts will be futile. Thankfully, most addicts, at one time or another, realize how miserable their life is. This is when they are willing to accept help.
>
> The better news is you can always change yourself. You can use Sacred Quantum Metaphysics to change the physical world—including yourself—so that you can be happy until an addict is ready to change. This will also make certain that you are not enabling the addict to continue their self-destructive behaviors.

Now you have opened the door to understanding the importance of free choice in the spiritual world, and in other human activities; next, you need to understand the reality behind the Law of Karma.

Your Heart's Desire—Karma

"I just want people to accept me for the person I pretend to be."
—Unknown

Most people have heard about Karma, but few of us understand the metaphysical principle behind it. You have certainly heard the phrase, "What goes around, comes around." This distorted view of Karma insinuates that a person who has harmed you will get a justified payback for their actions. This means it is almost like a punishment enforced by some unknown power.

Metaphysicians know Karma is better explained by "desires." Our Karma actually manifests itself by our wants, desires, choices, and decisions we make. This is not an outside punishment; it is each person voluntarily creating circumstances needed to learn from their actions. We choose these consequences freely, either consciously or unconsciously, by making choices based on our previous lessons and behaviors.

Karma is related to our material, three-dimensional world's "cause-and-effect"—also known as "action and reaction." It is the metaphysical equivalent to Newton's Third Law of Physics, which has been paraphrased as, "Every action has an equal and opposite reaction." In physics, we really do not fully understand what causes an equal and opposite reaction throughout our material three-dimensional universe, but we know it exists and can predict the effects.

In the ancient metaphysical wisdom, there is also an "equal and opposite reaction" to our thoughts, behaviors, and deeds. Similar to physics, we do not fully understand what causes it, but we know it exists and we can predict the effects. It is the metaphysical counterpart to the Law of Physics and why it is often called the "Law of Karma." In the "Meaning of Life—Practical Karma" chapter, you will have a better understanding of how Karma is manifested in real life examples.

Some people in the West resist the idea of Karma because it has been associated with Eastern philosophy. Christians sometimes teach what they call the "Law of Reciprocal Action." The essence is similar to the Law of Karma, but it is couched in a terminology easier for many Westerners to accept.

Personal Karma

How does Karma affect you personally? Whenever you interact with another person, you must experience the positive or negative consequences of your actions (equal and opposite reaction). You can either learn from your actions or experience the consequences (reciprocal actions) from them.

Obviously, it is much easier to learn our lessons intellectually, rather than to re-experience the consequences. Insight and learning are almost always preferable to trial and error, but sometimes we have little choice. If we do not learn the message that we needed to learn from our actions immediately, trial and error eventually teaches us the meaning we need to understand.

The spiritual is a purposeful, loving system. It does not operate mechanically or impersonally, like many people believe. If you have already learned your lesson, it would be absurd to go through an equal amount of negative "reciprocal action" as well. Once you have learned from your mistake, and understand the other person's hurt and pain, there is no reason for you to also experience the negative consequences.

If, however, you continue to be oblivious to the hurt and pain you have caused, then you will voluntarily choose to set up situations where you can experience the equal and opposite hurt and pain you inflicted on others. This is not punishment inflicted upon you, but it is a choice you willingly agree to in order to further your spiritual growth.

Attachments

Karma often expresses itself in what metaphysicians call "attachments." You can be attached to almost anything, including your fears, expectations, obsessions, desires, wants, needs, drugs, etc. When you have something to learn, you will make incredibly irrational and illogical choices, but they will give you the opportunity to experience your lesson. For example:

If after a series of disastrously failed relationships, you are still attracted to an alcohol-abusing partner, you are almost certainly dealing with Karmic attachments. If you insist on pursuing another alcoholic, you have not learned your lesson from your previous relationships. Metaphysicians say you are doomed to repeat it, until you can get rid of your desires and attachments (Karma). Now you're beginning to understand how your choices allow Karma to work in your life.

Metaphysics also tell us before you can reach enlightenment, you must get to a point of "no attachments," or what is called "no preferences." When you have no preferences, you certainly have rid yourself of all your desires, and thus you have resolved most, if not all, of your Karma. When you have resolved all of your Karma, you are a big step closer to allowing your enlightened master to emerge.

Positive Reactions

What is often neglected is that the Law of Karma (Law of Reciprocal Action) provides an "equal and opposite reaction" to the good things you do.

> For instance, if you are going to get niceness returned, you need to be genuinely nice. When you are genuinely nice to everyone, you will attract people into your life who will be genuinely nice to you. There is a major caveat here: It will not work metaphysically if you are nice to someone *in order* to get something in return. When you do something with the intention of getting a payback for your actions, you will not receive genuineness in return.

Nothing is ever lost or gained under the Law of Karma:

> If someone steals something from you, you have not lost anything in the long run. You might be making up for past actions—perhaps you stole something yourself and you now need to understand the hurt and pain you caused. Alternatively, perhaps you are creating a positive reciprocal reaction—which will bring more money or material goods to you in the future. You are either making up for something from the past, or stockpiling it into the future. Either way, you are one step ahead.

You have a much better understanding about the role of Karma and preferences in your life. When you get to "The New Sciences" section, you will get a much clearer perspective on how this ancient wisdom interrelates with modern scientific discoveries. Until then, simply understand that this is a very empathetic, supportive system, which allows us to perfect our character in the most compassionate, loving way.

Next we will examine what happens when you don't have enough time to get rid of all your attachments in just one lifetime.

Do-Overs—Non-Religious Reincarnation

"I don't mind dying. I just don't want to be there when it happens."
—Woody Allen

Before we get to the fascinating metaphysics of Reincarnation, we need to spend a moment refuting 1,600 years of misinformation. Some people think reincarnation is contrary to Christianity, which it isn't. In fact, reincarnation was a central belief in early Christianity, until it was removed by Roman emperors who felt it gave people too much freedom and self-control over their decisions. When you have more than one lifetime to learn from your mistakes, you do not need an emperor to tell you what to think.

If you are interested in this fascinating history, see "Appendix C—The Emperor's New Clothes—Historical Anti-Reincarnation." Reviewing these references isn't necessary for you to understand *Sacred Quantum Metaphysics*, and might sidetrack many readers, so they are not included here. Suffice it to say there are two clear examples of Jesus discussing reincarnation with the disciples—still existing in the New Testament today!

Metaphysics of Reincarnation

What do metaphysicians mean when they reference Reincarnation? I refer you back to the "Metaphysical Immortality—Consciousness Never Dies" and "Lotus Blooming—The Observer" chapters to remind you of your undying Spirit now temporarily inhabiting your current body. When you "break or wear this out," your consciousness or Spirit leaves your body behind.

Metaphysical Principles

Think of your human body as similar to a piece of clothing worn by your Spirit. When your clothes wear out, you replace them and put on new ones. Similarly, if we wear out one body, our Spirit can "put on" a different one. Since your Spirit is able to temporarily inhabit one body, why couldn't it subsequently incarnate into another one? This is the essence of how reincarnation works.

Modern Reincarnation

The Metaphysical truism, "We are spiritual beings having a material existence," is a great way of understanding the broader picture. You are an eternal Spirit who has chosen to incarnate into a human body to learn and evolve. Your spirit progresses through the tempering fires of experience and consequences, including Karma, eventually transforming you into an evolved, enlightened being.

Can you learn all the lessons you need to learn in a single lifetime? If enlightenment were fast and easy, lots of us would become Masters in one lifetime. Clearly this isn't the case because Awakened Masters are sadly too scarce, so obviously you require more than one lifetime to accomplish this arduous task.

Why do so many disciplines ignore the benefits of Reincarnation and demand their disciples withdraw from the everyday world? Since you are going to reach enlightenment eventually, you should be able to have a job, pay bills, raise a family, etc., and still pursue your spiritual path. You are lucky today because, with modern spirituality, you can still have the luxuries of our modern world, relationships, marriage, family, career, hobbies, creativity, etc., while you gain spiritual wisdom.

Spiritual Insights

When you understand Karma and reincarnation, some of the incomprehensible tragedies in life begin to make some sense. This allows us to comprehend how someone can come into a lifetime, suffer unspeakable abuse, and die prematurely. Perhaps this person in a previous lifetime caused the death of a young child. It would make sense that a spirit would come back and re-experience the abuse, not from the abuser's viewpoint, but from the child's viewpoint this time.

Metaphysicians tell us that sometimes a highly evolved being will choose to incarnate in a less than perfect human body. Sometimes they pick a mentally challenged child's body to learn the lessons of ridicule, dependency, and patience. There are thousands of reasons why a Spirit might choose a particular incarnation. When we get to the "Mysticism Explained—Applied Metaphysics" section, you will get a better understanding of why spirits choose different challenges. For now, suffice it to say that when you get the long view of many lifetimes, you realize the possibilities are endless.

With your basic understanding of why multiple lifetimes are essential for spiritual evolution, you next need to comprehend how the world can be altered.

Creating Reality—The Law of Attraction

"It is my belief that our purpose here is to develop our gifts of intentionality and to learn how to be effective creators."
—**William Tiller, Ph.D.**

What is the "Law of Attraction"? It is the generic name for attracting and creating anything you need and want. This simple idea uses metaphysical principles—and the recent scientific discoveries—to greatly enhance and empower the good things in your life: abundance, love, relationships, etc. The flipside is, if you have a spiritual need for a lesson (Karma), you will attract situations into your life to make those lessons clear to you.

The principle of Attraction has been around for at least two and a half millennia. Simply stated, whatever is focused on will manifest since there is an energetic or metaphysical positive attractive force (*philia*), and a negative repelling force (*neikos*), similar to the poles of a magnet in physics. Around 391 BC, Plato expanded upon these ideas by asserting "likes tend toward likes," which means positive or negative thoughts will correspondingly attract positive or negative results.

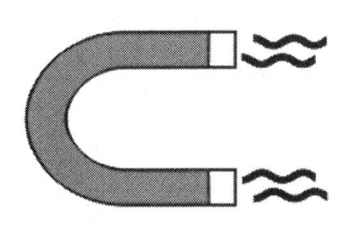

If the Law of Attraction were entirely bogus, don't you think it would have been discarded somewhere along those thousands of years? The fact that it wasn't rejected and remains a viable tool demonstrates many investigators decided the Law of Attraction was not only real, but essential. The deniers want you to believe there is nothing beyond the material, physical world, but they refuse to examine these claims subjectively.

Attraction Today

Some people get discouraged when the Law of Attraction doesn't seem to work for them. Unfortunately, they don't understand the concept in its entirety. This is because they do not comprehend the rules behind our spiritual universe.

If "like attracts like," then you cannot just wish for something and have it suddenly appear in your life. The Law of Attraction is a double-edged sword, because in order for you to attract something you desire, you first have to become "like" what you want to attract.

Dream for a moment: What would you like to manifest into your life? Material abundance? Friendship? Love? These things are all available when you are willing to understand the principles. Let's take a few of them and examine them one at a time.

Friendship

Maybe you are tired of being lonely and you would like to attract a friend. Have you ever heard the cliché, "In order to have a friend you need to be a friend"? According to the Law of Attraction, in order to attract a friend, you need to become a good friend to others. Once you become a good friend, you will attract good friends.

Metaphysically, there is a word of caution here: In order to "be a true friend" you need to be available as a genuine friend. Are you only being nice to others because you are going through the motions, attempting to manipulate the system to get what you want? If you are only acting friendly because you want something in return, you might as well save your effort. Since like attracts like, you will only draw someone who similarly wants something in return.

The Perfect Lover

Suppose you would like to find a lover who will share those intimate parts of being human. The intimacy shared between two human lovers can be beyond blissful. Most of us would like to find this ecstasy more often. When you want this in your life, the Law of Attraction says you must first become the best possible lover material for the other person, before you can attract someone like this into your life.

- If you desire a lover with sex appeal, you need to become as sexually attractive as you can for them. Everyone hates the idea of diet and exercise, but since "like attracts like," you need to take care of your body with healthy exercise and eating right, when your goal is to attract a sexy partner.

- How about the personality of your future lover? Do you want someone who is loving and caring? What are you doing to enhance and create more love and compassion within yourself?

- Do you desire somebody emotionally stable? Are you an emotionally stable person yourself? If not, work on it. You get the idea.

Unconditional Love

Conceivably, you rebelled at some of these thoughts and said to yourself, "I just want someone to love me exactly the way I am." What you are really saying is, "I want to be loved unconditionally." You are absolutely loved unconditionally—exactly the way you are—by the spiritual universe. This is not what you asked for, however. You are asking for a human lover, on this earth, in this lifetime.

Yes, people should love you unconditionally, exactly the way you are, but this is a totally unrealistic expectation to hope for in humans. Why? Most people are not very evolved spiritually, so the possibility that they are able to love you unconditionally is unlikely. Your most sensible option is to make yourself into the most attractive human lover you can be for a very ordinary human partner.

Creating Wealth and Abundance

So far we have looked at the Law of Attraction regarding relationships. Many times what people really want is to create material abundance in their lives. You will be happy to know this is actually quite simple once you understand the metaphysical principles behind it.

Perchance you would like to own a house instead of renting an apartment? Maybe you're just tired of eating oriental noodles every night because it is all you can afford? You now have your chance to change whatever it is you don't like, once you understand our complete universe.

Since humans can create wealth and abundance, there should be no poverty. We do have poverty, so what is it that we're doing wrong? Many people fail to create their own abundance because they are hindered by some very destructive attitudes.

Destructive Mindsets

- Perhaps the most damaging mindset is the constant drumbeat from people who want to keep you a victim and dependent. They want you to believe that you can never be rich because you are exploited by others. This is entirely wrong metaphysically, but if you stubbornly maintain this false belief, you will always be a "victim."

- Another destructive mentality is that you are powerless and need a government to give you everything you need. If you have this attitude, it will be very difficult, if not impossible, for you to ever create your own wealth.

- Some people refuse to consider that they are worthy of abundance because they have been told, and now believe, they are failures and will "never amount to anything." When you allow thinking like this to become ingrained into your personality, you need to create a new internal dialogue before you can turn your life around.

- When you have an attitude of desperation and lack, you cannot attract abundance. If you feel like you "need" something to be happy, Spirit will demonstrate to you that really do not "need" it after all. It will do this by making sure you don't ever receive it—convincing you that your life is just fine without it.

When you allow these damaging attitudes to manipulate your outlook, you need to rid yourself of them before the Law of Attraction will work.

Metaphysical Principles

Creating Wealth Out of Nothing

Underlying these falsehoods is the idea that there is only a limited financial pie, which must be divided up, with everybody getting a small share. Spiritually there are no limits to the power and energy the universe makes available to us, when we know how to access them. An everyday example will show you how to create wealth out of nothing:

Suppose you want to build a home for you and your family to live in . . .

First you need to build a cement foundation with rock, lime, sand, etc. In order to get these materials to you, people all over the world are paid to pull them out of the ground and ship them to you. Once the foundation is set, the house can be built.

There are thousands of different components of a home, which benefit many people along the way. All the sheet rock, nails, bolts, electrical, carpets, landscaping, paint, piping, roofing, heating, cooling, cabinets, plumbing fixtures, lighting, sewer lines, etc., were all provided by somebody who was able to partially feed their families from the money they get when you build your home.

Now, do you want to know the really astounding part? Even after all the people are getting paid, making money, and feeding their families, if you build your home efficiently, it is worth more than you paid to build it! You have just created wealth out of nothing for you, your family, and all the workers along the way.

Once you understand how something real and physical like a home can create wealth out of nothing, you can then understand how something like the Internet can create wealth out of electricity! Wealth is an unlimited resource that any of us can create, when you know how to do it. You can create wealth for yourself—and all of humanity—and you don't have to take it away from someone else. Do you understand now how Abundance is essentially an unlimited resource in a spiritual universe?

Since you are beginning to understand the Law of Attraction, next we need to examine some of the infinite abilities we can manifest.

Supernatural Understanding— Metaphysical "Magic"

"[Believers] . . . will do the works I have been doing, and they will do even greater things than these . . ."
John 14:12 NIV

What is it that past Masters were reportedly able to do simply with their minds? Some of those gifts are:

- psychic knowledge
- levitation
- control weather
- instant healing of themselves and others
- teleportation
- impervious to fire and pain
- ability to stop bleeding instantly
- manifesting material objects out of nothing

If they can do these things, you can do them also, with the proper knowledge, training, and practice. Different spiritual devotees were reported to be able to do many similar and diverse mysterious acts:

- Ascended master, Yoga Sutras (called the fully realized Yogi) was said to display evidence of "superhuman abilities" around 500 BC.

- There were spiritual masters called the Magi, who were documented as being able to project and manipulate an unseen force to transform the world around them. This is where the word "magic" originates.

- Buddha was reportedly able to access multidimensional planes and was said to have certain supernatural powers after he had reached Enlightenment.

- In Siberia, it was common knowledge that masters easily traveled between worlds.

- Jesus was reported to transform water into wine, control the weather, and levitate above the water.

- Other spiritual devotees have reported traveling between planes of space and time (dimensions).

Jesus said people would be able to perform "even greater" things than these. Why aren't they an everyday occurrence? The point is not to be critical, but if these are possible, why aren't we achieving them? Perhaps humanity didn't succeed in making these acts common before now because they didn't have the benefit of the modern scientific advances to guide them.

Traditional Spiritual Disciplines

After years of meditation or other disciplined metaphysical practice, many adherents have reported receiving supernatural gifts as the result of their efforts. These wise sages were subsequently asked to teach other students the techniques they had discovered.

Assuming the guru (*gu* = darkness; *ru* = light; literally bringing light out of darkness) was able to understand and explain his gifts, he would then need to formulate this knowledge into a step-by-step instruction that his students would understand and follow. Once the instruction was given and understood, the students' own trial and error experiences would need to be honed over several decades of disciplined practice. Since they didn't understand the science behind these wondrous activities, only a few dedicated adherents learned to duplicate these acts.

With modern scientific advances, you no longer have to stumble around utilizing trial and error to see what works, and what doesn't work. You now have a better understanding about what is possible when you are not limited to just our three-dimensional world. Are you ready to understand some of the spiritual potentialities?

Unlimited Possibilities—The Golden Chains

"It is man's destiny to ponder on the riddle of existence, and as a byproduct of his wonderment, to create a new life on the earth."
—**Charles F. Kettering**

Historical sages who guided new spiritual devotees into traditional metaphysical disciplines usually told them to avoid the "Golden Chains" or the "Golden Handcuffs." These are supernatural gifts that spontaneously appear as someone progresses toward enlightenment. These mystical abilities are so powerful and enticing (*Golden*) that they shackle the practitioner to the lowly earthly realm (*Chains*), holding them back from enlightenment.

What exactly are these "Golden Chains"? As people consistently practice spiritual techniques, they often attain the following "mysterious abilities":

- The most commonly reported characteristic is "permanent bliss and a profound sense of happiness."

- Spiritual seekers can attain "perfect wisdom and full awareness of the way consciousness works."

- Devotees attain "knowledge of the past and the future, including past and future lives."

- They are able to "read other people's minds" (telepathy), even gaining precise details of the motivation for these thoughts.

- They can create physical objects entirely from thought.

- Sages can transform one physical object into an entirely different one.

- Masters have changed physical reality simply by "conscious thought."

- Metaphysicians are able to levitate, also disappearing and reappearing again at will.

- They are able to instantaneously heal themselves or other people.

- They develop many other amazing gifts.

Would you like to accomplish similar feats? If your goal is reaching Enlightenment immediately, it is best to shun these supernatural gifts. If, however, you are like most of us, and you are primarily interested and manifesting alterations to our world and society, then these are important gifts or powers to be understood—and utilized. The "Mysticism Explained—Applied Metaphysics" section will explain how you can also accomplish similar deeds!

A word of caution: Just because you are able to accomplish these marvelous feats does not mean you will escape the karmic consequences for misusing them. If you only have selfish intent, you should not attempt any of these, because it will ultimately make your life much worse.

Now that you have a better understanding of what infinite abilities are possible, it is time for you to understand more about the metaphysics of the mind-body connection.

True Healing—Mind-Body Connections

"The individual may discover the I AM, he may know that within him lies all power to satisfy the soul, to fulfill its every need and desire."
—From *Life and Teaching of the Masters of the Far East*, **Volume 1, 1924**

For at least the last 5,000 years, history has recorded supernatural healing of disease, injury, or simple pain relief. Mind-body healing is a therapeutic technique originating in a wide variety of cultures across the world and passed down from generation to generation. If a particular treatment failed to be effective, it would not be taught to the next generation. It was a very efficient, self-correcting process.

When there was little or no other effective medical treatment except for medicinal plants, herbs, and "energy healing," people who understood how to use these techniques were in high demand. Specialists such as healers, herbalists, sages, etc., developed within each society, finding ways to ease the pain and suffering around them. These original "doctors" almost certainly didn't understand the science behind these miraculous healings, but they realized how effective they were. Not only are mind-body cures very low-cost and mostly pain-free, these treatments have little or no negative side effects. Luckily, many of these ancient cures survived into modern times due to the courage and persistence of very brave healers, who knew these remedies had great value. Some of them were subjected to criticism, harsh ridicule, imprisonment, or even death for healing patients during a time of scientific ignorance.

Do these mind-body healings work? Absolutely! While this chapter concentrates on the basic metaphysics of mind-body healing, there is the "New Medicine—Healing with the Mind" chapter in "The New Sciences" section, detailing phenomenal, recent medical discoveries. There is another basic listing and explanation for a few of the misunderstood healing techniques in "Appendix B—Healing Modalities."

If you want a sneak-peak of this modern research, science consistently verifies that about a third of patients are cured simply from the belief that whatever treatment they get will be effective (called the Placebo Effect). So just the mind of the patient has been proven to cure the person, which is a perfect example of mind-body healing.

So now you have been given a quick glimpse into our historical mind-body medicine; next, we will examine how your thoughts allow you to alter your reality.

Your Thoughts—Changing Reality

"It was the most beautiful and delicate crystal that I have so far seen—formed by being exposed to the words 'love and gratitude'... I can say it actually changed my life from that moment on."
—**Dr. Masaru Emoto from *The Hidden Messages in Water***

People who are familiar with this metaphysical topic will question why it seems to be so abbreviated. One of the new scientific discoveries, Quantum Physics, has massively expanded and clarified these principles; therefore, many of the fascinating details will be saved for "The New Sciences" section. First, you need to understand what has been taught for thousands of years before this quantum theory was discovered.

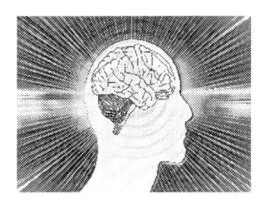

Metaphysicians know our thoughts have a profound effect on our body, mind, and the physical world. They have told us for millennia that we can "change reality with our thoughts," but this can sometimes cause us problems. Why? We need to be mindful of how we use our thoughts, being careful to make beneficial changes and avoid inadvertently creating negative consequences for ourselves.

Physical Effects to Your Body

A quick example will show you how needless negative thinking not only causes you mental suffering, but also causes physical harm to your health. Remember, none of us will have exactly these same thoughts, but most of us will recognize a similar line of thinking:

Suppose you are driving away from your home to go on vacation and you cannot remember whether you left the stove on. You start thinking how high your utility bill is going to be if you did leave the power on. Then you start to imagine even worse consequences . . .

You naturally begin picturing what might happen if the cabinets over the stove catch fire due to the relentless heat, which then would spread to other parts of the kitchen. You start preparing yourself for what damage might occur and how some of your irreplaceable, sentimental items might be lost forever.

You might construct an imaginary conversation about what you will say to the insurance adjuster to justify your claim. You know it is their job to pay you as little as possible, so you prepare a mental list of the valuables that could be lost. Often you will remember past memories of other confrontations, which either went well or turned out badly.

If you pay attention to your body, you will realize that your jaw is tightening, your heart rate increases, and you are gripping the steering wheel tighter, simply because you are creating this imaginary scenario! All this happened within your mind, regardless of whether you actually left the stove on. Remember, you don't even know for sure if there is a problem yet, but your imagination has created an enormous amount of stress in your body and mind.

It is important to comprehend this line of thinking, because it shows you how creating negative scenarios cause you mental, emotional, and even physical problems. Your reactions are immediate, and you can feel physical changes happening to your body. These physical reactions are just as real as if your home did catch fire. Your brain and body do not differentiate between your imagined scenario and a real crisis. This is how powerful your thoughts are!

Since your body reacts this intensely to negative thinking, why wouldn't it similarly have beneficial physical reactions to your positive thoughts? It is easier to recognize stressful reactions than it is to appreciate how positive thoughts—like love, compassion, and gratitude—can likewise create positive physical changes in your body. You need to realize both are equally real, and resolve that you are going to empower the positive physical manifestations and dampen the negative ones.

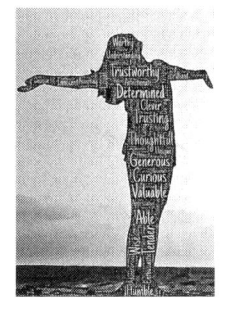

Loving, compassionate thinking will create positive reactions in your body, mind, and spirit. There are very real mental, physical, emotional, and spiritual consequences to our thinking. This is why metaphysicians caution you to always be aware of your thinking. One of the reasons meditation is encouraged is because it trains you to control your thoughts more effectively.

Troublesome Self-talk

Listen to your own internal "chatter" going on in your mind and pay attention to what you say to yourself in quiet moments:

> When you make a mistake—as all humans will—do you call yourself, "idiot" or "stupid"? What does this negative self-talk do to your confidence and self-esteem after many years? Most self-aware people recognize this negative thinking is destructive, and realize that they need to turn these thoughts into something positive before they create damaging attitudes.
>
> When people do something wrong, many people say to themselves, "I am always ___" (fill in the blank: clumsy, lazy,

impatient, etc.). This is very damaging because it doesn't allow you to change. You have just told yourself you will "always" react in a certain way. Moreover, this is usually very inaccurate. Is it true that you "always" react the same way? No, but you have just made it more likely that you will do it again in the future!

Similarly, some people say to themselves, "I never ___" (fill in the blank: prepare adequately, remember to . . . , think of . . . , etc.). Is it true? Probably not. The problem is, you have now made it less likely that you will ever change. If you feel like you need to give yourself a hard time over a mistake, wouldn't it be better to say, "Sometimes when I screw up I . . ." At least this gives you the opportunity to do it better next time.

Do you look in the mirror and tell yourself you "hate" this or that body part? Everyone has something that is less than idyllic when compared to some fantasized ideal. If you focus on minor flaws, you will likely create more imperfections from your thinking.

Now, you are beginning to comprehend how important your thoughts are. It is a good time to understand how metaphysics has predicted the true nature of this universe.

Select Your Frequency—The Vibrational Universe

"If you want to find the secrets of the universe, think in terms of energy, frequency and vibration."
—**Nikola Tesla**

This chapter will also be abbreviated because there are several chapters in "The New Sciences" section that expand upon this metaphysical principle. You still need to understand how enlightened Masters were able to understand the true universe before science revealed its own insights. Until we get to these later chapters, simply understand that somehow ancient wisdom revealed these possibilities millennia before our scientists were able to understand it.

Metaphysicians have long told us that variations in our physical world are simply differences in vibrational frequencies. Everything you see in your everyday three-dimensional world can be explained by these different variations. For example, the sounds we hear vary by the frequency of the vibrations received by our eardrums.

Light itself varies by vibrational differences. The colors we see are just different vibrational rates of light. For example, the color red vibrates from 400 to 484 THz, while violet is 700 to 789 THz. This is just the *visible light spectrum* which we are all familiar. Higher or lower frequencies of light, such as infrared and ultraviolet, exist but are invisible to the naked eye.

Electromagnetic Spectrum

| Radio Waves | Micro-waves & Radar | Milli-meter Waves, Telemetry | Infrared | Ultra-violet | X-rays & Gamma Rays |

10^5 10^6 10^7 10^8 10^9 10^{10} 10^{11} 10^{12} 10^{13} 10^{14} 10^{15} 10^{16} 10^{17} 10^{18} Hz

Low frequency
Long wavelength

High frequency
Short wavelength

Visible Light Spectrum

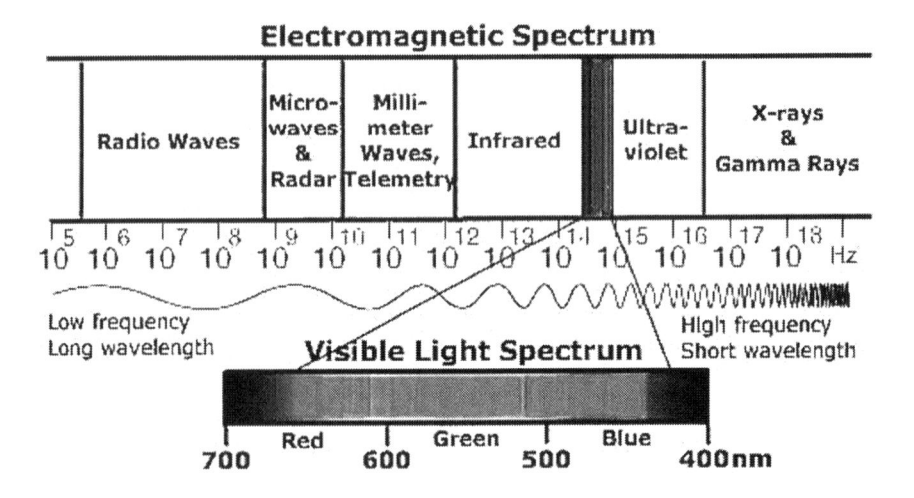

Red — 700
Green — 600
500
Blue — 400nm

Atoms and molecules, which make up our universe, are constantly vibrating. Depending upon the temperature, they vibrate faster or slower. We know that water at a high vibrational rate will convert to steam. Slow the vibrations down and it becomes liquid water. Slow them down even more and it becomes solid (ice).

The vibrational reality is what gives our material three-dimensional world the illusion of being solid, when we know it is just a moving, vibrating mass. Scientists tell that the differences in our material world are manifested by small differences in specific atoms, where the addition or subtraction of protons, neutrons and electrons physically changes reality. Masters of consciousness have verified these observations by being able to change reality just by increasing or decreasing the vibrational frequency of objects currently existing in our known universe (more on this in "The New Sciences" section).

Since everything in the universe has a different frequency, this includes you, your body, and your consciousness. You might have heard people discuss the "higher" feelings—love, compassion, acceptance, etc.—which refers to faster vibrational levels. Higher vibrational thoughts and emotions, like, supportiveness, gratefulness, tolerance, etc., allow you to attract higher emotions associated with enlightenment, like bliss, serenity, and ecstasy.

Metaphysicians will similarly discuss "lower" vibrational emotions of hate, anger, racism, etc. You will soon understand that negative thoughts like anger, hatred, and regret will create a very low vibrational rate, which allows even lower vibrational emotions like fear, panic, and depression to enter into your consciousness. This is why metaphysicians say you should always strive to keep your thoughts as positive as possible, which in turn keeps your vibrations high as well.

Now that you've been exposed to the Vibrational Universe, it is time for you to be introduce to the various spiritual realms.

Beyond the Veil—The Astral Planes

"Imaginary time is a new dimension, at right angles to ordinary, real-time."
—**Stephen Hawking**

Metaphysicians have long told us that there are different "planes of existence," which transcend our three-dimensional world. For millennia, these have been called the "Astral Planes," differentiating them from the materialistic world we live in. Our three-dimensional world, the one you currently inhabit, is considered one of the slower vibrational planes of existence.

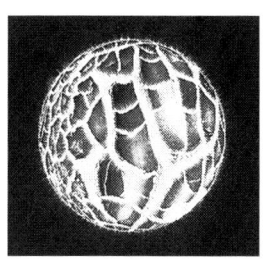

What then are the Astral Planes? It is easier to understand these in terms of what our modern mathematicians and scientists call dimensions (see "Appendix A—What Is a 'Dimension'?").

As you learned in the previous chapter, the physical world conforms to different vibrational frequencies. Metaphysicians tell us these higher spiritual dimensions vary by differing vibrational frequencies as well. As we go from this low vibrational, low-density material world into the higher dimensional Astral planes, the vibrations speed up.

Without getting too far ahead of ourselves, modern scientific discoveries (beginning with Einstein) have verified that there are many more dimensions than just our three-dimensional world. Mathematicians have long understood multiple dimensions mathematically, but it is only recently that our scientific discoveries have confirmed the existence of these different planes of existence.

METAPHYSICAL PRINCIPLES

Describing the Astral

The most common brief description people give when they travel to the astral planes and return is:

> They describe a beautiful "Crystal City" surrounded by an intense Unconditional Love, compassion, and acceptance—often called the Cosmic Consciousness or Divine Consciousness. Christians call this place Heaven. Others call it Nirvana or Paradise.
>
> There are planes where consciousness creates everything that exists within this realm. Alterations to this physical reality are instantaneous, but instantly disappear when the consciousness or thoughts change.
>
> Within this astral plane there is a place of great reverence, which can be readily visited, called the Hall of Knowledge (see "True Sight—Inner Knowledge" chapter). This is where people can access the Akashic Records. These details are important because some of the scientific research detailed in "The New Sciences" section has confirmed many of these observations.

How is it possible for you to experience these different dimensions? Metaphysicians have told us for millennia that you can raise or lower your own vibrational level to experience different levels of existence. In other words, as you raise your spiritual vibrational frequency, you can raise your consciousness to experience these higher dimensions. In the "Mysticism Explained—Applied Metaphysics" section, you will get a better understanding about how to do this.

Sacred Quantum Metaphysics

You have now reviewed the pertinent metaphysical principles and you are now almost ready to examine recent scientific discoveries. First, we need a more detailed look at why our current society is so resistant to change.

Our Divided Science

"There is a principle which is a bar against all information, which is proof against all arguments, and which cannot fail to keep a man in everlasting ignorance—that principle is contempt prior to investigation."
—Unknown

As mentioned earlier, the most historically important intellectual battle is raging today, but most of us don't even know it exists! Why? It has become an integral part of our established culture, therefore most people simply perceive it as reality.

Since the 16th century, it was beneficial for religion and science to separate from each other. Science wanted to be free from religious interference, which in those days could literally be painful and deadly. In return, the sciences would leave the otherworldly to the churches. This "duality" was a division between the spiritual and the material world.

Before we understood the true nature of the universe, the separation of religion and science had great promise. You will soon understand that this is a huge mistake. What evolved was a divided society, with entirely different ways of looking at the world.

It is important for you to examine this division in order to comprehend how to reverse this destructive trend, and get society back on track. Once you understand this separation, you will know how to counter it when you find it:

- One camp steadfastly refused to believe there was anything other than the static three-dimensional world of molecules, atoms, etc. They considered people who believed that there was a spiritual component to our universe were naïve and possibly superstitious. They thought the "mind" or "consciousness" was just an illusion, because humans were merely a material body and brain. People who believed this theory were called "Materialists."

Materialism theorized that there was nothing meaningful beyond matter—nothing worthy of study beyond the physical. They speculated that matter and energy, which are observable and measurable with our five senses, were the only significant part of our universe. They further assumed phenomena like consciousness and the "mind" were meaningless because they were not made from atoms, molecules, etc.

- The other part of our society believed that there was something more to life beyond mindless, impersonal atoms bouncing around. They probably did not know exactly what this "something" was, but they knew it existed. They grasped humans are so much more than just a body and brain—that consciousness and thinking not only existed but were powerful components of our reality. These people were generally called "spiritual."

The spiritual camp thought the mind, logic, and reasoning (consciousness) revealed the true nature of our complicated universe. They anticipated that new insights would be discovered, and then integrated into our evolving reality. Scientific discoveries of the 20th century have verified this spiritual approach.

When Newtonian theories confirmed planetary physics, scientists naturally believed Materialism would be the key to understanding everything in the universe. They believed phenomena relating to the mind, consciousness or spirituality, which were difficult to verify, were considered insignificant and not worthy of study.

It became a point of pride for many academics to separate from the dogmatic beliefs of the past by denying there was anything meaningful beyond the material universe. Materialists eventually postulated that the mind and consciousness were the meaningless side effects of the electrical impulses and chemical reactions from the neurons, synapses, hormones, etc., of the human brain.

You will soon understand that recent scientific breakthroughs have disclosed new insights into the true nature of our universe. As improbable as it may seem, these insights are sometimes ignored today, because they conflict with the common cultural mindset.

The Veil of Ignorance— Materialism

"He who knows nothing is closer to the truth than he whose mind is filled with falsehoods and errors."
—Thomas Jefferson

If you are one of those lucky open-minded people who believe spirituality and consciousness exist, it might be hard for you to comprehend that there is a huge portion of our society that tries to ignore it. Regrettably this is true.

Scan around your current environment: What philosophy dominates our current culture? In our attempt to remove religious edicts—a good thing—we made a terrible mistake by then removing the influence of consciousness and spirituality from many of our public policies. Since science has confirmed the essential spirituality of our universe, it is time to reverse this mistake.

I will give you some examples of the influences materialism still has on our society below. Most people reading these examples will not act like this, but there is a small portion of humans who are not guided by spiritual principles. It is important to examine these so that you can see how spirituality has largely been frozen out of our public policies:

- Governments: Materialists and anti-spiritualists have seized control of most of our political institutions and our public policies. Since according to this philosophy there is no value to life except some mindless atoms forming a body, then there is little reason why a non-spiritual government couldn't murder millions of people (if it can get away with it). Since there are no ethical standards or spiritual consequences, why should a politician tell the truth, or prevent the earth from being polluted (as long as no one knows)? Those who are skilled at maneuvering politics and politicians—even when they are criminals themselves—can receive fame and fortune through this manipulation. Secrecy and deception are essential tools for governments today, keeping people from being able to vote intelligently.

- Criminals: People who have no understanding of the spiritual ramifications feel like they can lie, cheat, and steal, if it means enjoying prostitutes, luxuries, and drugs with the money. Since humans are no better than animals, there is no reason not to sexually exploit children, or assassinate a competitor who is selling drugs on "their" corner (when they can avoid prison). Since there is nothing "wrong" with murder, then there shouldn't be anything immoral about torturing animals (if they can evade punishment).

- Courts: You can recognize the non-spiritual materialistic philosophy in our amoral legal system, where determining what is right or wrong is rarely considered. Pressure groups use the court system to remove spiritual references from public displays—and from public discourse, if possible. Our courts today have become a system of procedures rather than a "justice" system, even absolving criminals if they evade capture for a certain arbitrary amount of time (Statutes of Limitations). Considering there are no spiritual consequences, the most manipulative lawyer can free the guilty, or facilitate the lawful theft of an innocent person's assets. Legalistic extortion is common today, where people who are blameless pay other legal manipulators to have frivolous cases dismissed. When you remove consciousness and spirituality from law enforcement, all you are left with is force, punishment, and prison to deter criminal activity.

- Schools: Our public schools go to great extents to remove metaphysical topics from textbooks and the curriculum. Educators avoid topics that may be construed by anti-religious parents or administrators as promoting spirituality. It doesn't need to be an actual religious doctrine; if it simply alludes to something spiritual, it is usually avoided.[5]

- Media: While there are occasional fair presentations, the establishment is over-invested in ignoring metaphysical topics and promoting materialistic philosophy, even in the "news." When scientists examine spiritual topics, professional skeptics are almost always brought in to refute these modern scientific facts. When anyone famous promotes spiritual ethics, especially in politics or science, they will likely have their integrity questioned.

- Medicine: Do you suppose this historical anti-spiritual bias led to the effort to remove mind/body healing from medical research (see the Placebo Effect)? In the "New

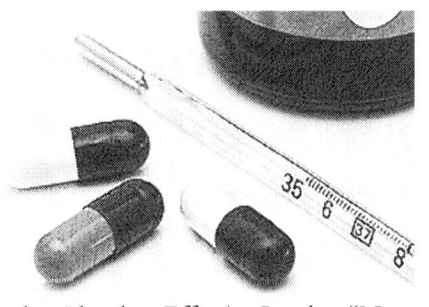

---

[5] There are some very promising signs this might be changing. Some schools have recently included "mindfulness" as an approved topic.

Medicine—Healing with the Mind" chapter and the "Mysticism Explained—Applied Metaphysics" section, you will receive many more details about this scientific mistake. There has been a somewhat successful effort to silence the medical community from expressing their approval of mind-body therapies—even though these have been proven very effective scientifically. Medical personnel have also been ostracized for discussing their own spiritual experiences (details later).

- Institutions: Our organizations will quickly finance research examining the material world, but will avoid investigating the spiritual and/or metaphysical. Anything having to do with the physical operations of the brain, for example, will be funded generously. This is true even though it has been proven scientifically that meditation, consciousness, quantum experiments, and the mind-body techniques can positively alter the brain better than pharmaceuticals.

Certainly the examples above do not describe the totality of our society today. They are only influences that manifest in the bizarre parts of our culture. It is important to understand the impacts so that you will be able to counter and circumvent them in the future.

Despite almost over a century of scientific discoveries proving a spiritual component to the universe, few universities have any full-time departments dedicated to this. Why? It is the career kiss of death for anyone to express their interest in researching metaphysical topics. When choosing a university to go to, evaluate campuses that not only show racial diversity, but also allow diversity of thought. The few universities that resist institutional groupthink are Harvard, Duke, Cambridge, Yale, Stanford, University of Arizona, and the University of Virginia. "The New Sciences" section will give you the incredible details and insights into these evolving disciplines.

The unfortunate part is many of the adherents to a materialistic philosophy are still in positions of power in our scientific and educational institutions. Why? The short answer is because much of our society has an innate aversion to anything that could possibly be considered religious.

For example, despite over a century of scientific discoveries such as Einstein, String Theory, Multidimensional Physics, Membrane Theory, altered states, Near-Death Experiences, Past Life research, Life-Between-Life studies, etc., some people are still trying to locate the source of our personalities within the human brain. What an incredible amount of wasted intellect, time, and money!

We must find a way to reintroduce the spiritual/metaphysical principles (certainly not religious dogma) back into our policies and society. The question becomes, how do we treat those who are not guided by innate spiritual ethics? Wouldn't it be better for society to convince politicians and criminals not to commit crimes in the first place? Instead of imprisoning those who are not spiritual, we must teach them why it is in their best interests to treat others humanely in a spiritual universe. Once they understand their personal consequences of harming others, they will no longer need to be told how to behave.

You are beginning to get a glimpse into how ingrained the outdated theory of materialism has become; now is a good time to understand why there is so much inertia in our society.

Piercing the Veil—Emerging True Science

"There is essentially nothing to matter whatsoever—it's completely insubstantial. The most solid thing you could say about all this insubstantial matter is that it's more like a thought; it's like a concentrated bit of information."
—Jeffrey Satinover, M.D.

Metaphysicians say we need to "pierce the veil of ignorance." It is as if there are blinders over the collective eyes of humanity. Once people close their mind, it is very difficult to get a new perspective or to see true reality. We know those blinders are difficult to remove, even when confronted with irrefutable scientific evidence.

Do you have a hard time believing that normally intelligent, rational, insightful scientists will refuse to believe the new scientific realities—and instead retain obviously discredited beliefs? It has happened many times throughout history:

- Recall the Flat Earth thinking of the past. Many believers, who were in positions of power, refused to accept the overwhelming evidence that the world was round. It wasn't until more open-minded scientists slowly replaced these stubborn believers that our society was able to move past the ignorance.

- Consider also the challenges Copernicus and Galileo each had convincing their scientific communities of their obvious truths. They came up with logical, even mathematical, explanations of how the cosmos operated.

> The established physicists and other "scientists" refused to open their minds, even when they could see the evidence. When intelligent, open-minded scientists were finally able to embrace the true reality is when those theories finally became "mainstream."

A quote from a modern scientist, who similarly faced brutal establishment opposition, will give you a better understanding of what open-minded thinkers face.

> *"A scientific truth does not triumph by convincing its opponents and making them see the light, but rather because its opponents eventually die and a new generation grows up that is familiar with it."*
> **—Max Planck, Quantum Theorist and Physics Nobel Prize winner**

You would think that we would have learned from history, but unfortunately this is very hard for mankind to do. It is even harder for today's academics to accept recent scientific discoveries than it was in Copernicus' or Galileo's time, because many of today's institutions enforce a strict groupthink to ensure conformity. No wonder our society is so dysfunctional, when so many people in a position of authority refuse to integrate scientific facts about the true nature of our universe.

Why is this important? When you pay attention, you will encounter people in your family and work who have a personal belief denying the reality of consciousness or spirituality. They will try hard to convince you that your spirituality and the powers of your consciousness are not real, even when you show them scientific proof. You need to be prepared for this resistance, because you will undoubtedly encounter it.

Seven billion people on our planet cannot continue to be held back by false scientific beliefs. We must evolve quickly as a species, and *Sacred Quantum Metaphysics* is the best hope we have to make it happen. The collective minds of science and educators are finally beginning to open up to the true nature of our universe. With your help, the obstinate holdouts may finally become convinced.

You have been given a peek into why mankind has been held back from attaining a fabulous future. Now is the time for you to understand the amazing recent scientific discoveries, which will allow humanity to evolve quickly.

The New Sciences

"One man's magic is another man's engineering."
—Robert Heinlein

Some people see the word "science" and are afraid it's going to be beyond their ability to understand. Do not despair. Everything written in this section is intended to be easy to understand, even for people who have no scientific or mathematical background whatsoever. There might be an equation here and there, but it is only to make a point, which you will easily grasp.

Why will this be so easy? You have already gained a basic understanding of many of the metaphysical principles, plus a glimpse into our divided society. This background will prepare you for understanding the underlying truths behind our universe, which these new sciences have revealed. Since you can understand the basic metaphysical principles, you will have no trouble at all understanding the science, because they are essentially the same.

Are you ready to begin your journey into some of the new science discoveries of the last century or so? If you are, this will knock your socks off. You will be given a basic outline of why our new sciences are, at long last, proving metaphysical principles. There is so much fascinating scientific evidence lately that has revealed the true universe has many wondrous aspects to it.

You will begin to understand how and why thousands of years of reports from metaphysical literature are not only possible, but how you can use science to make the same changes yourself! Remember, what we used to call "magic" or "miraculous" was just unknown science at the time.

Store Me Some Energy Please—Space-Time Continuum

"Gravity is not responsible for people falling in love."
—Albert Einstein

I would bet almost everyone has heard about Albert Einstein and how he was one of the great thinkers of the 20th century. Few people have taken the time to explain to you the real reasons why his discoveries were so groundbreaking.

What was it that made Einstein so incredibly different? His theories and equations were history-making, because what he discovered was totally against the accepted scientific dogma of the previous four centuries. After he published his world-changing insights in respected scientific journals, he was simply ignored by most physicists and academics.

One of the first to see Einstein's genius was another genius, Max Planck, who helped formulate Quantum Theory. If it were not for Max Planck, we might still be huddled in the ignorance of 400 years of scientific stagnation known as Materialism. Lucky for us, the truth finally did come out.

Why was there so much resistance to his theory? Earlier we briefly discussed the divided society, and how physicists and academics erroneously believed there was only the three-dimensional material universe. Then here comes Einstein disproving materialistic philosophy. How? With his ideas of space-time continuum and the interrelationship between matter and energy (described in lay language below).

Most of you have heard about Einstein's famous equation $E=MC^2$, but do you know it verified some very surprising metaphysical principles?

Without getting technical at all, let me break down this equation for you in simple terms:

- The amount of Energy (E) contained in any object is equal to (=) the Mass (M) of this object multiplied by the speed of light squared (C^2).
- To make this even simpler, just realize the speed of light squared is a very, very large number.
- Restated: E = M multiplied by this big number.
- The important part of this equation is E = M (Energy = Mass).

Einstein's genius was he discovered that matter is energy and energy is matter. Thus, all matter—everything we think is solid—is simply stored energy!

He proved it is possible to convert matter into energy, and likewise energy can be stored into matter. When you change matter into energy, you have a very large amount of energy being stored up in a small piece of matter—because it is multiplied by that very large number C^2. This is the principle explaining how an atomic bomb is possible: A tiny piece of uranium, with very little mass, can produce a spectacular explosion when its matter releases all of its stored energy.

Many centuries of false scientific beliefs were overturned when Einstein discovered matter, molecules, electrons, etc., to be a fleeting manifestation of energy, certainly not the essence of our universe. This is why his discoveries were so groundbreaking!

Connections to Metaphysics

It does not take a mastermind to connect how Einstein's theory and metaphysics have both reported matter can be transformed and then re-formed again.

Einstein also theorized that the fabric of space is changeable and can be folded and manipulated, which is what metaphysicians have told us for thousands of years. After Einstein's incredible discoveries, we are beginning to understand the science behind some of the unexplained abilities of metaphysical Masters.

For example, sages have often been observed dissolving matter and then recreating it into a different form of matter—as Einstein predicted. The question becomes, "How were Masters of the past able to manipulate matter and energy to transform our physical reality?"

When Einstein published his famous Theory of Relativity, he concluded there must be at least one additional dimension—the fourth dimension of time. This combination of our ordinary 3-D world plus time was called the "Space-time Continuum."[6] You can now recognize the similarities between Einstein's extra dimension and the metaphysical "astral plane." It is probable that the metaphysical term "astral plane" and the mathematical and scientific term of "space-time continuum" are likely different terms for the same reality.

It is interesting to note that 3,000 years ago metaphysical literature predicted the scientific facts surrounding the Big Bang. The Rig Veda, part of the Hindu ancient wisdom, reports the beginning of time very similar to our current understanding. The Vedas were reportedly read by many great modern thinkers, including Quantum theorists, Einstein, and Nikola Tesla.

---

[6] Understanding dimensions is not easy, and thankfully not absolutely necessary for you to understand Sacred Quantum Metaphysics, but can be quite enlightening. If you would like to comprehend what a dimension is, and what the differences between dimensions are, I encourage you to go to "Appendix A—What Is a 'Dimension'?"

Democritus, the father of modern science, reportedly obtained his ideas that the entire universe made from atoms from metaphysical sources 2,500 years ago. He was reportedly studying with the Magi before coming back to Greece with his discoveries.

This is only the beginning of the connections between metaphysics and science, so hold on for the ride of your lifetime! Now is the time for you to understand the true nature of our universe.

What Lies Beyond—The Hidden Universe

"Nature confuses the skeptics and reason confutes the dogmatists."
—Blaise Pascal

I have some friends who say, "Unless I can see it or touch it, it does not exist." They express this as if it's something meaningful, but this is simply a way to close their minds to the vastness of the cosmos. Even before the recent scientific discoveries, we knew there was much more to our world than what can be seen or touched.

Your eyes may seem like miraculous organs, but they are actually very inadequate and inefficient filters of a small portion of what is out there. As mentioned before, we know there are ultraviolet and infrared light spectrums that your eyes cannot see, but we know they exist. How about microwaves and x-rays? Can you see them? No, but everyone certainly knows they are real.

Few people would deny that microwaves, x-rays, or ultraviolet light exists, but they still refuse to consider how much is out there that is unseen/metaphysical. Since there is this much information about our material three-dimensional cosmos that is completely outside of our ability to perceive them with our five senses, can you imagine how much more we are missing? First, let's consider how much is out there that we *can* see and touch:

> Think about how big the Earth is: it is mostly covered with water but still has enough territory for about seven billion humans—with room to spare. As big as the Earth is, our planet is very tiny compared to other planets in our solar

system, and most of these have multiple moons circling them. All of those planets and moons are circling around a star we call our Sun.

Now as big as the Earth is, it would take 300,000 Earths to fit inside our Sun. When you add up the Sun plus all the planets and moons in our solar system alone, it is a vast amount of matter. Remember, the Sun is only one star. As big as our Sun is compared to our planet, it is really minuscule compared to some of the other stars out there. For example, VY Canis Majoris is between five and nine billion times the size of our Sun. Now imagine five billion Suns each containing 300,000 Earths—all in one star. This is a huge amount of matter.

Next, consider that there are hundreds of billions of stars similar to our Sun in our Milky Way Galaxy alone. Astronomers speculate there is a likelihood of one or more planets much bigger than Earth, possibly with multiple moons, orbiting around each of those stars.

Astrophysicists tell us there are hundreds of billions of other galaxies similar to our Milky Way. Each one of these galaxies likely contains hundreds of billions of stars similar to our own Sun. These stars might have multiple planets, and those planets likely have multiple moons.

When you add up all this matter—the entire Earth, plus other planets in our solar system, plus all the material in the hundreds of billions of stars, planets and moons in each of those hundreds of billions of galaxies—it adds up to quite a bit of matter doesn't it?

Sacred Quantum Metaphysics

All of this matter is only 4% of our universe! 96% is something other than molecules. Of that 96%, about 70% of the known universe is "Dark Energy," and the other 26% is "Dark Matter." They call this "Dark," not because it's negative, but because it is unseen/metaphysical and does not consist of matter, molecules, etc.

Ignoring Reality

This certainly shoots a big hole in materialism that believes the only significant part of our universe is atoms, electrons, etc., doesn't it? Since 96% of our cosmos is not physical matter, how could anyone think the only important part of the universe is material? These new scientific facts do not stop some people from ignoring reality.

As recently as 2009, a denier of spirituality ignored the recently discovered 96% nonmaterial universe and proclaimed Materialism was still valid! Now do you understand why we keep referencing this antiquated theory, since a major portion of our society stubbornly refuses to believe recent scientific advances? Maybe you have heard one definition of psychosis, "Insanity is doing the same thing over and over again and expecting different results." There is a scientific corollary to this stating, "Scientific insanity is knowing a theory was proven false, time and time again, but still clinging to the hope it is true!" This is a very interesting look at the human psychological concepts of denial, rationalization, and delusion at work, operating right before our eyes.

Embracing Reality

Instead of ignoring 96% of the cosmos, wouldn't you think people would seriously investigate this metaphysical part of our universe? You would think so, but this means thinking independently, and going against the ingrained institutional groupthink, which is hard for any human to do.

You are lucky since you can perceive the true universe without the institutional biases, so that you can be part of the catalyst for change. People will not like it when they are challenged to examine their underlying beliefs, but it must be done for the good of humanity. This is why it's vitally important that you are there to help them make the transition.

There are some creative and innovative researchers who are opening up the realities of the metaphysical 96% of our cosmos. Without getting too far ahead of ourselves, is it possible this Dark Energy is the same elusive energy Metaphysicians have used to transform the world for many millennia? Of course it probably is, but the important thing is just to keep an open mind about this possibility for now.

So now you are beginning to comprehend the vast enormity of the true universe. Next it is important to get a glimpse of the Quantum world.

Your Quantum Leap— Quantum Physics Simplified

"Quantum physics . . . is the physics of possibilities."
—**Amit Goswami**

When people hear the word "Quantum" they tend to skip over the information, mainly because other people say how unbelievably confusing it can be. You will be happy to know that quantum mechanics is actually very easy to understand when you do not close your mind to the true nature of the recent scientific discoveries.

Whether you call it Quantum Theory, Quantum Mechanics, or Quantum Physics, these are different terms describing essentially the same reality. In short, Quantum Mechanics provides a description of how energy and matter can behave at small atomic or subatomic levels. What is important to remember is, when changes are made at very small levels, they eventually change the larger universe.

I am not a quantum physicist. You will be happy to learn I am going to explain the important parts of Quantum Theory without using formulas or equations! Lucky for you, you don't need to understand physics, mathematics, or the events occurring at the atomic and subatomic levels to understand the Quantum world.

Pre-Quantum Science

Why was quantum mechanics necessary? Physicists realized classical physics does not explain the phenomenon witnessed when examining events at small atomic levels. They tried to describe what they were observing as best they could.

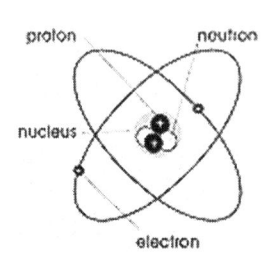

For example, according to classical physics, it is impossible for electrons to continuously orbit the nucleus of a molecule. This is because they would eventually lose energy and then collide with the nucleus. This does not happen, so they had to search deeply to find an explanation.

Quantum observations were confusing to some scientists, because they were intent on conforming them to their beliefs of materialism and classical (Newtonian) physics. Researcher Steven Weinberg said, "There is now in my opinion no entirely satisfactory interpretation of quantum mechanics." Physicist Richard Feynman said, "I think I can safely say that nobody understands quantum mechanics." Not understanding that science was ignoring 96% of the universe, many theorists could not comprehend why it didn't fit into the theories they were taught in school.

Quantum theory is actually very easy to understand when the totality of the true universe is taken into consideration. With the realization that the vast majority of the universe is not material molecules, atoms, etc., we can finally begin to comprehend the true wondrous nature of our fascinating cosmos.

True Quantum Observations

As with any theoretical branch of science, there are competing theories, and quantum theory is no exception. The goal of any theory is to match, explain, and eventually predict our real world experiences. Any theory failing to explain or predict how various real life phenomena occur will eventually be discarded.

There is one quantum theory that conforms to the observed experiments, and it also explains many of the metaphysical principles

Sacred Quantum Metaphysics

outlined earlier in the book. The other competing theories don't completely explain the documented quantum occurrences and they certainly don't explain the metaphysical reports from the last few thousand years. Perhaps this quote will give you an understanding from someone who ought to know:

> *"I regard consciousness as fundamental. I regard matter as derivative from consciousness."*
> **—Max Planck, called the father of quantum theory.**

What previous theorists failed to take into consideration was there is another variable that makes its influence obvious at the subatomic level—Consciousness. What do we mean by consciousness? Consciousness is simply another form of energy, existing independently of the human body and brain. When true consciousness—the Observer or Essence Mind—expresses itself through the human brain, it is called the "mind." The mind is a sluggish, ineffectual distortion of our true consciousness.

Quantum observations show subatomic particles are altered when they are "observed." Experiments demonstrate this "reality" is actually a set of possibilities until a consciousness observes it, which then transforms our physical world into a single concrete reality.

When you combine Einstein's revelations, showing matter is simply a form of stored energy, with the insight that it is the energy of consciousness that solidifies reality, you realize how important consciousness is to our universe.

Consciousness, which is energy, can never be created or destroyed, but can be transformed into other forms of energy. This energy can be stored into physical matter, but it all starts with consciousness. Consciousness then is the prime source of everything!

Uncertainty Principle

Another important part of quantum theory is Heisenberg's Uncertainty Principle, which predicts we cannot simultaneously measure the position and the momentum of subatomic particles. This means that very little can be predicted at the quantum level. If you remove the real influence of consciousness, as the materialists attempt to do, no Quantum observations, including Heisenberg's Uncertainty Principle, make sense. When, however, you include the influence of consciousness, you find this unpredictability completely understandable, because the Observer is what is altering the real world, moment by moment.

If you follow the debates, people say quantum mechanics is the "end of causation"—the end of cause and effect. Cause-and-effect still exists; we just needed to add in the influence of consciousness to reliably comprehend subatomic changes. These then transform the greater universe. When you realize that the consciousness of the Observer is actually changing the physical reality, you begin to understand thousands of years of metaphysical reports—including the principle of the Observer.

Non-local Entanglement

Einstein subsequently theorized about what has become known as quantum non-locality and entanglement. Two or more particles become so interrelated (entangled) that when one changes its direction of spin, the other changes its rotation at the same instant—even at great distances (non-locality).

There are many scientific studies demonstrating the real-world application of quantum entanglement:

> For example, the brains of two individuals were monitored while they were meditating together. After the meditation,

they were separated into different locations and their individual brain scans were monitored. One meditator was then shown a visual stimulus. The astounding part is the other meditator's brain showed a similar reaction even though there was no visual input. Their brains still showed a distinct connection (entanglement), even though they were now separated (non-local) and received different stimulation.

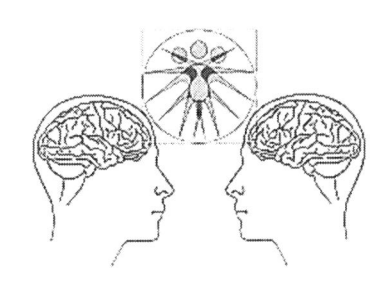

Metaphysical Connections

Metaphysicians have long told us, when the Observer is involved, changes to the physical universe are possible. Now quantum mechanics is confirming it. You are uncovering some insights into why positive thinking and prayer have always been consistent metaphysical recommendations.

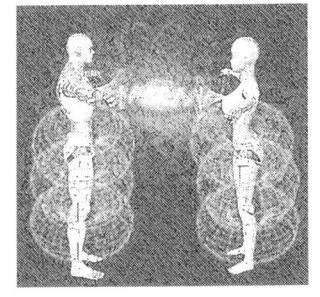

If you are insightful, you will see the associations between these quantum observations and many of the metaphysical principles discussed earlier. Do you suppose it is a complete coincidence that quantum theory discovered the very valuable influence of consciousness, and the metaphysical principle of the Observer predicted it? Einstein and quantum theorists found a wave, such as light, could also be described as an energetic particle, which varies according to its "frequency." Do they seem to be confirming one of the great metaphysical principles of the Vibrational Universe?[7]

With these insights, you have the key to understand how metaphysical Masters and sages have altered the world for thousands of years. Since consciousness has been proven to alter the physical reality at very small levels, then it is entirely possible that this is the mechanism for manifesting larger changes to our universe. Fasten your seatbelts, because this is only the beginning!

So now that you have an opening into this very real and exceedingly wondrous quantum world, it is time to start to understand how science is verifying even more details of the metaphysical principle of the Vibrational Universe.

---

[7] For more connections to the Vibrational Universe, see the next chapter on String Theory.

The Essence—String Theory Simplified

"There is a whole realm of physics called the hidden sector, which is given to us by Superstring theory; it's a world of its own. . . . This is probably what you call mind."
—**Superstring researcher**

What exactly is String Theory? In the 1980s, String Theory emerged to show all particles and all forms of energy were one-dimensional "strings" vibrating in a multi-dimensional universe. This may seem exceedingly complicated, but it really isn't when you recall the metaphysical principle of the Vibrational Universe.

String Theory verified what metaphysicians have told us about our universe for many millennia. It reveals every form of matter or energy is the result of the different vibrations of these strings. Strings vibrate in multiple dimensions, and depending on the frequency, might appear in our four-dimensional Space-Time as matter, light, or gravity.

The frequency of the vibrations is what determines whether it is matter or energy, verifying Einstein's famous equation of how it is possible to store energy into matter and vice versa. The only difference between matter and energy is the frequency of the vibrations. When you change the vibrations of something, you change its form.

As the vibrations go from pure consciousness, which is the essence of high vibrational level, to lower frequencies, energy is created in our multidimensional universe. Once this energy has been created, the vibrational levels can be further lowered to begin to create matter and mass by storing this energy into atoms and molecules (see "The 'God Particle'—The Higgs Boson" chapter). This is how you create reality with your Observer consciousness.

Similarly, when the slower vibrations of matter are increased, it converts the matter into energy. When the vibrations of energy can be slowed down, it forms into matter. Metaphysicians have claimed this is possible for thousands of years, and now String Theory has allowed us to understand the science.

So now that you're beginning to understand how simple it can be to change the physical three-dimensional world, this is a good time to figure out how many dimensions exist.

The Brane New World— 11-Dimensional Space

"What I thought was unreal now, for me, seems in some ways to be more real than what I think to be real, which seems now to be unreal."
—**Fred Alan Wolf PhD**

In the previous chapter you have learned that String Theory has verified the metaphysical principle of the Vibrational Universe. As scientists and mathematicians analyzed String Theory, they realized there were five mathematically consistent theories explaining String Theory. These five facets, once thought to be competing theories, are actually consistent subsets of vibrating strings in 11-dimensional space.[8] Thus, if the mathematics are correct, it means that our cosmos must consist of eleven dimensions.

Since physicists and mathematicians have concluded that there must be at least 11 dimensions to our universe, they call this the "Membrane Theory," sometimes shortened to "Brane Theory," or abbreviated even more simply to "M-theory." [9]

How important is M-theory? Physicist Michio Kaku has called M-theory the likely ultimate "Theory of Everything," which has eluded theorists, including Einstein, for the last hundred years. Physicist Stephen Hawking said, "M-theory is the *only* candidate for a complete theory of the universe." This shows you the incredible importance this 11-dimensional space discovery has for the future of mankind!

---

[8] For a better understanding of what a dimension is, please go to "Appendix A—What Is a 'Dimension'?"

[9] Supergravity theorists also confirmed our universe must contain at least 11 dimensions, further validating M-Theory.

The New Sciences

Metaphysical Connections

It is not necessary to understand M-theory in order to implement Sacred Quantum Metaphysics, but it is important to recognize the relationship between M-theory and metaphysics.

Metaphysicians have described multiple dimensions for many millennia calling them the Astral Planes, Seven Astral Realms or Seven Levels of Heaven. Now that science and mathematics has verified that there are 11 dimensions, the question becomes, how did ancient metaphysicians discover this before modern science? It is likely that they had access to the metaphysical powers of Inner Knowledge, or they accessed the Akashic Records. If they could access a profound transcendent knowledge base (similar to reports from Nikolai Tesla and Albert Einstein), you can do it also.

You are aware of our three-dimensional world of solids, where each has height, width, and depth. This describes everything you see, touch, and measure in your physical world.

Einstein's continuing genius was understanding what we call "time" is the fourth dimension. Although mathematicians have long predicted the existence of extra dimensions, Albert Einstein made the term commonplace by describing our four dimensions as the Space-Time Continuum.

If you add Einstein's four dimensions of Space-Time Continuum, plus the metaphysical "Seven Astral Realms," described for thousands of years, what do you get? That's right, eleven dimensions—or M-theory! Isn't it nice that science has finally caught up with thousands of years of metaphysical thinking? But we have to ask, where would humanity be today if researchers had paid attention to this ancient wisdom 500 years ago?

Scholars are just beginning to realize how foolish they were to have rejected this wisdom out of hand, with just unproven speculation (materialism) to replace it. The idea that the only important part of our universe is the three-dimensional world, when there are at least eleven dimensions, eight of which are entirely nonmaterial, is completely absurd. Once again you understand how this false science sadly prevented mankind from progressing to its highest potential.

Now you know that this fascinating 11-dimensional universe exists, the question becomes, "Where did matter come from?"

The "God Particle"—The Higgs Boson

". . . scientists believe that science must be . . . based on . . . matter. . . . Quantum physics showed us that we must change that myopic prejudice of scientists, otherwise we cannot comprehend quantum physics. So now we have science within consciousness . . . based on the primacy of consciousness that is gradually replacing the old materialist science."
—Amit Goswami

Scientists realized that there must be some mechanism for converting energy into matter, even though sages and masters have been doing it for thousands of years. Confirmation of the Higgs boson—the "God Particle"—and the associated Higgs field was reported on March 14, 2013 from CERN at an announcement from research completed at the Large Hadron Collider. The particle itself does provide a fascinating glimpse into how our universe really works.

This critical discovery confirmed there must have been something converting the pure energy of the Big Bang (the start of the new universe) into the first atom. This early universe initially contained only energy, so something had to be added before there was any matter. The interaction with the Higgs boson is what allows energy to slow down, acquire mass, and become matter—perhaps allowing space-time. Scientists calculate it took our cosmos 380,000 years—more than a third of one million years—before the Higgs boson allowed the first atom to be created after the Big Bang.

Quantum evidence mandates that the only thing which could be added is consciousness, hence the sensational but inaccurate name "God Particle." Remember, we know from quantum theory that consciousness is the prime source of everything, so it must have been consciousness that transformed this early energy into the first atom.

Could masters and sages have inadvertently tapped into this "God Particle" in order to make the supernatural creation of matter out of nothing, which metaphysicians have mentioned for many millennia? Certainly it is possible.

What gives materialists a huge headache is, "Where did this consciousness come from?" It certainly was not human consciousness, since humans will not be created for another 13.5 billion years. The logical assumption is it might be the infinite Observer consciousness, independent of a human body, which is responsible for this transformation.

Since science has verified that the Higgs boson exists, you can utilize it too. According to the Vibrational Universe, as the frequency of consciousness reaches a certain lower level, energy is formed. Lower the vibrations even more, and energy begins to create matter. This gives Sacred Quantum Metaphysics the framework to use consciousness to create physical matter out of energy—by accessing the Higgs boson.

Since you are beginning to understand how you can create matter out of energy, it is time for you to understand how science is proving that consciousness can make physical changes to your own body.

New Medicine—Healing with the Mind

"Is mind over matter real? The short answer is yes. There been thousands of different experiments conducted over the years, which show this to be the case..."

—**Alexandra Bruce**

For 5,000 years, people were finding solutions to their health problems, healing of disease, injury, or simply painful conditions, using techniques passed down from generation to generation. Those effective procedures were continued and passed on to others, while those not producing successful treatments were discarded in favor of more effectual techniques. These ancient healers witnessed these ancient cures working incredibly well, so there was not much reason for them to go out and find additional cures. You have almost certainly heard the admonition, "If it isn't broken . . . don't fix it."

Then came a time when scientific researchers arbitrarily rejected these proven cures and took medicine into a predominately materialistic direction.[10] For example, effective herbal remedies that were passed down from generation to generation were studied by modern pharmaceutical companies to create modern drugs. They then patented these chemicals, preventing others from duplicating these formally natural cures. Also,

---

[10] Many of these proven healing modalities are still around and some of them are described in "Appendix B—Healing Modalities."

Western medicine fought for years against the introduction of traditional Chinese medical techniques—like acupuncture and acupressure—even though the beneficial results were verified.

Since the widely accepted false belief was that consciousness had little importance and the only significant part of a human was the material body, of course you would eliminate the mind from medicine. What an incredible mistake this was!

Before I get too much farther along, it has to be acknowledged that there are some incredible advances made by studying the natural three-dimensional world—for instance, killing bacteria with antibiotics and discovering viruses. I do not want this discussion to take away from those phenomenal advances, but the whole purpose of this book is to show you what needs to be changed in our society, not to rehash advances. Certainly there have been many advances, but medicine should have integrated these new findings with the very effective cures from the past.

After hundreds of years of Western medicine trying to remove the mind from medicine, recent scientific advances proved it is the essential component of our universe. We now know that the materialistic research only examined an insignificant 4% of the cosmos.

Medicine then began to rely only on the cures verified exclusively by the scientific method. When you think about it, the standard model is a very limiting way to help people stay healthy, because it only looks at 4% of our universe. There were some very effective historical treatments discarded because they weren't easily studied under this new standard, while those which could easily be studied—predominantly surgery and drugs—were examined extensively. Unfortunately, this has led us to the inadequate healthcare system we have today.

Sacred Quantum Metaphysics

Medicine next tried to find the physical causation for everything, including mind and consciousness. When you remove metaphysics from the healing process, it follows that there must be something within the body or environment causing the problems. This led to treatments such as "bloodletting" with leeches (remarkably still in use today) and lobotomies in psychiatry. In 2000, the American Medical Association Journal reported that the third leading cause of death, after heart disease and cancer, is mainstream medicine errors. Not only has our medical community failed to evolve with the new sciences, but they have persistently resisted integrating the new scientific discoveries into medical practices. Now you can see how distorted our healthcare has become.

The Placebo Effect

Science discovered that a certain number of patients are healed simply by their belief that the treatment they receive is effective—called the "placebo effect." These patients are healed even when there is no actual treatment, or if the "medication" administered is an inert sugar pill. The number of people who find relief from their symptoms and/or are cured of their disease from the placebo effect vary widely, but they generally range from 35% to 52%.

Metaphysicians have known for thousands of years that the mind can heal the body, but under a materialistic mindset there has been a concerted effort to exclude these mind-body healings from research. They try to eliminate the influence of the mind, so they can test the effectiveness of their treatments—usually pharmaceuticals or surgeries. By discounting and ignoring this effective mind-body healing, investigators have mostly removed spirituality from medical research.

It would seem far more reasonable to research how one-third to one-half of the patients are curing themselves through this free or low cost mind-body treatment, then scrutinize why the other half to two-thirds of these patients are not responding! This approach would allow all of us to better understand the inner workings of the mind-body connection, and would also allow science to begin to understand more about the 96% of the unseen universe.

Understanding True Medicine

Before science understood the true nature of the universe, we passed laws mandating we must get our treatment from a "practicing doctor" and our medicines from a pharmacist. Then they needed a heavy-handed enforcement arm, using our police and courts, to force conformity to "standard" medical practices. This way, if someone didn't follow the accepted procedures, they can lose their medical license. The advances of science, and the well-being of the patients, needed to take a second place to maintaining the medical community's groupthink—even though we now know it was based on faulty science.

Why is this important? How can the healthcare industry justify charging you a lot of money for treatment when your own mind cured you? In order to get you to ignore these largely pain-free, low cost, no side effect cures, they will do everything possible to convince you that these cures are not real, even when science proves otherwise.

How effective is the medical industry in their attempt to convince you *not* to try alternative treatments? Instead of deciding you will try a pain-free, no side effect, mind-body cure to your problem, most of us will decide to risk taking prescription drugs or let the hospital take a knife and cut us open. If we do not die from these procedures, we might spend weeks in recovery. To mitigate the pain, people often take painkillers, many of which are addictive or have substantial side effects—potentially ruining your life for years to come.

When you view these two alternatives and see how prevalent surgery and pharmaceuticals are in our society, you realize how effective the brainwashing has worked to get most of us to ignore the safe, pain-free, mind-body solutions. I predict in a few decades, when more mind-body techniques are accepted, our children will ask in bewilderment, "You mean they used to take knives and cut people open? And they thought this would cure them? How bizarre!"

Science discovered that it made a huge mistake by completely removing all mind-body treatments from medicine. We don't want to make the same mistake by eliminating all effective Western medicine treatments. We need to scientifically examine which treatment works best in a particular situation.

While Western medicine sometimes did produce cures and relief of symptoms, there are times when this fell very far short:

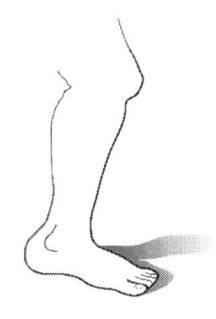

For example, there was a recent study determining the effectiveness of arthritic knee surgery. Three groups of patients were randomly divided. One group had traditional extensive surgery to repair the knee. The second group had a partial surgical treatment. The third group had only a minor incision in the knee but no surgical treatment. All three groups reported the same improvement in knee functioning, equal reduction in pain, and similar overall satisfaction with the results of the "surgery." Obviously, from these examples you realize that what is giving these patients relief from their knee problems is little more than the expectation that what the doctor was doing was effective (the placebo effect).

It would seem logical for medicine to concentrate on curing the huge portion of patients using the mind-body approach, prior to doing anything as radical and intrusive as surgery and/or pharmaceuticals. When more studies like this can be verified, we may look back on our current condition of medical technology as the barbaric era of needless cutting and bloodletting—similar to how we look back at the "science" of lobotomy to cure patients of their mental disorders.

Psychosomatic Excuses

When doctors did not find the causes of a person's illness, they often hid the inadequacy of their treatments by telling the patients that it must be "psychosomatic"—meaning their physical problems were caused entirely by the patient's mind. They refused to study how the mind would help cure their patients—which has been proven in many cases—but they are all too willing to blame the patient's mind when the cause of a condition stumps them. This gives you a glimpse into the contempt materialistic medicine holds toward the mind.

There are documented cases in criminal forensics when a doctor could not find the cause of a person's deteriorating health and it was labeled psychosomatic. After an autopsy was conducted, it was determined to be arsenic poisoning. This is arguably an extreme case, but it shows you how doctors will try to blame the patient when they cannot uncover the cause of the symptoms.

Health Insurance Distortions

One of the most intrusive ways of enforcing materialist control over our healthcare system is through health insurance. Insurers can mandate what is an "approved" treatment and what is not. If you, as an informed and consenting adult, believe an alternative treatment may be more beneficial with less complications, your treatment will not be paid for—even when your doctor agrees! An example will show you how much control they can have over your decisions:

I have a friend who went through a tough time financially and she had to let her health insurance lapse. When she got temporarily sick, instead of finding alternative solutions to her problems, she suffered through the illness. When I told her there were many free or low-cost alternative treatments like Reiki or Healing Touch (see "Appendix B—Healing Modalities"), it was like I was speaking a different language. In her world, you needed to have health insurance, which would then pay a major portion of her medical bills. If you didn't have health insurance, you could not get medical treatment.

I told her that if she tells the doctors she will "self-pay," her doctor might negotiate the price of the office visit, since they didn't have to wait for payment after billing the insurance company. She still would not listen and endured the illness. Luckily it wasn't fatal.

Metaphysical Insights

Since your body reacts positively to the placebo effect, the mind can also create similar negative changes in your body and your health. We have already examined how worry, fear, and resentment can cause immediate negative reactions, so it is important to understand how your thoughts can negatively affect your overall health.

If you have any question at all about how your thoughts can transform objects, I refer you to the book *The Hidden Messages in Water* by Dr. Masaru Emoto. In his research, he proved that when water was blessed by loving, positive messages—or with negative emotions—it changed the crystalline structure, which can be photographed.

When something as crucial as water can be influenced by positive or negative thoughts, it is obvious that your thinking can make physical changes to your body. Now when you consider that the human body is 80% water, what do you think the effects will be on your body over a long period of time of constantly giving yourself negative messages? When you are examining your internal negative chatter, you need to ask yourself, "What is this doing to the 80% of me that is water?" Now you are beginning to understand how important your thoughts are to your health.

The Future of Healthcare

Since modern research is still trying to eliminate any hint of consciousness from medical research, very few studies are being done comparing surgery and pharmaceuticals to the proven effectiveness of mind-body healing. Even though we neglected these free/no-side-effect healings for the last few centuries, it doesn't mean we need to ignore them any longer. As more mind-body studies are performed, we will finally understand the connections between mind-body healing and our new scientific discoveries.

We are starting to understand the new sciences, which totally reject the idea of the body and brain being the only important subject for study. A promising sign is that many medical institutions, especially Health Maintenance Organizations, are including "complementary" treatments such as chiropractic, acupuncture, massage, etc. Unfortunately, unless there is a concerted effort to reevaluate the previous faulty science, medical personnel will believe what they were taught, and then they will teach future generations the same flawed medicine.

You now know how important consciousness is to your health, so you can begin to envision how you can create a much more humane healthcare. You will be instrumental in creating a future where these pain-free, no side-effect healings can occur more often, while surgery and pharmaceuticals are only used in very extreme cases. This is one of those areas in our current society that desperately needs people like you to open up the system, encouraging preventative medicine, rather than reacting to people who get sick.

You are beginning to understand our healthcare system; now you are ready to understand recent scientific research regarding what happens when you almost die.

Over and Back—Near-Death Experiences

"Once you accept your own death, all of a sudden you are free to live."
—Saul Alinsky

Metaphysicians have reported over many thousands of years that when our body is nearing death, our consciousness—the real eternal part—separates from the body, and has some very profound experiences. One of the most compelling pieces of recent scientific research is the verification of these events from people who have had what is now called a "Near-Death Experience" (NDE).

These reports were one of the first scientific confirmations proving consciousness can exist independent of the human body. Remember, one of the basic metaphysical principles is your consciousness never dies. Your body will eventually wear out or get damaged beyond repair, but your consciousness never ceases.

When the dividing line between life and death became so tenuous because of modern medical advances, people returned from conditions that would have killed them 100 years ago. When they returned, they often reported consistent experiences.

The first serious researcher to document Near-Death Experiences was Doctor Raymond Moody in the early 1970s, who wrote the book *Life After Life*. His book documented many people's experiences after they were seriously injured or had "died" during an operation. Before being revived on the operating table—or otherwise becoming reunited with their body again—they reported a very consistent set of experiences during the time their consciousness was separated from their human body

The New Sciences

After Doctor Moody's book, many other researchers have reported similar findings. At the last count there were over two million such reports documented from the past few decades. Now there are many multiple reports from all over the world, which can be compared to each other. These reports proved to be very similar, regardless of the person's religious beliefs or cultural background. This is astounding when you consider the vast differences between cultures and their differing religions.

Typical NDE Experience

Not everyone who has experienced a Near-Death Experience has had all these experiences detailed below, but Near-Death Experiences generally fall into some fairly consistent broad categories:

People are usually aware of their surroundings when they are declared "dead." They typically experience floating above their body entirely pain-free, sometimes looking down and seeing frantic attempts by medical personnel to revive their body. They almost always report an overwhelming feeling of peace and unconditional love surrounding them—something they don't experience while on this earthly realm. On occasion they report a super lucidity (high intelligence with sharp, clear thinking) once they are freed from the inadequate human brain.

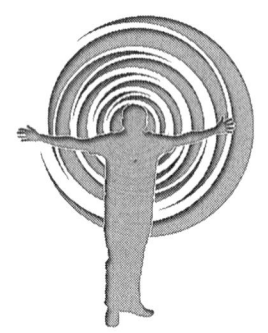

The out-of-body person is able to hear and see everything that's going on, but he/she is unable to communicate with the people still in our three-dimensional realm. Many times the person hears or sees activities far away from their body, even hearing conversations of medical personnel or living loved ones in other rooms. People who have been blind since birth can suddenly see perfectly.

Sometimes relatives who had previously died will appear to greet them and make them less afraid. They usually notice that they can travel in ways impossible to do with a physical body; for instance, going through ceilings and walls.

Most often they will see a tunnel of light drawing them to it, and then into it. At the end of the tunnel they encounter a loving "City of Light" or a "Crystal City," full of love, compassion, and acceptance (see "Beyond the Veil—The Astral Planes" chapter). The most common description for this place is they have gone "home." They frequently realize that the spiritual realm is the natural place for the spirit to be, while our three-dimensional earthly realm is the dreary aberration.

If the experience lasts long enough, people encounter what they call a "Being of Light." Depending on the person's beliefs and culture, they might call this entity Jesus, Moses, Allah, Krishna, or other spiritual names. This Being seems to know each person intimately, and each person comes away from this encounter knowing they are loved completely and unconditionally. People who have attempted suicide come away from this encounter filled with sadness for their actions, but are also certain of how deeply they are loved spiritually.

The out-of-body people might ask this Light Being questions and they will receive answers telepathically. They say these answers are the only answers possible, given their now-complete understanding of reality. Frequently, the person's response is, "Of course"—hinting that they already knew the answer, but had forgotten it during their human incarnation.

If the Near-Death Experience continues, this Being will show them a love-based, holographic life-review of the important events in the person's life. Not only does this person re-experience the events, they also report they receive the details of reactions from the other people impacted during those events and how it affected them. This review is not for the purposes of condemnation, but rather a loving support for any mistakes that were made.

Eventually this out-of-body person is given the choice to go back—and suffer the ramifications of the injury or surgery, or they can choose to stay in the Spiritual Realm. Others are told, "It is not your time," and they are instructed to return. Obviously, anyone who is being interviewed has returned from the Spiritual Realm. Once the decision is made, they are immediately snapped back into their human body, instantaneously feeling pain or other bodily sensations.

Someone who was told it wasn't their time is frequently resentful for having to be back in their human body. Some become bitter for having to leave this beautiful, unconditionally loving place.

Sacred Quantum Metaphysics

The experience is often a life-changing event for this person. He/she will usually have a renewed sense of purpose and direction and rarely fears death. Sometimes they become internally spiritual, even when they were devoutly religious, agnostic, or atheistic prior to this. They know without a doubt there is "life after death" and there is an incredibly loving place that they will go to after their body dies.

NDE Deniers Futile Arguments

One way deniers discount Near-Death Experiences is to assert that after Doctor Moody's book came out, it skewed the future reports of Near-Death Experiences, and this is why they are so amazingly consistent across the world. This is absurd, because there have been very similar reports like this for thousands of years. Plato reported a very similar account from a man who woke up on a funeral pyre, just before his body was to be burned. Another account was found in the obscure early Christian Gnostic scrolls from Nag Hammadi. It is absurd to think all the people who Doctor Moody first interviewed had somehow read Plato's account or had been influenced by the Gnostic scrolls.

Another way Near-Death Experiences are dismissed is to say these are simply hallucinations from a brain losing oxygen. If this were the case, the reports from these people would be as bizarre and irrational as dreams normally are for any two of us. Do you know any other person, much less thousands of people all over the world, who have the exact same dream you have? The fact that Near-Death Experiences do not vary wildly is one great piece of evidence tending to confirm that people who report Near-Death Experiences are witnessing something very profound and real.

Some skeptics shut their minds to Near-Death Experience evidence, supposing they are simply creations from the person's wishful thinking. If this were the case, these reports would be geographically and culturally influenced by what people would expect to see when they were facing death. For example, in Western cultures, we should see many reports of Pearly Gates, streets of gold, and St. Peter at the gate, but we do not.

Since Near-Death Experiences actually contradict what people were taught in their cultures, this is evidence that there is some common experience happening among them. For example, why would people across the world come up with a description of a holographic life-review from their wishful thinking? Again, this is entirely absurd. You would assume an atheist would come back into their body with no spiritual experience whatsoever—but they report the same experiences as agnostics and devoutly religious people! None of these groups experience anything close to what they thought would happen, which further validates these experiences as being real.

Perchance you heard that when a certain spot of the brain is stimulated, the person experiences something similar to a Near-Death Experience. Just because there is something similar, does not mean it negates the reality of what these people are reporting. This may simply be the mechanism whereby the true consciousness is released out of the "prison" of the human body during a Near-Death Experience.

There are many reports from people who show no brainwave activity, but they are aware of—and remember—conversations and activities going on around them. None of the doubters who believe that we are simply a material brain have ever been able to explain how thousands of people can recall events when there are no brainwaves to record them. The skeptics just ignore this evidence. The obvious conclusion is that awareness and consciousness exist independent of the body and brain.

A case in point is the very thorough work done by Eban Alexander, neurosurgeon and neuroscientist, who for fifteen years was a highly-respected associate professor teaching neurosurgery at Harvard Medical School. In his book *Proof of Heaven*, during a near fatal episode with meningitis, he had a very profound and extensive Near-Death Experience.

During Eban's NDE, he returned with many wondrous insights. He received these experiences during a time when he proved (by his medical charts) that he had no brainwave activity whatsoever. Doctor Alexander's own doctor concurs that there was not any conscious brain activity or hallucinations generated from the brain, because there were literally no electrical impulses being generated in that portion of the brain.

He is one of the few scientists to have such a profound Near-Death Experience, who is able to read his own medical charts, and prove irrefutably there was no consciousness generated from the material human brain during this time. He counters all the arguments that the deniers attempt to use to explain away NDEs in Appendix B of *Proof of Heaven*. I highly recommend his point-by-point proofs, especially when you encounter someone who is adamant that NDEs are not real.

Verifying Metaphysics

Now let us examine this NDE science and compare it to the different aspects of metaphysics, which you studied earlier. Maybe you've heard that when you're drowning, your "whole life passes before your eyes"? Obviously, the person who is reporting this did not actually die, so the origin of this report is most likely related to a typical NDE "life-review."

Why would somebody, in his or her life-review, need to experience how the other person felt? Since our main spiritual purpose is to love and learn from our experiences, it would be entirely consistent with Karma to understand what the other person sensed during our actions. Do you think it would be "wishful thinking" to want to experience another person's emotions? Not likely.

This research confirms the metaphysical principles of out-of-body awareness and reincarnation. NDEs prove that your consciousness can exist while out-of-body. Wouldn't it then be possible for your consciousness to exist long after your body dies? It would certainly be possible for your Essence Mind to inhabit another human body in the future.

The NDE reports of a spiritual place of unconditional love, existing outside of our three-dimensional world, fit perfectly with the metaphysical concept of different dimensions or astral planes. Can it be that sages have been able to access these extra dimensions, then report the details to their fellow spiritual seekers when they returned—calling it Heaven, Nirvana, or Paradise? Certainly it is possible, because many modern people who have had NDEs are significantly transformed spiritually.

Conceivably, early metaphysical masters were one of the lucky ones to have a spontaneous NDE and then returned to teach others about their experiences. Is it plausible that someone who fasts for forty days and forty nights might get close to death, have a Near-Death Experience, and bring back some profound insights about the true nature of spirituality?

Metaphysicians have told us that once we can be released from the dense human body, our vibrations increase so that we can travel to these higher Astral dimensions. This explains how consciousness can travel around and observe our earthly world during a Near-Death Experience, but cannot be seen or heard by those still confined in a human body.

Another interesting interrelationship with these reports and the new sciences is that when people do return from a Near-Death Experience, they often express, "Time does not exist there." Remembering Einstein's Space-Time Continuum, where the fourth dimension is time, you realize that if time does not exist there, it must be outside of our normal three-dimensional perceptions—in the fourth dimension or higher.

Sacred Quantum Metaphysics

These are just a few of the similarities between what spiritual sages and masters have reported, and what is now being verified by Near-Death and scientific research. Hold on tight, because this is only the start!

Now that you have begun to open the fascinating Pandora's Box of science verifying metaphysical principles, it is important that you understand an easy way to empower your consciousness.

Altered States of Consciousness

"During periods of relaxation after concentrated intellectual activity, the intuitive mind seems to take over and can produce the sudden clarifying insights, which gives so much joy and delight."
—Fritjof Capra, Physicist

Over many millennia, mankind has stumbled upon effective ways of changing the world. As those successes were duplicated, more people started using these techniques and eventually began enhancing them. Unfortunately, most of this knowledge was previously restricted to the disciples of some very secretive wisdom traditions. When these techniques used to alter physical reality were carefully examined, the common component was that they were almost always accomplished in an altered state of consciousness.

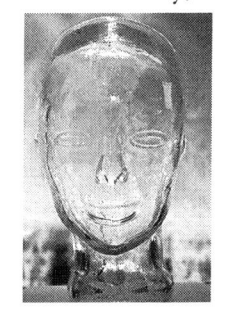

What is an "altered state of consciousness"? The simple definition: An altered state of consciousness is an alternative awareness that is different from your normal awakened state of thinking. What does normal, awake thinking mean? When you pay attention to your thoughts, you will see there is an incessant stream of thinking, consuming almost most of your waking hours. Some people call it "chatter"—meditation traditions call it the "monkey mind." An altered state might be daydreaming, watching a movie, reading a novel, meditating, visualizing, lost in thought, chanting, praying, affirmations, or formal trances (many of these are illuminated below).

Chatter is something so common and normal that most people don't notice it unless they start looking for it. In an earlier chapter on meditation, you were given some techniques to quell the chatter down, at least for a few minutes. You can also quell it by putting yourself into a formal trance.

Since altered states have been around for thousands of years, why are they included in this New Sciences section? Since previously accepted false science believed that consciousness was the meaningless side effect of the human brain, researchers tried to exclude anything related to consciousness, including altered states. It was only recently that human mindfulness was openly studied by science and academia, so that people like yourself can utilize them quickly and easily.

Understanding Your Ego

Your normal state of consciousness is called the "ego." It is what separates "you" from the rest of the world, and all other human beings. Whenever you use the words I, me, my, we, our, etc., you have just separated yourself from other people and the rest of the world. When you are consumed by your ego, you are thinking about how you are different from other people, not how you are connected to them.

Anything that is temporary and changeable, like profession, status, emotion, relationship, etc., is part of the ego. Your ego obsesses over something that has happened in the past, and worries about the future—neither of which you can change today. The ego is concerned with animal instincts, material wants, physical needs, and our base emotions like anger, fear, and hate. This is why spiritual traditions work to dampen down the ego.

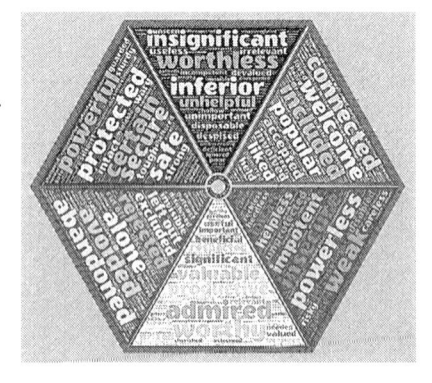

This is not to say that the ego is necessarily bad. In our modern world we need to separate ourselves from those around us. The ego is what keeps track of the possessions that we need to survive on this planet. It is the ego that plans for the future and prepares for the worst.

If I, we, me, etc., is the ego, what else is there? As you learned earlier, there is your true consciousness—the Observer or Essence Mind—which always has existed and always will exist. One of the easiest ways to enter an alternative awareness is to "observe" your ego. When you watch your ego, instead of having your ego control your thinking, you have just accessed your Observer.

The ego can be understood as the thoughts coming from your true consciousness, which are filtered down through your inadequate human brain. This filtered, distorted thinking, which includes chatter, is called the "mind." An alternative awareness is how your ego's chatter is dampened down, and exactly how you can access your true awareness (Essence Mind).

Using Affirmations

A simple way to dampen down your chatter, and produce an altered state, is by using affirmations. What is an affirmation? It is a positive thought or statement intended to manifest changes to yourself or the world around you. Remember, quantum and other scientific truths prove that consciousness is what changes the three-dimensional world at subatomic levels. Affirmations are one way to use these scientific realities to create alterations.

Combining the Law of Attraction and Power of Positive Thinking, people have found that they are able to alter reality by consistently repeating affirmations. Some people advise that an affirmation only has to be presented once and then it becomes a reality. Modern neuroscience has found that we need to repeat an affirmation over and over until the newly created neurons become reinforced, and thus become established. Small changes are instantaneous, and larger transformations become evident after affirmations are repeated consistently enough.

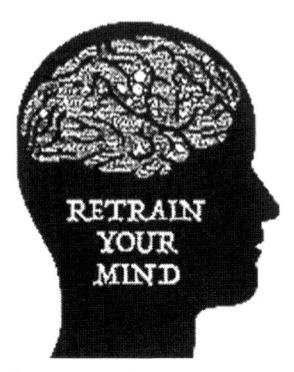

The science of neuroplasticity shows that when you think new thoughts, your brain creates new neural-pathways. It takes about three days for a new pathway to become established in your brain. A single affirmation will create a new pathway, but it will be weak. In order to strengthen this connection, the neuron needs to be reinforced by thinking similar thoughts over and over again. This is why affirmations should be repeated.

There is another problem with a one-time affirmation: we then go on to the next affirmation, and then the next, and the next. What this does is distract our consciousness from concentrating the full power of the Observer for a long enough time to make the physical change we desire.

When using affirmations, metaphysicians say to always keep them positive. Always state what you want; never what you don't want. Research shows that subconscious mind functions by creating mental images. It cannot create a mental picture of a negative.

For example, if you say, "I don't want to lose my job," your subconscious mind cannot visualize "don't," so it only creates the mental image of, "I . . . want to lose my job." As you can imagine, this is a very bad affirmation when you have a family who is counting on your income! A better affirmation would be to say, "I am valuable at work, and they reward me generously for the good work I do." Same idea, it is just a different form, which your subconscious is able to visualize.

Similarly, you should never say, "I don't want a divorce." Your subconscious mind only hears, "I . . . want a divorce." A better affirmation would be, "I love my spouse, and my spouse loves me." The outcome will be the result you want, but this time you will create the reality you actually desire.

It is important to understand the difference between the subconscious mind not being able to create a negative, and the conscious mind giving yourself negative messages. For example, if your conscious mind is telling you that you "can't" do something, you will find a way *not* to do it. You might procrastinate until it is too late, or your self-confidence will be so low you won't attempt it at all. Either way it is your conscious mind undermining your efforts.

Since you know the power of positive thinking works, you should realize the power of negative thinking also creates negative results. Find a way to dampen or eliminate your negative thinking, before you create a future that you do not want. A real-life example will make it a little clearer:

When my kids were little, I would take them skiing. Before I explained the danger, as we were riding up the chairlift, my kids would sometimes yell at a skier traveling down the slopes saying, "Don't fall!" They thought it was funny when the skier would look up and immediately fall down in the snow. The poor skier's unconscious mind would only hear the word "fall," and never the word "don't," which meant the person's subconscious mind would picture a fall, and almost always go down.

There is another good side to this forming of new neural pathways in your brain: we can similarly remove negative, counterproductive thinking permanently. When we stop thinking degrading or self-limiting thoughts, those established neural pathways eventually atrophy, and are ultimately replaced by productive and self-empowering conduits. You are literally rewiring your brain, either positively or negatively, every moment you are awake—so make sure you are consciously making it the best it can possibly become.

The New Sciences

Personal Technique

Some of you have asked how I use affirmations. I hesitate to describe this because I don't want you to think this is the best way to do it. Please just use this as an example, and find whatever method works best for you.

When I'm grasping for something to focus my mind on during meditation, I will adapt Ben Franklin's ditty, repeating, "I am happy, healthy, wealthy and wise." As I breathe, I will pull air in, saying to myself, "I am happy." As I exhale, I will push away anything interfering with my happiness: anxiety, anger, sadness, fear, etc.

On the next breath, I will pull air into my lungs with my thought, "I am healthy." Then as I exhale, I will push away any pain, distress, stress, disease, or condition interfering with my best possible health.

When I next inhale, I will say to myself, "I am wealthy." As I exhale, I will push away anything hindering the Law of Attraction: desperation, lack, doubt, etc.

Finally, on my next inhale, I will say to myself, "I am wise." Then when I exhale, I push away anything impeding wisdom: ignorance, close-mindedness, judgment, etc.

I repeat the process until something more important seems to focus my consciousness away—maybe a specific health problem that I want to be healed or cured of. Then I would concentrate on the "I am healthy" part, as I breathe in health, and exhale away whatever disease or injury I need removed.

It ultimately makes the meditation time to be over exceedingly quickly. I can guarantee you it does make physical transformations, if repeated consistently enough.

Visualization

By using your imagination to envision a mental picture of something you would like to enhance in your life, you can make it happen. As you just learned in the affirmations discussion above, the subconscious mind creates images from the words that you repeat to it. Obviously, it would be much simpler to create the images directly by your imagination, instead of using verbiage, which may get misinterpreted. This is why Visualization is such a powerful technique.

Suppose you would like to add something into your world, for example, a partner to share your life with. You can envision it as a common, normal part of your everyday lifetime. When you create this mental image, with enough detail and often enough, it sets quantum consciousness and the Law of Attraction into action to create it.

When you are visualizing, it is important to be in a relaxed state of mindfulness, presumably from the position of the Observer. It is always much more effective when it is done from the spiritual/Essence Mind part, rather than from the ego. As mentioned earlier, it is hard, if not impossible, for you to change the world from the position of your needy ego. Once you cross over from an alternative awareness into ego thinking, the process generally shuts down—unless you are very skilled at this practice.

Einstein used visualization to get insights into true reality. He called his visualizations "thought experiments." He told reporters that he gained his understanding of relativity by visualizing what he would be experiencing when he would ride on a light beam across the universe.

Top athletes often use visualization by picturing an upcoming race or event, including as much detail as possible. The body responds to this visualization by preparing the athlete for the actual competition. Studies with CAT scans or PET scans show the same areas of the brain light up from either visualization or from the actual physical activity. This scientific discovery shows mental visualization is as beneficial as physical training—and may be even better, because visualization does not cause injury and conserves the athlete's energy.

There is the common caveat when visualizing: "Be careful what you visualize, because you may well create it." The best way to predict the future is to create it, so you can visualize something beyond your capacity to handle it. Many people who win the lottery wish that they had torn up the ticket knowing what they know today about how their life has changed! When you're going to visualize something, be sure that it is something you really want, and that it is spiritually good for you.

Never visualize someone else getting harmed. This is obviously not the way to transform the world into a better place. Visualizing harm has to be made from an ego, instinct-driven consciousness, and usually terminates your mindful state. This ego-driven consciousness is incompatible with the altered state of the Observer, which is needed to actually change reality.

Prayer

I know some people will see the title of this sub-chapter and cringe. Many people shy away from the word "prayer" because it has been so consistently connected with organized religion. It is critical to separate the principle of prayer from the different religious traditions that promote it. Prayer is just a thought conversation with a spiritual higher power or your higher self.

For thousands of years, people have recommended the power of prayer. If there was no benefit to this practice, don't you think it would have faded away in the last 10,000 years or so? Then again, if there was some truth behind the power of prayer, don't you think it would be studied and verified scientifically by now? There has been recent scientific research verifying the effectiveness of prayer—but I bet you haven't heard about it!

Sacred Quantum Metaphysics

Dr. Daniel J. Benor reviewed 131 controlled scientific trials with 56 of these verifying the efficacy of prayer—even upon things as simple as common bacteria. More recently, Dr. Mitchell Krucott at Duke University analyzed recent research to determine whether prayer worked or not. He concluded, "All of these studies, all the reports, are remarkably consistent in suggesting the potential measurable health benefit associated with prayer or spiritual interventions."

There is an old saying, "Prayer is when you talk to your Higher Power; Meditation is when you listen." Since prayer is carrying on a conversation with your higher self or higher power, then it is always good to meditate so that you can "listen" for any response you may need to comprehend.

It is apparent that when you are in prayer, by definition you are in an alternative awareness. When you are praying, you are communing with something beyond yourself and outside your current materialistic world. Could it be that you are tapping into the 96% of the unseen universe, which cannot be seen, touched, or measured? Someday we will know exactly how prayer works, but until then we clearly know it *does* work.

What does it mean to have an "answered prayer"? There are two parts. The first part is, you must ask for what you want. You cannot have an answered prayer if you are not asking for something specific. Before you can ask for something, you need to be clear about what you want. The other part is you must believe it will work, and this is one reason for presenting Dr. Larry Dossey's research. You must believe it will work, before it will work.

There is a common misconception around prayer that says changes can be made in another person without their knowledge or consent. People say, "I will pray for him or her." As you now know from the chapter on Free Will, nothing spiritually can be done by force—only by permission. When a person doesn't want to change, prayer is not going to convert him or her into a mindless robot. Obviously, you can always use the power of prayer to make changes within yourself, because you are obviously giving yourself permission to change.

There is another important part of this. Some people say that we should pray for those who hate us or want to do us harm, for instance: terrorists. The problem with this is that prayer cannot change another person who does not want to be changed. Metaphysicians tell us that when we send energy, including prayer, to a non-spiritual, hateful individual, we will just be empowering this person's hate—making it stronger. The more productive action would be to send this love and compassion to any high vibrational individual close to this hateful person, conceivably a relief worker. This will empower the spiritual people, who then counter the terrorist's negativity, without empowering the negative person.

Dreaming as an Altered State

What exactly is a dream? Metaphysicians believe all of us are higher dimensional spiritual beings, temporarily inhabiting a three-dimensional body and brain. It would be absolute torture for a high-vibrational spirit to be trapped within a human body for a few weeks, much less a lifetime, without any ability to escape from time to time.

In order for us to cope with the intense loneliness we experience being away from the spiritual realm, we must release our spirit from the sluggish, low vibrational human body and brain and return to our true spiritual essence periodically. This is what happens when you *dream*. When you dream, you are definitely away from your ego, and this is one definition of an altered state of consciousness.

In a dream, you get out of your body and travel to the higher planes of existence, deeper dimensions, or Astral Planes. Metaphysicians tell us that anything you think of in these higher dimensions is instantly created by your consciousness into a temporary physical form. This explains how you can carry on a conversation with dead people, perceive dinosaurs near your childhood home, or why you can be attacked and then have no injuries when you wake up. These physical forms instantly dematerialize when your true consciousness thinks of something else.

Science previously disregarded how important dreams were to human beings. Then research showed that when someone is not allowed to dream for an extended period of time—allowed to sleep but constantly awakened when dreaming occurs—they experience vivid waking hallucinations.

Some people believe a dream is just a random firing of neurons, creating irrational hallucinations, while sleeping. History is full of reports of people who have been able to attain unbelievable insight and wisdom while dreaming, like the scientist who received the details of the double helix DNA molecule in a dream. There are stories of exceptional individuals throughout history who interpreted and gave meaning to other people's dreams. Obviously, taken as a whole, there must be some mechanism within a dream that has some significance.

The New Sciences

Becoming "One" With Your Activity

Do you remember a time when you became so absorbed in what you were doing that you "tuned out" the rest of the world? It might have happened while you were in deep contemplation, creating art, reading a book, listening to music, gardening, or even watching TV. You have likely experienced this ecstasy at one time or another, if you are lucky. Many people call this "getting into the zone."

This is different from most relaxed states because you are actively engaged in your waking activity. Many of us think an alternative awareness is something when you almost become unconscious. This is far from true, particularly when you consider affirmations, visualization, and becoming so absorbed in your activity you tune out the world. The true commonality in any alternative awareness is that you are away from your ego-driven thoughts.

Remember the earlier discussion about "Happiness is impossible except in the here and now." When you are so concerned about resentments, regrets, anger, memories, etc., of the past, you lose contact with being one with your activity—being in the moment. Similarly, you cannot be distracted with worry, to-do lists, doubts, planning, fears, expectations, or preparations and be able to experience the elation of tuning out the world for a few moments. When you exclude the past or the future from your thoughts, and just enjoy being in the here and now, you will find contentment in any activity.

Research (including neuroplasticity) confirms that the more you practice tuning out all your distractions, the more your mind allows it in the future. The more you practice it, the easier it becomes. If you pay attention, this is your Observer experiencing the ecstasy and joy of tuning out the world, by becoming absorbed in your experience. It is this blissful state that any of us can find—when you allow yourself to "observe" it.

Multiple-Person Altered States

Ascended Masters were able to focus the conscious mind to make alterations to the physical world. This is the result of spending decades perfecting control over their spiritual and mental facilities. For those of us who have not perfected this skill, we can do the same when two people work together to accomplish the same results. This is called a multiple-person altered state of consciousness.

If you don't want to spend decades learning to focus your mind to be able to change reality, the two-person altered state is an easy shortcut for you to reach the same miraculous results. What is the difference between a single person and a multiple-person alternative state of awareness? Meditation is a perfect example of a single person's alternative awareness—it is something you can do while you are alone. Hypnosis is the perfect example of a multiple-person altered state; one person guides the experience while the other person maintains the altered state (see the following chapter).

All of you can now enter any number of altered states and be in the moment and joyful. It is even better when you're able to access your Observer and watch yourself being serene. It is here where the incredible power of altering the world is manifested. Next you need to understand how to focus an altered state.

Mesmerizing Possibilities— Hypnotic Journeys

". . . hypnosis allows us to . . . consciously enter the subconscious realm. . . . You are able to do this, because you regularly move through four states of brain activity every day."
—**Joe Dispenza, D. C.**

For over 100 years, people have been using trance states to provide instantaneous physical healing, as well as an instant relief of a person's emotional difficulties. Every aspect of being a human has been shown to be improved or easily transformed by hypnosis.

Hypnotic trances have been proven effective for non-pharmaceutical, non-allergenic pain relief, like childbirth. Hypnosis is also effective in ending addictions, removing anxiety and depression, treating insomnia, emotional healing, improving memory, smoking cessation, drug-free weight control, to name just a few important uses. The magical part is that when you have made changes through an altered state of consciousness, they become permanent, without intrusive drugs or surgery.[11]

While the very powerful process of hypnosis was discovered prior to Einstein, it was only recently that the full power of this fabulous tool was researched. The incredible potential has really only been perfected within the last forty years or so. The next few chapters will explain to you the most significant insights.

---

[11] There are two quality organizations who can refer people for hypnotherapy training or to qualified therapists: the National Association of Transpersonal Hypnotherapists and the National Guild of Hypnotists.

Why It Works

The essence of hypnosis is an altered state of consciousness, where your normal ego awareness is temporarily put aside. It is then that the hypnotist can focus your attention on allowing instant emotional or physical improvements, spiritual insights, enlightenment, or even profound access to the spiritual realms.

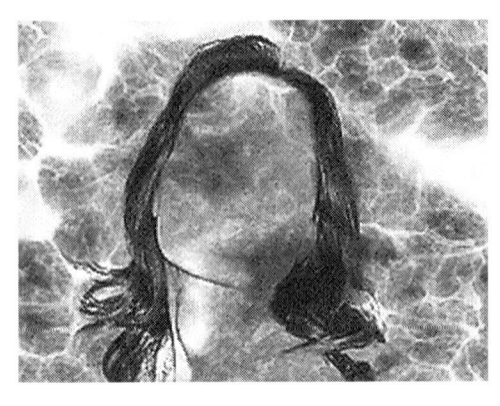

Hypnosis is nothing like what you see in the movies or on stage. It is simply a very relaxed state. People go into a similar relaxed state many times during the day, especially when watching a movie or reading a novel. It is important to note that you don't do anything specific to enter this alternative awareness; it just happens naturally.

Another perfect example is when you are driving a car along a route you travel frequently, like to work and home. After doing this many times, you will find yourself pulling into the driveway, and you don't remember the last three or four miles. You realize your mind is allowing you to daydream or concentrate on something more important, while another part of your brain watches out for the traffic lights, turn signals, brake lights ahead, etc. If there is anything demanding your immediate attention, such as an erratic driver, you are instantly brought back to your conscious awareness, ready to swerve or slam on the brakes. You don't consciously enter or exit this form of hypnosis; it just happens spontaneously.

Understanding the Mind

In order to understand why altered states are so effective, it is important to understand the differences between the conscious, subconscious, unconscious, and Observer parts of your mind:

The **conscious** is the part of the mind that is aware, analytical, and decisive. You have some control over your thoughts, but obviously not 100%, as you learned from the meditation chapter. You can never completely control the incessant chatter interrupting your thoughts, but you can temporarily direct your thinking.

There is another part of your brain that you do not consciously control, called the **unconscious**. It controls your pain awareness, heart rate, hormones, etc., completely outside your normal everyday awareness. Almost everything your body does to keep itself alive, including reflexes, regulating temperature, and fighting infections, even while you are sleeping, is controlled unconsciously. As you learned in previous chapters, this does not mean your mind cannot influence these activities, but they function perfectly well without any conscious thought.

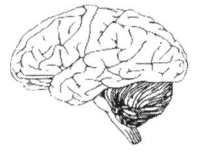

Psychotherapists say there is another part of the mind called the **subconscious**. This controls our attitudes, desires, preferences, emotions, feelings, opinions, attachments, etc. Many people believe our "chatter," which constantly interrupts our conscious thoughts, comes from the subconscious part of our mind. If you remember the discussion on Karma, the subconscious mind is where you make the decisions based on what is good for you as a spirit, not necessarily what is best for you as a human being.

Our important Karmic lessons are revealed and experienced from our desires. These are considered subconscious motivations. You may intellectually realize you have the capacity to make different choices, but you "choose" not to. This is why the subconscious thoughts of self-criticism, fearfulness, dread, anxiety, etc., can be so insidious, because they happen outside your conscious awareness. The good news is you can learn to counteract those negative thoughts using altered states.

There is a fourth level of consciousness, verified by quantum experiments, which is so new that most psychological textbooks don't even mention it, called the Essence-Mind or Observer. This is the true consciousness that is able to observe the other three forms of consciousness. Simply perceiving the other three forms of the mind allows you to access the Observer—as you begin to watch for their influences.

Any alternative awareness circumvents the ego by allowing access to parts of the mind outside of a person's conscious awareness, including the subconscious and unconscious mind.

Metaphysical Insights

More recently, hypnosis has been found to be one of the most effective ways of uncovering spiritual insights. What exactly does this incredibly effective technique do for you? Here are some examples:

Hypnosis is one of the easiest ways to directly access the Akashic Records. This is where you can access everything that has ever happened to you. Anything you would like to understand about yourself is recorded in the Akashic Records.

When you desire to understand some of your past-life influences, hypnosis is likely the best way to open up these memories. You have already been exposed to the science proving consciousness survives the death of the human body, so these memories are easily available.

Since you can access conversations that happened while you were a baby (example given in a previous chapter), what else would you be able to access? Early childhood memories, traumas, etc., may be important for some people. Other people feel inexplicably drawn to certain people or cultures, and they want to understand if there are any karmic influences at play. Everything can be remembered here, when it becomes important to you.

These are just a few of the metaphysical insights that can be made through hypnosis, but you should also remember that any altered state can make physical changes to your three-dimensional world.

Two-Person Altered State

Study after study has shown a two-person altered state of consciousness, like hypnosis, helps people make positive changes in their behavior and their attitudes. The person to be healed is put into an alternative consciousness (trance) while the mindfulness of the hypnotist is directing the actual transformations. One person can maintain a relaxed state, accessing the Observer, while the second person uses their conscious mind to guide the first person toward the desired goals.

This is not to imply that hypnosis is the only suitable avenue to provide the benefits of two-person transformations. In the medical field, the doctor is influencing the patient's passive mind, explaining the instant, non-intrusive healing called the placebo effect. Look at the different alternative and energetic healings including Reiki, Healing Touch, acupuncture, faith healing, etc., to see similar, multiple-person transformations. [12]

Science has allowed us to understand how several people working together can magnify the ability to make transformations, quickly and easily. Remember, Quantum Entanglement shows how two different people can connect to each other's brains. This shows that when two or more people are working together, the power is magnified.

Quantum science has provided a viable explanation how you can make permanent changes to the world. This works because an alternative awareness allows direct access to the unconscious and subconscious mind. The Essence Mind is what creates the immediate and lasting healing.

Society's Resistance

Why haven't hypnosis and other altered states of consciousness become more accepted in our modern society? The beauty of hypnosis is a person can find instantaneous relief from physical or emotional problems, almost always without any negative side effects whatsoever. The cost for these treatments is usually hundreds of times less than more intrusive surgeries, pharmaceuticals, etc. Since the cost is so much less, and there are no major side effects, you would think this would be the preferred therapeutic treatment. A quick story will give you some insights:

---

[12] See "Appendix B—Healing Modalities."

Sacred Quantum Metaphysics

When I was building my practice, I went to a medical office building to rent some office space. Before I got the paperwork signed, the word got out that a hypnotherapist might be renting an office in the building. The traditional medical practices were in an uproar because a mind-body therapist was going to be in the same building. Why?

The doctors did not want their patients to get the idea that there was an easier, cheaper, and more effective alternative to what they were providing. This example shows how a powerful special interest keeps information about effective mind-body healing modalities away from your awareness.

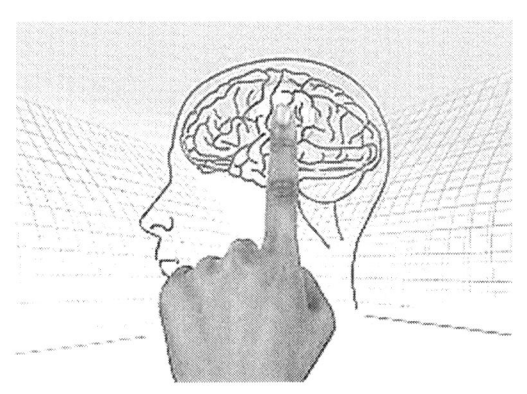

Sometimes the best indicator for an altered state is when there is a physical symptom, but the doctors have no clue what is causing it. It is prudent to eliminate any purely physical causes for a condition first, before alternative solutions are tried. The tragedy occurs when people automatically follow recommendations for an intrusive surgical procedure or a lifetime of pharmaceuticals without a second opinion.

What is especially sad is when patients are told that there are no solutions to their condition, when in fact there are often many alternative treatments available—costing far less and having little or no side effects.

So now you've been exposed to a very powerful altered state of consciousness called hypnosis. Next you need to understand how our recent scientific advances have uncovered evidence of reincarnation.

Trips Down Memory Lane— Past-Life Evidence

"I have witnessed incredible healing, as patients get rid of both emotional and physical symptoms after they recall the past-life roots of their illnesses."
—**Brian L. Weiss, M. D. Afterword,** *Many Lives, Many Masters*

The next important piece of research to be discovered was the very extensive examination of what is now called "Past-life Recall." Reports of people remembering previous lifetimes have been chronicled for thousands of years, but it was only in the last 50 years or so that we have had sufficient numbers to document and scrutinize these reports. We also needed the mass media's ability to disseminate this information widely enough to allow investigators all over the world to compare notes.

People often ask, "If past lives are real, why don't we recall them?" Many children under about eight years old do remember their past lifetimes. Unfortunately, parents will often ridicule the child and make them feel stupid when they mention a previous life. Over and over, people report remembering a previous existence, either spontaneously or through altered states of consciousness.

Access to past-life memories is especially difficult from your ego consciousness, because you only have your inefficient human brain to filter the information into your awareness. It would be impossible for your inadequate brain to readily access 100% of the memories that you have had since the day you were born, much less all your experiences in multiple past lifetimes. This is why an alternative awareness is the perfect avenue for uncovering this information. Unless these memories are recovered through an altered state of consciousness, they will remain stored away in the Akashic Records.

Serious researchers began taking a hard look at whether they could prove or disprove these reports. Let me just give you one example of a very thorough university study:

> Dr. Ian Stevenson of the University of Virginia documented reports collected from 5,000 children from all over the world for over 30 years in at least 20 countries. These children reported remembering a previous lifetime. In order to prove or disprove these reports, the researchers recorded all the remembered details and then went through census and other archives, which verified many facts these children had reported.

These children were able to recount accurate, intimate details of another person's historical lifetime. Scientists will never say definitively that past-lives do exist, but they can say a previous lifetime was the most logical explanation for why these children had specific details of someone else's history.

The events that are most easily remembered are the ones carrying the most important significance or have been reinforced over time. If it is something that you have remembered periodically, due to its emotional impact—regret, resentment, shame, etc.—it will be readily available to your memory. This illustration will demonstrate the process:

Suppose that on your sixth birthday you got a pony, which you were desperately wanting. Every time you see a pony, you recall getting your own pony. You will be able to access this memory, as long as you keep reinforcing it, by recalling it from time to time.

On the other hand, if you had an uneventful sixth birthday, you will not remember it consciously, because you did not have this memory reinforced periodically over the years. As you know from the discussion of the Akashic Records, every detail is still recorded there. If you want to go back and recall your uneventful sixth birthday, you can certainly do so.

Dr. Joe Dispenza describes this process perfectly in his book *You Are the Placebo*:

"Therefore, if we repeat what we learn enough times, we strengthen communities of neurons to support us in remembering it the next time. If we don't, then the synaptic connections soon disappear and the memory is erased. This is why it's important for us to continually update, review, and remember our new thoughts, choices, behaviors, habits, beliefs and experiences if we want them to solidify in our brains."[13]

For therapists and other healers, when a client remembers a previous lifetime it often allows instantaneous healing of the client's problems. If there were nothing at all to these past-life experiences, how is it possible that these people will find instantaneous healing for their problems? Obviously, if these memories were not real, or were not otherwise meaningful, there would be no significant healing taking place. Certainly since the healing is instantaneous and beneficial, Past-life Recall must be taken very seriously for anyone interested in alleviating human problems.

---

[13] Page 58

The New Sciences

Past-life Examples

Some people will have a suspicion that they are being influenced by a previous lifetime, but they are unable to access enough details to fully understand it or to avoid the negative consequences. Let me give you a detailed example, because I know this is foreign information to many people:

> A client experienced what doctors described as symptoms similar to epileptic convulsions. Doctors could not find any physical cause for the seizures, so they referred her to me. She wanted to find the true cause of her symptoms, so we decided to access the Akashic Records to find the "source" of her convulsions.
>
> When we go to the "source," it might reveal an event from her current lifetime, such as a head injury. Other times the source of the problem may stem from a previous lifetime that is still influencing her today.
>
> When we went to the source of her problem, what she uncovered was a past-life memory. She was a teenager in the 1960s who got involved in the drug culture and ultimately overdosed from those drugs. The physical symptoms that she experienced as she died (in her previous lifetime) were very violent spasms leading to her death.
>
> She realized that she was carrying forward these seizures to remind her how out of control she was in her drug overdose. Even though she was not consciously aware of why she was doing it, she kept these physical seizures reoccurring to

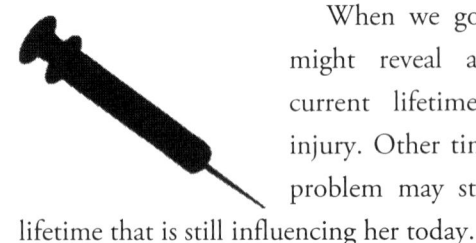

remember to be strong and not succumb to drugs or any similar addictions in her current lifetime.

After she remembered this past-life, she had no reason to continue having the seizures, because she now rationally understood the reasons for her symptoms. The convulsions instantly stopped. As of the latest follow-up, she is totally without symptoms and regained a normal life.

Once a person is able to access the Akashic Records, any number of details can be uncovered about a previous lifetime. An easy example would be someone who is afraid of heights for no apparent reason. Going to the "source" of the problem might yield a past-life memory of being pushed off a cliff, which, once remembered, will remove the fear forever. Other examples are of someone who had taken a vow of poverty or chastity in a monastery or nunnery, then found monetary abundance or a satisfying sex life eluding them in this lifetime.

Personal Example

Will you allow me to give you a very extensive personal example? There are a lot of details here, but there are some important lessons to be learned from it, so bear with me . . .

Ever since I was a little child, I would get into a shower and this thought would enter my mind, "Thank God I'm born at a time when I can have hot showers!" I would get startled, look around the room, as if this thought came from somewhere outside of myself. I would actually ask myself, "Where did this thought come from?"

Even when I was raising my own children, I would still get into the shower and say to myself, "Thank God I'm born now." This didn't interfere with my life, but it bothered me enough to have a fellow hypnotist take me to the "source" of those thoughts. What came out was completely unexpected:

> I saw myself in a previous lifetime—in a different culture—which was quite startling because I didn't believe in reincarnation then. The hypnotist said, "Look down and tell me what you are wearing." I saw these animal skins wrapped around my feet and I said, "I have moccasins on." I immediately thought this must be an American Indian lifetime.
>
> He next said, "Go to a childhood activity and tell me what you see." I saw myself carrying two buckets full of grain and garbage out to a corral where farm animals were eagerly waiting for me to feed them. I saw crops beyond the corral, so I assumed I was part of a ranching and farming family.
>
> I remembered this being a very isolated existence, and these animals were just about my only "friends," so I became emotionally attached to them. I remembered going inside for dinner, and there on the table was one of my "friends," who had been glad to see me just a few days before. My father was the one to butcher these animals, but I still had to eat what was prepared. Eating the meat from the animal was very hard for me, but of course, I had no choice.
>
> The hypnotist then said, "Go to a celebration and tell me what you recall." I saw myself with a bunch of other scruffy-looking men, and we were all celebrating because we had just captured a town and its small castle. I remember thinking, this couldn't be an American Indian lifetime, which didn't seem to

make much sense to me, but fortunately I allowed the experience to continue.

Everyone was celebrating, drinking the stores of alcohol and dividing up the spoils from the conquest. There was a portly, middle-aged man tied up in the corner of the main dining hall. The rest of my fellow raiders were being very cruel to him, and there was another room full of people who were destined to be sold off into slavery. I hated being part of this cruelty.

I remember thinking that I didn't want to be there. I wanted to be home with my wife and children, but I had to be there. I also knew that I wasn't a slave, but I still had no choice and was somehow duty-bound to be there.

Eventually this lifetime advanced to the time I died and passed out of that body. I was in an open Viking boat crossing the ocean when a torrential rainstorm soaked me to the bone. It turned into a huge blizzard and I eventually froze to death. As my spirit was leaving my body, I remember thinking, "I was cold this whole lifetime."

I told you before that I am a very skeptical person. When I finished this experience, I thought it must be bogus, because there were too many things that didn't fit. There were the American Indian moccasins, the ranching and farming, the capturing of the castle, etc., which didn't seem to be compatible at all. I am just grateful that I didn't shut down the experience, because I would have missed out on important insights.

The good news is, I didn't get in the

shower anymore and have the strange thoughts about "thank God I'm born now." It was instantly gone. This is the beauty of Past-life Recall—the healing is instantaneous. For me it was a very useful twenty minutes of my life, just to be rid of those strange, nagging thoughts. So I just put it out of my mind, grateful for the instantaneous healing I had received.

I hadn't really thought much about this experience, mainly because it just didn't seem to make a lot of sense to me. Then my Higher Self was nagging at me to attend the local museum exhibit on the Vikings. Archaeologists discovered a Viking king's buried funeral boat, and they learned a lot about the culture and traditions. They then sent a display of these artifacts around the world. Thankfully I relented and went to this exhibit to see what my Higher Power wanted me to understand.

What the archaeologist had discovered was that Vikings were mostly farmers and ranchers. They would only go "a Viking"—their name for going on these raids (not what they called themselves)—when their king or warlord had protected them. They were obligated, as part of that society, to go on these raids as a form of tax to pay for their family's protection. Suddenly, the very bizarre notion that I wasn't a slave, but I was required to participate in the raid, was verified by the archaeology.

They found that most of the treasure came from selling captured people into slavery. This display also mentioned they would celebrate if they would capture a nobleman, because they could hold him for ransom. This explains the man tied up in the corner of the room. He was secured in the open to ensure his safety, which guaranteed the ransom.

One of the first glass displays contained my animal skin shoes—the ones I had originally called "moccasins." All of these details, which initially didn't seem to make sense to me, were perfectly consistent with this culture and verified by the archaeological evidence. I believe this was my higher power telling me to pay attention to Past-life Recall as a healing modality.

Many researchers have documented incredible previous lifetimes with the use of two-person altered states of consciousness. It might be a tool for you when using Sacred Quantum Metaphysics to help heal the world. Are you ready now to learn about some fascinating research uncovering the details of what happens after we "die"?

"Going Home"—Remembering the "Afterlife"

". . . (when we) can see ourselves as creative, eternal beings creating physical experience, joined at that level of existence you call consciousness—then you start to see and create this world that you live in quite differently."
—Ed Mitchell

This chapter is not just my opinion; it is the result of many creative scientific researchers, who have tried to uncover the mysteries of what happens after we "die." I know the term "afterlife" is hard for many people, because as soon as it is mentioned, we conjure up all kinds of images about heaven, hell, judgment, sermons, and regrets. Please put these aside for the time being, because when you can be open to the information, you will discover some wondrous and comforting evidence.

The first important scientific study was reported by Whitton and Fisher in their 1986 book, *Life Between Life.* They detailed what they called the "void separating one incarnation from the next." This "void" appears to be what various traditions term as Heaven, Nirvana, Paradise, astral planes, deeper dimensions, etc.

I told you earlier I am a skeptic and this is a perfect example: When I first encountered Whitton and Fisher's book, I discounted it, because they called this between-life realm the "Bardo"—which is a Tibetan term for the afterlife. I was concerned they were just promoting their religious beliefs and looking for evidence to back them up. Even though I found it fascinating, I initially set the research aside.

In 1994, Dr. Michael Newton published his amazing research in his book, *Journey of Souls*, detailing "case studies of life between lives"—which revealed details of what we generally call the afterlife. I went back and compared both of their findings. I was astounded when both researchers had discovered very similar results independently of each other.

"Replication" is a threshold for research when at least two independent researchers reach similar conclusions. This prevents either researcher from distorting their findings. When two independent researchers arrive at parallel findings, most likely they've uncovered a deep truth about our universe—as is the case with these two studies. This is when I decided I needed to examine this research, now called "Life-Between-Life" or LBL, more thoroughly.

The Typical Life-Between-Life Journey

A quick synopsis of what was discovered over the last few decades will give you a better idea of the LBL details:

> Most experiencers recount this realm as one filled with unconditional love, forgiveness, and support—not one of judgment, punishment, or torment. They usually feel like they were "going home"; this is the place that we all originally came from, and our earthly existence is but a temporary aberration.
>
> They often describe a razor-sharp lucidity with direct, clear thinking. It is a deeper consciousness, somehow different from the human brain and mind—probably the Essence Mind or "Observer." When people return from an LBL journey, it is very difficult to describe their experiences, because the human language has few words for what they have just witnessed.

People often experience higher beings, whose purpose is to help each spirit evolve and learn from the experiences. Communication with these beings is instantaneous and telepathic. Depending on the culture, they may be called guides, angels, guardian angels, etc.

Sometimes people encounter another group of higher beings called the Council or the Council of Elders, whose purpose is to give advice and help each person evolve as a spiritual being. They often report being part of a group of like-minded spirits, generally called a "Soul Group," who sometimes mutually agree to incarnate together to help each other evolve more quickly.

The most fascinating insights usually pertain to decisions that someone made preparing for their current incarnation—what their purpose in life will be, what family they will choose, etc. You will get more insights into how these decisions are made in the example below, but now you have a few of the details of this fascinating realm.

Metaphysical Insights

If a huge number of LBL memories reported visions of "pearly gates" and "Saint Peter," we might conclude people were just imagining what they expected to find. Since these reports were consistent across the world, and were completely different from the established cultural or religious teachings, we can conclude they were experiencing something very real and profound.

I realized these LBL regressions could be a very powerful healing technique for my clients. Since neither researcher was teaching their techniques at the time, I had to find my own way to get my clients into this realm. Since everything that has ever happened to a person is recorded in the Akashic Records, this would be a good place for my clients to remember their insights.

The good news is that the Akashic Records are easily accessible through various altered states of consciousness, like meditation and hypnosis. I continued to access the Akashic records for my clients until I was truly fortunate in 2001 to train with Dr. Michael Newton (researcher and author of *Journey of Souls*), learning his techniques when he started teaching them to qualified hypnotherapists.

I said earlier that I did not want this book to be about me, but I can only vouch for my own personal experience. My hope is that a personal example will help you to understand:

> Metaphysicians tell us that we ultimately choose the family we incarnate into. This idea was very hard for me, and I struggled to understand why I would have picked my dysfunctional family. My dad was an alcoholic and my mom was always on the verge of insanity. Three out of four of my older half-siblings were also close to insanity. If I chose the family I am going to be born into, what possible reason would I have to pick such a dysfunctional one?
>
> Among many diverse spiritual insights, we can recall the time when we are getting ready to incarnate and we are making major life choices. When I got the opportunity to experience the Life-Between-Life Realm, my

main intention was to disprove the absurd idea that I had any choice in selecting such a dysfunctional family, or alternatively, to understand why I would pick it.

Much to my chagrin, I was able to recall that I did agree to be the youngest child in this family. Why? This is very difficult to explain, but for the evolution of my Spirit, it was the perfect place to learn and evolve. I needed to learn about alcohol abuse, and I wanted a deeper understanding of human insanity. This was probably my unconscious (karmic) motivation for pursuing a Psychology Degree.

Observing these two parents and my half-siblings up-close and personal allowed me the best perspective to learn about alcoholism and insanity. By trying to figure out why they would behave in such a bizarre manner, I eventually did find some understanding and then compassion for their plight. I never would have been able to grasp the nuances of those conditions if I wasn't exposed to their chaos and confusion.

Understanding the true nature of my choices, and realizing that I'm not a victim of circumstances, has given me a beautiful, peaceful perspective on my journey toward enlightenment!

You are lucky to have been born at a time when the science of hypnotherapy, meditation, past-life research, and near-death studies facilitate these spiritual journeys. Now that you've been introduced to the metaphysical wisdom traditions, plus the major scientific advances over the past few decades, you're now ready to put both of these together to explain the many metaphysical "miracles."

Sit back and enjoy!

Mysticism Explained—
Applied Metaphysics

"All that was great in the past was ridiculed, condemned, combated, suppressed—only to emerge all the more powerfully, all the more triumphantly from the struggle."
—Nikola Tesla

When you first picked up this book, you were undoubtedly motivated to better your life and transform the world. This is exactly what the rest of this book will address. Previously, you examined general metaphysical principles. Next, you opened your mind to why our society is so unevolved. Now you just examined recent scientific discoveries verifying metaphysical wisdom. You are now ready to understand how to make the changes for yourself, not based on some unproven theory or wishful thinking, but based on *Sacred Quantum Metaphysics*.

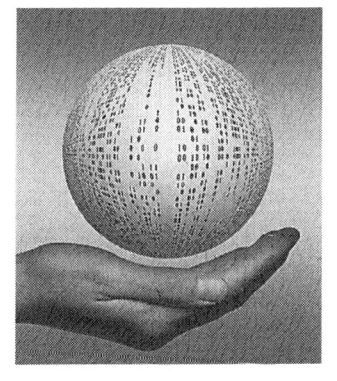

The following chapters will explain techniques that enlightened masters used to manipulate the material world. We will clarify the secrets of nature behind these previously unexplained phenomena, so that you can accomplish similar feats—eventually significantly exceeding them, and thereby propelling mankind forward. You have the advantage of recent scientific discoveries to focus your efforts without spending decades in trial and error practice. With you, and others like you, accomplishing wondrous deeds, the future is going to be glorious indeed!

First a quick caveat: There will be examples given, referring to well-known supernatural deeds, some of which have first appeared in ancient Scriptures. Please look at those examples as a common source of information that everyone can ponder. No disrespect is intended by not attributing any act to a divine source; similarly, nothing here should be construed as an endorsement of one philosophy over another.

Are you ready to examine what some of those wondrous accomplishments are?

Unlimited Potentia—Supernatural Abilities

Potentia definition: force, power, might—ability, capacity—authority, influence, sway

As mentioned earlier, metaphysicians warn spiritual devotees to avoid the "Golden Chains" of manifesting miraculous abilities if they desire immediate enlightenment. If, however, you are like most of us who understand that we have a long way before we can become an Enlightened Master, you might as well take advantage of these gifts. Assuming you are intent on trying to manifest changes to your life or the universe, these are important powers to be understood and then perfected.

What are these supernatural gifts? The first three listed here are already explained in previous Metaphysical Principles or New Sciences chapter(s) referenced in parentheses:

- Metaphysicians say spiritual seekers can attain perfect wisdom and full awareness of the way consciousness works ("What's to Know?—The Akashic Records").

- Previous devotees have attained knowledge of the past and the future, including past and future lives ("Trips down Memory Lane—Past-Life Evidence" and "'Going Home'—Remembering the 'Afterlife'").

- They are reportedly able to read other people's minds (telepathy), even gaining precise details of the motivation of their thinking and thought ("Your Quantum Leap—Quantum Physics Simplified").

The New Sciences

The remaining attributes of these "supernatural abilities" will be given extensive explanations in their own chapters below:

- The most commonly reported characteristic is a profound sense of happiness and constant bliss ("Cease Suffering—Precious Moment Example").

- Another of those apparent abilities is being able to manifest physical objects entirely from the conscious mind ("Give Me A . . —Manifesting Material Objects").

- Skilled spiritual adepts are able to transform one physical object into another material object ("Pick Your Reality—Transforming Physical Objects").

- Being able to "create reality with our thoughts" is one of those clear metaphysical principles ("Changing Reality—Applied Quantum Physics").

- Metaphysicians are reportedly able to levitate, also disappearing and reappearing again at will ("Gravity Pushes—Levitation").

- The reports of Masters who perform instantaneous healings of themselves or another person ("New Medicine—Healing with the Mind" and "Appendix B—Healing Modalities").

- Other amazing gifts ("The Wow Factor—Paranormal Abilities").

- Understanding the evolution of consciousness into an enlightened master ("The Meaning of Life—Practical Karma").

Sacred Quantum Metaphysics

Today's Potential

When you look at all the magical actions performed by Sages in relation to the new sciences, these previously thought of "miracles" are actually very understandable. Masters seem to have more abilities than the rest of us because they apparently are able to focus their consciousness at will. After years of spiritual discipline, Sages appear to remain in their normal state of consciousness and to perform what you might call the mystical. They can decide what they want and then immediately manifest it. The rest of us, because we have not honed our minds sufficiently, could not do this until today.

The evidence shows that it is very difficult for everyday humans to transform the physical world from a position of ego, desperation, fear, or status seeking. Until we are able to develop our minds sufficiently, we will be better off reaching an alternative awareness with the help of another spiritually minded person. The two-person altered state of consciousness technique is available to almost everybody, especially after the last chapter. This way we don't need to discipline our minds with decades of arduous practice to gain the benefits.

Do you understand now why it is important to find a shortcut like *Sacred Quantum Metaphysics* so that mankind can evolve quickly? With the help of another spiritual devotee, you will be able to match, and eventually exceed, the consciousness of enlightened sages. Exactly how successful you will be will depend on how committed you are to learning and practicing these techniques.

Another word of caution is due here: Just because you are able to accomplish these marvelous feats of magic does not mean that you will escape the karmic consequences for misusing them. If you use this process with the goal of self-promotion and selfish desires, you will only make things worse for yourself. First, it will usually be a waste of time, because you cannot manifest these gifts except from a pure spiritual consciousness. Second, you will pay dearly for self-seeking manipulation.

Are you ready now to create unlimited ecstasy and joy in your life? Remember, a very wise man said, "Happiness is impossible except in the here and now"—the present moment.

Cease Suffering—Precious Moment Example

"He that falls in love with himself will have no rivals."
—**Poor Richard's Almanack**

First, a quick review. We are normally so distracted by everyday activities that we rarely take any time just to enjoy what we already have. As we discovered earlier, part of self-created misery is worrying about the future and agonizing about the past. When you are doing this, you are missing out on current moments which should make you happy. The past is gone; the future is but a possibility—and you cannot do anything about either of these now. You have just wasted valuable time and energy and missed the opportunity to find happiness in the present moment.

Your brain obsesses over past events, presumably so that you will not make the same mistakes again, thereby increasing the likelihood you will avoid harm. Likewise, the brain fixates on potential threats, keeping you vigilant.

Constantly being worried about future dangers, or agonizing about past mistakes, keeps us continually in stress. We are so accustomed to this stress that we hardly notice it. Most of us know that these higher levels of anxiety can have devastating physical and mental consequences in the long-term. Here is a perfect example of the metaphysical principle "we create our own happiness," because we can choose not to create this stress. Before you get to the end of this chapter you will have a perfect tool for removing these "two tragedies in life."

Be Open

This may be one of the best tools you will *ever* receive for creating more happiness in your life, so do not skip over it. As was mentioned earlier: It is the natural human tendency to read about how people create their own suffering, and we immediately think of other people—certainly not ourselves—to whom it might pertain. This is your ego distracting you away from the ancient wisdom. Don't let this happen to you.

Remember, it is not your sister, your uncle, or your best friend who will benefit from learning this exciting tool; it is you. If you are going to attain the wonderful ecstasy and peace that sages have experienced over the centuries, then you must pay attention to how this technique can help you to be happy. You're the only one who can remove your own self-created suffering, and the only way you can do this is to observe your true thinking. When you do this, you will find the same elation and joyfulness which Masters have told us is possible for any human being.

Other Distractions

Before getting to the Precious Moment Example, you need to examine some of the other ways that you distract yourself away from being in the moment, besides thinking about the past or the future. One example is when you feed your ego with the trappings of material goods and status:

> All of us need to purchase things to survive: food, clothes, household goods, etc., but you create your own suffering when you expect any new purchase will give you long-term happiness. Most of us have experienced a momentary burst of joy when acquiring something new. Think back about how fleeting this happiness really was. It only lasted a moment or

two while it was fresh, then it became another insignificant object in the background.

Believing a purchase will enhance your social standing only creates more disappointment. Many of the people in your life will never notice it. So in reality, you have spent time, energy, money, and your mental resources to obtain something that really will not enhance your status or make you happy for a long time.

Metaphysicians know that when someone is distracted by material possessions, they rarely enjoy being in the moment.

Another way to distract yourself from your moments is by means of a favorite TV show, movie, or social website. The question is, do any of these things really make you happy? You decide for yourself, but obviously you aren't enjoying your moments when you are preoccupied by another person's life—real or imagined—on the TV screen or on your computer.

Watching TV has become so natural in our society that we rarely think about how destructive it is. Remember, the ancient Romans realized that the occupied masses would be very docile if they were well fed and entertained. Every major Roman city put on "games" to pacify the populace.

Western society is certainly well fed, and our TV has become the modern "coliseum." If you watch the daily news, you will be getting an over-abundance of death and violence—worse than any gladiator would provide. Are you similar to the Roman citizen who became docile and pacified by watching endless blood and gore?

Suppose you are watching sitcoms instead, where people are constantly being ridiculed and put down. You are not doing much better. You are creating more separation between you and your fellow humans than you would ever allow consciously, if you thought about it seriously. Think about what all this negativity does to the budding Enlightened Master inside of you!

In your busy day, when you finally have a minute to calm down, do you pull out your cell phone and occupy your mind with texts, social media, or current events? Yes, all of us need to stay in touch with our electronic modern world. All I am saying is that you should not allow it to consume your thoughts and behavior. You should control it and not let it control you, by allocating limited time to participate in it.

Metaphysicians know that it is very difficult to experience happiness when we are distracted away from what's happening in the here and now. Focusing on someone else's life certainly isn't being in your moment. This distracts us from any real peace and happiness of being in the here and now, and when those moments are gone, they are gone forever. Since we cannot get those beautiful moments back, why do we allow ourselves to be distracted from them? Most of it is just our own self-created suffering.

You have the choice to create more pleasure for yourself. Once you understand this, it is easy to put yourself back on track. It is easier than you think, once you understand the principles behind it.

Your Perfect Tool

As promised, now is the time for me to give you an easy method for increasing your happiness. It is simple to understand, and the effectiveness of this procedure has been backed up by many studies. Don't short-change yourself by skipping over this example. It will become one of the most important tools that you will ever have in a lifetime to create profound happiness.

Whenever you find yourself thinking about the past: resentment, regret, guilt, shame, bitterness, anger, revenge, etc., or agonizing over the future: worry, fear, expectations, to do lists, etc., consciously stop and recreate this example below. It is simple and easy to instigate anytime you

Sacred Quantum Metaphysics

find yourself distracted by the past or the future. You can also follow this example when you find yourself consumed by thoughts of watching TV, tapping into social media, or other electronic distractions. This can be your ticket away from being bored while waiting in line, driving in traffic or otherwise engaged in less than meaningful situations.

Simply read the example below and then take just thirty seconds to experience it.

> Take in a full deep breath and exhale it slowly. Mentally examine everything currently around you at this exact moment. Gaze around your environment and notice some details of whatever is in front of you—things you normally would be ignoring. Pay attention to the shadows and the contrasting reflections as you look at whatever you are focusing on. Observe every object around you as if it is the first time you've seen this object before. Carefully examine how the light hits each object, making shadows behind and around it. Notice the textures of the objects, walls, furniture, etc. Some of them may appear shiny and smooth, others rough and dull. Don't judge anything you are seeing, just experience it for what it is.
>
> Listen carefully for any sounds around you. You might hear human activity going on around you or the hum of machines in the background. You might hear animals, birds, dogs, etc., doing what animals do. Maybe you will just hear the sound of silence. Don't put any emotions or judgments into it; just soak in the sounds as part of the moment.
>
> See if you can feel parts of your body that you would normally be ignoring. Pay attention to your face, mouth, and jaw. Many of us hold tension in our face, especially the mouth

and jaw. Do you feel any pressure where your body contacts the chair, floor, or bed?

The weight and the texture of your clothes, shoes, etc., will be noticeable when you pay attention to them. If you feel any pain, don't allow yourself to go back to remembering how the pain came about. Just pay attention to the sensation. See if you can feel your body connecting to the rest of the world through your skin. Scan your body for any tingling or vibrations in your torso, arms, legs, feet, or hands.

Take a second to see if there are any smells you would normally be ignoring. Do you recognize any particular scent? Don't make any judgments as to whether you like or dislike a particular smell; just be aware it is an aroma you had previously neglected.

Next pay attention to your mouth and tongue. Do you feel the air going in through your mouth? Is there anything you can taste? Sometimes the smell you noticed earlier has a flavor you can still perceive. Maybe you took a drink earlier and you have a residual essence still present—if you pay attention to it.

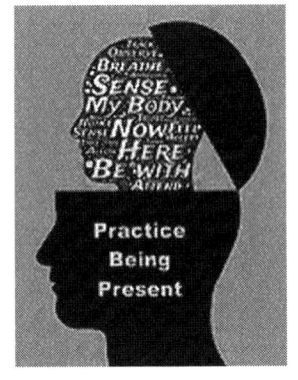

Now take in all these sensations at once and realize the incredible beauty you found. In just a quick few seconds, you became aware of things you normally wouldn't be paying attention to. Remember, enlightened masters always report the beauty of being in the moment. Experience what they have experienced, and be grateful you have found it also.

Next, pay close attention to how you feel now that you focused on the present moment. Chances are you have found peace and comfort. Your mind has gone from hectic to calm. You will realize that you have found true happiness—and you've literally created it out of nothing! The amazing part is this is something that has been around you all along, but in your frantic lifestyle, you unconsciously ignored it.

All it took was a few seconds of effort to create some peace, comfort, and happiness in your life. We hardly ever take the time to do this, and we need to ask ourselves, "Why not?" The good news is that the science of neuroplasticity proves that the more you experience these moments of happiness, the easier you can create them—and the happier your whole life will become.

What you have just done is simply excluded everything extraneous that normally keeps you busy and that continues to keep you wasting your mental energy and time. Now that you have re-centered yourself, you have more mental capacity and energy to accomplish the things which are really important in your life, even the tasks you consider drudgery.

Use these techniques to turn your self-created misery into newly found happiness—anytime you wish! Remember, "You are your thoughts." Do not let your mental chatter take you away from what is truly important. You are in control of your life, when you believe it.

So now that you've been able to experience being in the moment, it is time you learned how Masters are able to use this altered state to transform energy into physical matter.

Give Me A . . .—Manifesting Material Objects

". . . anything you imagine it will create for you. And you learn. Your intention causes this thing to materialize once you're conscious enough and you learn how to use your intentionality."
—**William Tiller, Ph.D.**

For millennia, metaphysicians have created physical objects out of nothing, often in front of huge crowds. For example, there are reports of a Master being able to sprinkle down sparkling particles on a crowd, simply by waving his hand in the air.

Assuming these masters were not magicians using sleight-of-hand, it is not difficult to imagine how they could do this based on the recent scientific discoveries. Using Einstein's equation $E = MC^2$, they probably converted their conscious thoughts into physical energy. This energy can be further stored into matter, creating something as simple as sparkling dust.

There is a subset of research called Psycho-energetic Science—a fancy new name for an old metaphysical principle—where mass can be converted into energy, which can be transformed back into matter. When you realize physical objects are not solid at all, it is much easier to imagine how changing reality is possible.

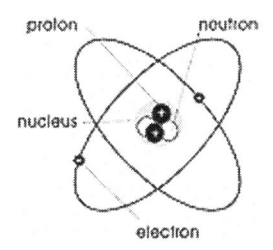

You have certainly seen the neat little diagram of an atom. It depicts a nucleus with tight little spheres of orbiting electrons, like the picture below. It is complete illusion!

First of all, if the nucleus of the atom was increased to scale to the size of a soccer ball, the first electron might appear 20 to 40 miles away. This is why we say most of our three-dimensional material world is actually just so much "fluff."

You can now understand how so much mass and gravity can be condensed into such a small space when it collapses into a black hole—all the fluff is removed. The equivalent of 20 miles of space between the nucleus and the first electron gets packed down so far the electron is right next to the nucleus. It loses those 20 miles of "space," but of course it retains all the weight and mass of the previous atom.

Also, the electrons do not orbit like they told you. Electrons appear out of nothing, then disappear out of existence, and then reappear somewhere else around the nucleus. Where do the electrons go? We don't know for sure, but metaphysicians have told us for many millennia that matter goes in and out of other planes of existence, or what our mathematicians call dimensions. Recent quantum discoveries propose an alternate theory: the electrons are simply created out of energy—conceivably by consciousness— and then reconverted back into energy when they disappear.

People often wonder, since material is so much fluff, why can't you just put your hand or arm through a table or wall? The answer is, "You can!"—at least you should be able to. There are reports of Masters going through solid walls, mountains, or ordinary objects entirely unfazed and unaffected. How can this be possible?

Quantum mechanics shows us that physical changes happen at the subatomic level (the fluff) by consciousness. If you wanted to put your arm through a material object, it is possible to use consciousness to convert part of the material object into energy, put your arm through the energy, and then withdraw your arm. Then you would simply convert the energy back into the original matter to fill in the hole.

Sacred Quantum Metaphysics

Were past Masters naturally able to access what today we know as Dark Energy to make these changes? Just because we recently proved 96% of the universe is non-material doesn't mean metaphysicians did not have access to this energy. It has always been the vast majority of our universe; we just didn't know it until recently.

Remember, String Theory and the Vibrational Universe shows us that different types of energy, as well as what differentiates energy from matter, are simply fluctuations in the frequency of vibrations. Raising and lowering frequencies should be child's play to any of you, once you understand what is possible. Three well-known examples of metaphysical phenomena will give you a better idea of what is possible, either by higher powers or metaphysicians:

> One example would be the Jewish miracle of Hanukkah, when a small amount of lamp oil lasted many days. It might be done scientifically in several ways:
>
> One way would be to add extra lamp oil into the lamps—using consciousness to create energy and then convert this energy into oil.
>
> The other simpler way would be to use consciousness to create energy, which would then be used to create photons (light) coming out of the lamp, without the use of any kind of oil whatsoever. Either way, the result is the same—just a simple physical manipulation of scientific principles.
>
> Another example would be the miracle of the "loaves and fishes" mentioned in the New Testament when a small amount of food fed thousands of people.
>
> It should be a simple proposition to take consciousness, convert it into three-dimensional compatible energy, and then use this energy to create bread and fish.

Alternatively, consciousness could be used, via quantum entanglement and non-locality, to give the other humans the sensation they were full and well fed. Both ways, you have consciousness creating changes in the material three-dimensional world.

The last example is: Buddha creating a physical walkway in order to transverse the sky. Assuming this was not a misreporting of teleportation or levitation (future chapter), the physical bridge across the sky might be created by focusing consciousness into energy, then storing the energy into materials, which create the physical bridge across the sky.

Now it is your turn. What can you imagine you would like to change in the physical world? Would you like to magnify the lamp oil example (above) into creating free energy for everyone, like Nikola Tesla envisioned? Can you envision creating enough food, even if only bread and fish, for anyone on our planet who is hungry?

Do not limit what you would like to create. Would you like an antigravity propulsion system to explore interstellar space? The point here is for you to dream big, and then find the scientific principles needed to accomplish it. Remember, you will be given concrete steps needed to put this into practice; until then, realize that metaphysically, unless you can envision it . . . you will never create it.

Now you are opening the door to understanding how matter can be created out of Quantum consciousness; next, you can begin to understand how the Masters have been able to transform one object into other physical objects.

Pick Your Reality—Transforming Physical Objects

"It's a good thing that my dog does not create reality. By his stares, I'm sure he would turn me into a dog treat at the first opportunity."
—**Unknown**

For millennia, metaphysicians have been able to convert one form of matter into another, like turning water into wine. How is this possible? Again, it is easier than you might imagine when you thoroughly understand the recent scientific discoveries. Is it possible that past Ascended Masters were able to perform truly unbelievable feats, simply because they were able to convert matter into energy, and then back into matter again, as Einstein's $E=MC^2$ proves is possible?

Let's recap how our three-dimensional world is constructed. Understanding our material world gives you access to how those changes can be made:

THE NEW SCIENCES

If you look carefully at the chart, what creates different forms of matter is the addition or subtraction of protons—the top number of each square. Quantum discoveries show consciousness can convert one molecule into another one by adding or subtracting various subatomic particles, including protons.

Let us examine the historical reports of turning water into wine using recently discovered scientific principles:

> Since water is simply stored energy—as Einstein proved—consciousness can turn it back into energy, and then re-form it again into liquid, but this time by adding alcohol molecules. How difficult would it be to use Quantum principles (next chapter) to add a few extra protons, electrons, etc.? Not hard at all.
>
> If you prefer, divine power can use the same scientific principles to convert water into energy and then reconvert it into wine. Remember, these are the same scientific principles put into place when our universe was created, so they are available to any form of consciousness—divine or spiritual.

Now it is your turn. Could you be like alchemists who were reportedly able to turn lead into gold? Would you like to transform the Earth's pollution into fertilizer? You might like to alter the HIV virus into an inert substance. Maybe you will be the one to use Sacred Quantum Metaphysics to accomplish these things, and then show the rest of the world exactly how it is done.

You now have the basics about how to convert one object into another; are you ready to clearly understand how quantum theory supports your endeavors?

Changing Reality—Applied Quantum Physics

"I regard consciousness as fundamental. I regard matter as derivative from consciousness."
—Max Planck, the father of Quantum Theory

With the discovery of Quantum Theory, the exact nature of how mankind's consciousness can directly affect and change the physical world has been verified. How? As you know, consciousness can be converted into other forms of energy, which can then be stored into matter ($E=MC^2$), but it all starts with consciousness. Consciousness is the prime source of everything existing in our three-dimensional world.

What is this consciousness? Your Observer consciousness, which is independent of the Ego, is what is able to transform the material three-dimensional world. This Essence Mind, which is energy, can then create other forms of energy. These energies can then transform physical matter, which we know is a form of temporarily stored energy.

The next step is to measure how much consciousness is changing our physical reality. The observable and measurable effect of consciousness is only documented at small quantum levels, but we know the effect is very real. Based on thousands of years of metaphysical reports, consciousness does make profound changes to the entire physical universe, but these transformations are hard to measure and quantify unless multiple people work together.

In trying to analyze the influence of consciousness on the everyday world, there are many variables that are altering the outcome. Obviously, everyone else's consciousness is similarly modifying the three-dimensional universe, sometimes conflicting with, or negating, your best intentions.

This is why innovative researchers will organize large numbers of meditators and then show measurable improvement in crime statistics. When just a few thousand people cooperate, it can be documented to affect society as a whole. This is why you need to practice Sacred Quantum Metaphysics. You are now beginning to understand how powerful your consciousness actually is. If many thousands of people start focusing their consciousness in a concerted, positive direction, it will instantly change our society and culture for the better.

Time and the Creation of the Universe

What is the nature of this Observer consciousness? You first need to ask, "What consciousness created the stars, supernovas, etc., which existed for the billions of years before humans began to think?" Then the ultimate question is, "What consciousness existed before the Big Bang, which is what created our three-dimensional universe?" There must have been some sort of consciousness existing from the beginning of what we call "time."

Many people say that we cannot know what existed prior to the Big Bang, but what Einstein called "time" is simply the fourth dimension.[14] Since "time" is simply another dimension—similar to our three dimensions—then it is certainly possible that this higher dimension, along with our Essence Mind, existed previous to the Big Bang, which created the three dimensions. The Observer consciousness exists independent of your physical body, and could certainly exist independent of our Earth, life

---

[14] See "Appendix A—What is a 'Dimension'?" for a more in-depth perspective.

forms, etc., and any other three-dimensional objects created after the Big Bang.

Is there any evidence to back up such an idea? Remember, people returning from various spiritual journeys report that "time does not exist" in the Astral Planes. If time does not exist in the Spiritual Realms, these deeper dimensions must have existed prior to the creation of our three-dimensional universe—when theorists believe time began.

Can you tap into your Observer to be able to remember the time before the Big Bang? Once you are able to access the Akashic Records, you will have access to the true nature of all the details of our cosmos.

Quantum Entanglement and Non-locality

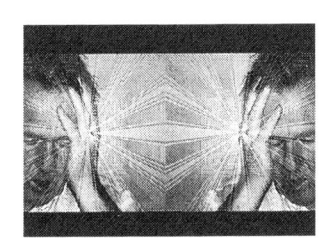

Einstein then theorized what has become known as quantum non-locality and entanglement, which has now been verified. This means two or more people can become intimately connected (entangled) to each other, even when they are at vast distances apart (non-locality).

Consciousness must be the ultimate energy source used to convert and store energy into matter, by entanglement and non-local influences. It is clear that all research is pointing to this conclusion. Metaphysically, your personal Observer is what ultimately changes your reality. The more people you can cooperate with, the better the result (see "Your Glorious Future" chapter)—and mankind desperately needs your efforts and insights right now!

The discovery of these Quantum insights eventually explained many of the metaphysical phenomena documented over thousands of years. As you begin to understand the science behind these events, you realize ancient masters most likely didn't know why consciousness changed our three-dimensional universe, but fortunately for us, they discovered that it worked. The trick is for you, the future enlightened master, to learn to use your consciousness in such a way that you can access ageless wisdom and make reality change in the direction you want.

You have scratched the surface comprehending how quantum theory can allow your Observer to change reality. Next you will be fascinated by how Masters are able to circumvent gravity.

Gravity Pushes—Levitation

> *"... perhaps the (Quantum) collapse occurs precisely at the last possible moment; and it always occurs precisely at the level of consciousness, and perhaps, moreover, consciousness is always the agent that brings it about."*
> —**David Albert, *Quantum Mechanics and Experience*, 1992**

I will explain levitation, partially from recent scientific advances, but also from the perspective of metaphysical adepts who have reported how they were able to accomplish this feat. These first-person accounts give us a fascinating glimpse into the true nature of our universe.

Many witnesses have reported that metaphysical Masters were able to levitate at will, sometimes traveling vast distances before returning to Earth. 2,500 years ago, the Buddha was observed, in front of a huge crowd of people, instantly transporting himself across a 100-kilometer-wide raging river to the other bank. Jesus was reported to be able to "walk on water," which certainly sounds like levitation.

Historical Levitation?

Ancient Egyptians were able to move millions of multi-ton blocks to create the Great Pyramids, possibly by using sound to levitate these blocks. Another ancient civilization in Peru was able to fit multi-ton blocks of stone together with such precision that not even a human hair can fit in

PERU

between them. Does this mean these ancient civilizations were able to levitate these blocks? Certainly the proposition that this could be accomplished with crude stone tools and without the use of the wheel strains credibility. It seems entirely plausible that there was ancient technology lost through generations of modern scientific neglect.

Historians have always assumed that the Great Pyramids were built by slave manpower. Is it possible that these ancient civilizations somehow learned how to harness antigravity to create these wonders? This is one of those areas you need to research for yourself, if you have a keen interest in it.

What *is* clear is that a very scrawny man created the Coral Castle in Florida, all by himself, by balancing multi-ton blocks of stone. He told people he was able to accomplish this because he rediscovered the "Secrets of the Egyptians." He never disclosed those secrets before he died, even when bullies surrounded him, beating him up to force him to reveal his discernments.

Someone reading this who is interested in duplicating these amazing accomplishments—and will certainly become famous from it—can go to the Akashic Records and glean the historical facts. Everything is recorded there, so this is available to anyone who is willing to pursue this knowledge. Conceivably, the two-person altered state of consciousness would be used to get the exact details.

Levitation Techniques

The following explains how levitation can be accomplished, using metaphysical principles and the new scientific discoveries. There are at least two ways levitation can be accomplished:

> Sages and masters have reported that they were able to levitate by increasing the vibrational frequency of their

consciousness and subsequently found themselves levitating, sometimes by accident. Combining the metaphysical principle of the Vibrational Universe with the science of String Theory, you can increase the frequency of your thoughts by focused awareness. This technique will take practice and training to manipulate consciousness this extensively, but since others have been able to do it, you can do it also.

Another technique is using what scientists call "antigravity" particles. When you use Quantum principles—your Observer—to create or accumulate antigravity particles, it would give you a reservoir of energy to counteract gravity. The advantage to this technique would be to allow mankind to eventually explore interplanetary space, once these particles became easily harnessed. An altered state of consciousness can take you to the Akashic Records to get more details on the nature of antigravity particles.

You have just been introduced to how you can levitate objects and yourself around the three-dimensional world; let's spend some time understanding how to heal the physical body.

Future Medicine—Real Healing

"If you practice something over and over again, those nerves have a long-term relationship. If you get angry on a daily basis, if you are frustrated on a daily basis, if you suffer on a daily basis, if you give reason for the victimization in your life, you're rewiring and re-integrating that neural net on a daily basis..."
—**Joseph Dispenza, DC**

If people understood the awesome healing effects of the mind, it would turn the whole medical community upside down instantly. When scientists and other researchers seriously study the science behind these pain-free, no side effect cures, it will open mankind's eyes to what is actually possible.

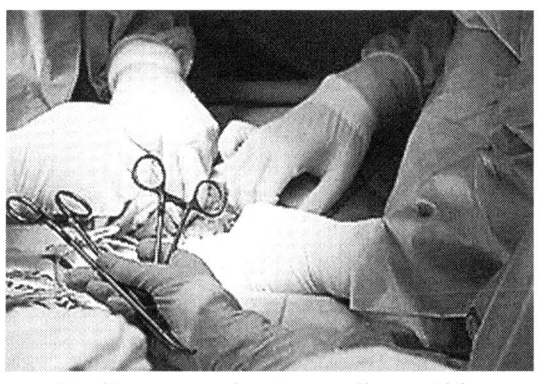

Science discovered that it made a huge mistake by categorically removing all consciousness-related healings and treatments. We don't want to make the same mistake today by categorically removing all Western medicine treatments, which might be effective. The important part is to examine which is the most effective treatment possible, without biases in favor of one philosophy over another.

The likely result of reexamining mind-body healings would be there would be little need for multibillion-dollar pharmaceutical companies, extensive hospitals, recovery facilities, etc., because for the most part people will heal themselves. Why would this be a problem? Powerful vested interests are intent on keeping things the way they are.

As you have seen in the examples given in the "New Medicine—Healing with the Mind" chapter in "The New Sciences" section, we have created a medical system where people think there is only one acceptable approach to healthcare. Since the insurance company often pays the bills, they can dictate what is an "approved" treatment and what is not. Even if you and your doctor believe an alternative treatment would be preferable, the insurance company can refuse to pay for it.

Mind-body Techniques

Now you can comprehend how the new sciences are combined with metaphysical principles to fully utilize the true mind-body techniques. Here are a few techniques to accomplish effective mind-body healing:

- If you remember the discussion of Herbert Benson's meditation protocol, he ingeniously added a visualization component to traditional meditation. The patient would clearly and intensely visualize a time when there was no disease or injury. During this protocol, the mind is somehow able to reconstruct the body without the disease or injury in the future—likely using Einstein's equation along with quantum theory. Remember, it was proven scientifically that there are many cures from using Benson's simple technique, including changing a person's genetics.

- There are many other treatments, such as Reiki, Healing Touch, Reflexology, yoga, etc., (see "Appendix B—Healing Modalities"), which can provide substantial relief and/or cures at minimal costs, compared to modern intrusive medical treatments.

- An additional way to treat physical problems would be to surround the disease or injury with the higher vibrations of love and compassion. When those higher vibrational levels are incompatible with the disease or injury, healing will result.

- In the earlier chapter on the Akashic Records, Edgar Cayce used them to find simply amazing cures for thousands of individuals—almost always without drugs or surgery. Since he came up with nontraditional cures through the Akashic records, you can do it also.

- A more difficult, but certainly feasible, way of healing would be to focus consciousness on the diseased or injured body part, convert it into energy, and reconstruct it into new tissue, using Einstein's $E=MC^2$.

If you think these treatments are impossible, they certainly will be unachievable for you. Do not sabotage yourself before beginning!

New Medicine Example

A practical step-by-step example of how to use the new sciences to make major changes in the medical and psychological world will make this clearer. Any time you are dealing with human decisions and motivations, it is necessarily a very complicated process, so always keep your mind open to new innovations.

> Suppose that you would like to create a world where people are innately empowered and do not become addicted

to drugs or alcohol (mentioned early in this book). Remember, as in other areas of the spiritual universe, you can never change another person without expressed consent, so people need to agree to accept the help.

Before beginning, you need to understand the progression of addiction. What are the factors that lead someone into addiction? Understanding why people become addicted allows you to comprehend how to defeat it. Anytime someone is attached to something materialistic, like drugs or alcohol, you know they are overwhelmed by their low-vibrational three-dimensional body. You can always harness the 96% of the cosmos to raise their vibrations out of the lowly, earthbound levels, which substance abuse necessarily creates.

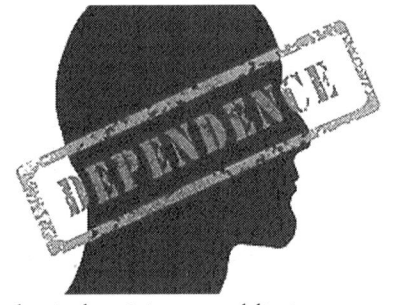

Perhaps you decide that there is a genetic or physical origin to addiction; you can focus on the purely physical causes. Einstein's $E=MC^2$ or Benson's meditation protocol can be used to individually alter the genetics or chemical imbalance which caused the addiction.

Conceivably, you decide that the best way to end dependency is by providing spiritual solutions; you can use the different metaphysical principles to alleviate it. Certainly you could go to the Akashic Records, like Edgar Cayce did, and find simple cures for whatever is controlling each person. Is self-forgiveness or forgiving someone else the key? Is your addict consumed by fears or unfulfilled expectations? You get the idea—but remember the metaphysical solutions presented earlier!

Maybe there is a past-life or karmic reason this person has chosen self-medicating. You can provide relief through a two-person alternative awareness or meditation. You have previously been shown that these will provide instant relief for this type of malady.

As more addicts get sober, the benefits to society will magnify and ripple out into our culture, helping even more people. Children will no longer have an addict as their primary role model and will not follow them into the downward spiral. Those who have been cured of their addiction will likely have a heart for helping other addicts, and will join your effort. Eventually the criminal drug gangs and drug cartels will simply disappear out of our society—and into a historical footnote.

Ultimately, the medical and psychological professionals will take notice and acknowledge an astounding transformation has solved what they once thought was an insurmountable problem. They will then begin acknowledging and using the 96% of the previously ignored universe to make changes in many other people's lives—not just addicts! As more inexpensive spiritual remedies are found, more hospitals and medical personnel will be practicing these techniques to cure the remaining diseases.

Future Medicine

So what is the future of medicine? Since modern research is still eliminating consciousness and spirituality—the placebo effect—they continue to ignore 96% of the universe. It is obvious that we will never understand what is possible when medicine stubbornly focuses on only 4% of reality. It is essential for the well-being of all of humanity to change this quickly.

The New Sciences

Lucky for all of us alive today, many of us are beginning to understand the true reality. Can you envision a world when scientists are willing to "follow the evidence wherever it leads," as science was intended to do? Only the very enlightened ones will do this at first, but the rest will come around eventually, because the ones who use the 96% of the universe will receive the Nobel Prizes.

Next we need a medical profession that will use mind-body healings first and rely on the materialist treatments like surgery, pharmaceuticals, chemotherapy, etc., as a last resort. The free healings from the placebo effect—which are 100% effective for the patients who respond to it—could be used as templates for future healings. We can then research why the mind failed to cure the rest of the patients. We would also gain insights into the inner workings of the entire human condition.

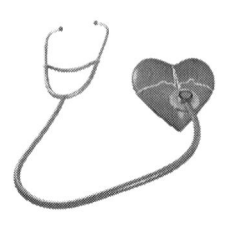

You can subsequently envision a psychological and psychiatric community utilizing the previously ignored 96% of the spiritual universe to help clients emotionally and psychologically. This will be instrumental in putting aside most of the materialistic practices that rely on hospitalization, pharmaceuticals and behavior modification for most conditions. These Western medical solutions might still be needed for the short-term, but eventually most everyone will become skilled in changing their own mind, body and genetics.

More studies assessing the proven effectiveness of mind-body healing techniques will be instigated by our mainstream institutions in the near future, benefiting all of mankind. The advances of science, and the well-being of the patients, will no longer take a second place to maintaining the controlling groupthink over medical research.

Next, we need to open the minds of all doctors, because they must reevaluate their basic assumptions adopted at the time when medicine was first created in the 16th century. If they do not, medicine will continue to ignore 96% of the universe, and it will continue to teach future generations the same inadequate science.

What You Can Do

It is the inertia created by the outdated attitudes still ingrained in our institutions that prevents mankind from achieving its full potential. Since you are open to the new scientific discoveries, you can envision how to create a much more humane healthcare system. You will be instrumental in creating a future where these pain-free, no side-effect cures can occur much more often, and the outdated drugs and surgery will be reserved for emergency situations. Thanks to all of you, we will get there eventually.

As you perfect your Sacred Quantum Metaphysical techniques, you will develop your creative and spiritually tuned mind to discover even more effective ways to heal people. As you find cheaper, faster, and easier ways to heal humanity, please remember to document these, so that other people can build on your successes.

Now that you have a glimpse of the future of medicine, it is important to begin to understand the science behind the paranormal—or what many people understand to include psychic abilities.

The Wow Factor—Paranormal Abilities

"Man's capacities have never been measured; nor are you to judge of what he can do by any precedent, so little has been tried."
—**Henry David Thoreau**

For the last 5,000 years, there have been documented reports of paranormal abilities. The outdated "science" since the 16th century couldn't understand the metaphysical mechanisms behind these miraculous feats because they were only looking at the observable 4% of the cosmos. Luckily, in the last hundred years or so, we have been able to look past this limiting viewpoint.

Ignoring Reality

When the scientific and academic institutions wanted to believe that there was nothing spiritual to our cosmos, they simply refused to study these phenomena, explaining them away as aberrations or superstition. When researchers would scientifically investigate metaphysics and find "statistically significant" results, they ignored these now scientifically proven facts. Remember, simply because a study has proven something scientifically does not mean the scientists will allow themselves to believe it.

It is perfectly understandable why supposedly objective scientists will ignore hard science. When they do lend credence to research that runs counter to the accepted groupthink of their colleagues, they open themselves up to the same ridicule and professional isolation that they have put other researchers through.[15] They cannot risk losing everything in order to be scientifically impartial. Therefore, it is easier to avoid controversy and follow the safe intellectual pursuits supported by their colleagues.

Modern Advances

Recent discoveries have provided a wonderful glimpse into the science behind the ancient wisdom revealed in the many centuries of metaphysical reports. You have already been exposed to levitation, mind-body healing, transforming matter, changing reality, etc., in previous chapters. Let's examine a few of the remaining metaphysical "miracles" one at a time.

Are you able to access pertinent information about another person's physical, mental, emotional, or spiritual condition? Edgar Cayce was able to do exactly this, by tapping into the Akashic Records during a trance. Since he was able to do it, you can also do it, by using Sacred Quantum Metaphysical techniques. You will then have access to everything that has ever happened to anyone. There is one important caveat: you must have a person's permission to access their personal information.

What about the phenomenon of telepathy, or the ability to directly access another person's consciousness? This should be one of the easiest connections to make, since Quantum theory shows both persons' thoughts are similar energy and should be accessible to each other, assuming both people are open to the information. This connection is possible through the Quantum principle of "non-local entanglement," where distinct and separate phenomena interrelate with each other.

---

[15] Perhaps these scientists would benefit from reading about the metaphysical principle of Karma.

Sacred Quantum Metaphysics

Quantum entanglement scientifically explains how "psychic readings" work. Entanglement allows direct access to all types of consciousness, which include someone's hopes, desires, experiences, past-lives, spiritual purpose, guidance, and karmic influences. This does not mean everyone who purports to be able to do this actually can, but those who are able to use Sacred Quantum Metaphysics techniques, especially the Akashic records, will have true access to spiritual knowledge.

Does quantum theory also explain accessing the consciousness of people who have passed over to the other side? We know studies have proved beyond a reasonable statistical threshold that communication with the consciousness of a deceased person is possible; therefore, quantum theory is the best explanation for it. Remember the earlier discussion of the research done by Gary Schwartz of the University of Arizona in his book, *The Afterlife Experiments*? He proved scientifically that the thoughts of a person somehow continue to exist even after his or her body dies. Since it is possible to access the consciousness of people who have died, then it should be a much easier process to make contact with the consciousness of someone who is still living on this planet, through psychic readings and telepathy.

One last thought about foretelling the future. Many of us want to know what the future holds. Metaphysicians tell us that nothing about the future is certain—there are only probabilities. Without this malleable future, we would be similar to programmed robots with no Free Will, Karma, or the ability to evolve toward enlightenment—violating important metaphysical principles. Thus if you attempt to access your future, you are probably only acquiring the most likely possibility, so do not count on predictions with 100% certainty.

THE NEW SCIENCES

It is such an exciting time because you no longer need a "seer" to give psychic insights about yourself, your past-lives, etc., because you can get direct insights by accessing unlimited information yourself. You have direct access to almost any knowledge you may need, for any purpose.

Now you have a glimpse into the scientific understanding of psychic phenomena. It is time to look at how your everyday life is affected by Karma.

Meaning of Life—Practical Karma

"What if we're more than this? Could it be that we're really unique, very special, very powerful beings in disguise? What if we're delegates of miraculous potential, born into this world to fulfill a beautiful destiny—one that we've simply forgotten . . . ?"
—**Gregg Braden's** *Deep Truth*

Let us take a moment to review what we have discussed so far: We are a consciousness that never dies, we incarnate to be separated from the unconditional love of the spiritual realm, we make mistakes and learn from those mistakes, so we can evolve spiritually to become a future enlightened master. It sounds pretty simple, but in reality, it is the "learning from our mistakes" which makes living so hard.

One of the major ways to understand Karma is to pay attention to our preferences, which is how Karma influences our life. In an earlier discussion, you were presented with the idea that there is a spiritual "equal and opposite reaction" to all of our actions. Metaphysicians tell us that our conscious and unconscious desires, choices, and decisions, fulfill our karmic destiny. You think you are making great choices, but later discover there are negative aftereffects. Then you tell yourself, "But it seemed like such a good idea at the time!"

Karmic Examples

Let us examine a very potent example (which has a very inspiring ending), to demonstrate how something from the past can still influence you today:

The New Sciences

A man came to me for a "Past-life Reading" to verify his intuition regarding his previous lifetime. In his past-life, he was a guard at a concentration camp in Nazi Germany. He did many awful things to the people who were imprisoned there, not entirely out of his own hatred and animosity, but often from the orders from his superiors. He believed in the philosophy of Nazism and certainly did not fight against what was being done to these people.

Before he died (in this previous lifetime) he began to comprehend the magnitude of the hurt and pain he had caused. He held an enormous amount of guilt over the things that he had done. This guilt had caused an enormous amount of suffering for him until the day he died.

When he "passed over" into the Spiritual Realm, he was greeted with disappointment and sorrow, but not any significant condemnation. Perhaps this was because he was already so remorseful for what he had done. There was the loving acceptance of him as an eternal soul, who had made some incredibly awful choices. There was no mistaking the sadness from what he had done. From the perspective of an infinite spirit, he realized Karma had placed a huge burden upon him.

This man decided to incarnate as a minority, and with a physical deformity. I have no doubt this was his attempt to make up for the pain and suffering that he had caused the other people. He willingly took on the deformities to learn compassion and understanding for those who were less than physically perfect.

There are three important parts to remember from this fascinating story:

1. If this man can be forgiven for his choices, the rest of us should have no problem at all being forgiven for the mistakes we make as humans.

2. Even though there is a loving, supportive Spiritual Realm, this in no way absolved him from the consequences of his decisions and actions.

3. When we can start to understand the hurt and pain that we have caused, and express a sincere desire to make up for them, we can begin the process of making amends for our past actions.

For this next example, I want to thank Katy for her permission to reveal what happened in her Life-Between-Life Journey. Without her permission, this information is legally confidential, and could never be disclosed:

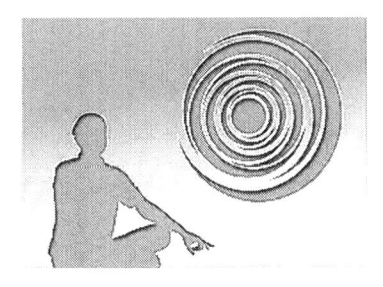

Katy was not at all interested in discovering insights about her birth family or tapping into the Akashic records. She was mainly interested in what her true purpose in this lifetime was.

She had previously determined there were several past lifetimes with her current husband and wondered why they decided to incarnate together again. In one of these previous lifetimes, he was a pastor and she was the pastor's wife. He had become entwined into the church's beliefs and became very judgmental when implementing its religious dogma. When he was a pastor, he was fearful of rejecting the conventional religious dogmas, because "they might be right."

When she remembered her time before she incarnated, she remembered her main purpose in this life was an agreement to assist her husband to find a spiritual, rather than a religious path. She was instrumental in allowing her husband to develop many spiritual and metaphysical gifts. When she realized she had accomplished her goal she said, "My work here is done."

This doesn't mean her lifetime ended, because she still had many other things to accomplish. It just meant that she was finished with her most important goal.

Distorting the Truth

The real tragedy is that we don't teach people in our society the importance of the spiritual universe, especially the Law of Karma. We rarely advise people how it is in their own benefit to be loving and kind toward their fellow humans. We also don't explain that when they do something that violates or hurts other people, they still must accept the spiritual consequences of their actions—even if they are never caught and punished here in the human world.

Most of us understand the negative Karmic ramifications of stealing, raping, or murdering someone, but let's examine an example of what most of us would perceive as simply nonviolent mischief:

> Some teenagers are so bored they think it exciting and cool to create a computer virus, which will hack into and infect operating systems. They are never taught that there is a spiritual consequence to their actions, so they don't even think about the long-term negativity they are creating.

By infecting millions of computers, these teens inflict an enormous amount of pain and suffering on untold millions of people. It is likely that they will never get caught by law enforcement, but they cannot escape the metaphysical "equal and opposite reaction" consequences for their actions.

Metaphysicians tell us they must suffer the same amount of misery as the millions of people all over the world have suffered, and they have just signed up for many lifetimes of intense despair and misery—unless they can find a spiritual solution.

The metaphysical remedy for this is to completely understand the violation and frustration that they have caused, and then to sympathize with all the maliciousness they created and inflicted on their fellow human beings.

This remedy from their karmic consequences isn't taught by our media, schools or parents, so these poor teens are each doomed to experiencing an equal amount of pain and suffering as they have caused. It is simply too horrific to imagine—one person having to experience that much retribution over a stupid prank, but that's what happens without spiritual insights.

We desperately need to get to the point where everyone is aware of the true spiritual nature of our universe, so that humanity may evolve out of the darkness of our previous non-spiritual mindset.

Non-spiritual Punishment

If all we are is a mindless blob of molecules, which eventually dies and stops existing, then there is really no good reason for us to behave or treat others benevolently. Unless there is a karmic "equal and opposite reaction" to our actions, there is no reason why we shouldn't rape, murder, and steal, assuming we won't get caught. If humans do not have innate spirituality, then there is no reason why we shouldn't sell addictive drugs to children, if it means more money for us. Since our lives are nothing more than a mechanical body and brain, there is no reason why we shouldn't kidnap women and hold them as sex slaves; perhaps even their children. This describes the attitude of many criminals today.

Without a spiritual deterrent, the only remedy society has to require good behavior is by threatening prison if someone misbehaves. When society's only recourse is punishment, we must next enact a never-ending set of "laws" to force people to behave humanely. The problem is that we have more people breaking laws than we have people enforcing them. Therefore, we require a massive prison system to isolate and punish those criminals who do get caught. This describes much of our law enforcement today.

Most criminals feel there is little risk of punishment for their illegal behavior. Since criminals are not taught there is a real spiritual benefit to behaving well, they continue to hurt their fellow humans. Without the understanding of spiritual ethics revealed in the new scientific discoveries, including Karma, we have no ability to convince them to treat others ethically, except to threaten prison if they do not.

It is obvious that not harming someone certainly benefits the person who was never harmed, but it simultaneously provides wonderful spiritual benefits to the would-be perpetrator. Over the long-term, giving our fellow spiritual beings respect, love, tolerance, etc., brings more of these into our life, making our life much more consequential and happy. The reality is that your consciousness does not only change physical reality, but it can also change your Karma. Unfortunately, the beneficial consequences of our good choices are not taught in our schools or society, so most humans don't learn that it is in their long-term benefit to choose kindness over selfishness.

This is how spiritual education will make our society better. Since there is an equal and opposite reaction to your actions, you don't have to behave out of fear of punishment. As you realize your neighbor is just another budding enlightened master in the making, you realize that to rape, murder or rob another spiritual entity is mainly hurting you. When you add the spiritual component to your ethics, you realize that you treat others with kindness because it is in your own best interest to do so. You don't need the threat of prison to force you to treat others lovingly.

Divide and You Will Be Conquered

One of the most potent karmic risks occurs when we divide ourselves from other human beings.

> Suppose that you have an internal hatred or dislike of a whole group of people. If you feel this way, metaphysicians

tell us you have just doomed yourself to another lifetime when you will return as a member of this group. Perhaps you hate gays, blacks, whites, Irish, Middle Easterners, Muslims, Christians, prostitutes, policemen, you name it, you will need to return to experience what this group of people had to go through. You agree to do this willingly so that you can learn compassion, sympathy, and tolerance—because, in reality, they are future enlightened masters just like you.

For instance, one way politicians divide and conquer us is by racial differences. Race is only manifesting genetic heritage, which is entirely materialistic and essentially meaningless in terms of the evolution of an individual spirit. Since we choose our birth family, race is simply a matter of choice. Remember, since all of us are just temporary spirits inhabiting our temporal bodies, then race is one of the least meaningful aspects of incarnation. If someone has an intense dislike of people based on their racial background, reincarnation as a member of this race will be selected, to comprehend everything positive and negative their culture has experienced.

Most of us recognize that our society is divided by gender politics, which divides people into groups based on sex or sexual preferences. Metaphysicians tell us that we can decide to incarnate as either gender, therefore whatever sexual organs we have are really meaningless in terms of our spiritual progress. The other gender is simply another spirit, temporarily encased in a mortal body, just like us. For example, when someone expresses loathing for women in general, they will need to come back as a woman to experience similar loathing firsthand.

One more way that people are divided—and conquered—is by their nationality. Is it really significant that someone is born on this side of the border rather than the other side? People will fight and die over an imaginary line (border) drawn on a map. In our anti-spiritual culture, we are told that borders are extremely important, but it is truly meaningless in terms of spiritual evolution. If someone denigrates a particular nationality, they have almost certainly doomed themselves into coming back as a citizen of that country.

Another big division for humans is religion. Even small differences in Christian philosophy have ended up in prolonged wars between Protestants and Catholics. The twentieth century is full of atheist governments massacring people, simply because they believed in religion. People today decide whether someone should live or die, based on what religion they follow. This type of religious prejudice mandates that the person will return as a true believer of the religion they now despise.

Suppose that you've listened to the constant drumbeat from the "news" about how horrible liberals or conservatives are. You will likely choose to incarnate again to be the liberal or conservative you disdain. Why? If you dislike any group of people, you realize the best way to learn compassion and understanding for this particular group is to become one of them. Once you "walk in their shoes," you can understand why they think and act the way they do.

Applied Karmic Metaphysics

What difference does it make if we include spirituality or not in structuring our society? When we embrace spirituality, we have finally included the spiritual 96% of the universe. Our previous refusal to account for spirituality in our sciences and institutions has led to today's problems. Let's examine a few of the distortions mankind has created:

> When governments and political ideologies deny a spiritual component to the universe, there is no reason why humans

should be treated as any differently than dispensable farm animals. Since humans are only here to be exploited and taxed, then they become meaningless casualties to someone else's pursuit of power and control. This is how Hitler murdered 7 million people, or Stalin massacred 50 million of his citizens, so easily. When political leaders don't understand the 96% of the spiritual nature of our universe, which few of them do, there is little reason to treat humans humanely, since they are merely meaningless blobs of atoms and molecules.

Does our lack of understanding of spiritual ethics have any consequences in our modern society's obsession for war? Of course it does. What disincentives do we have to keep another country from invading us? The only deterrence, in a materialistic society, is to maintain a bigger threat, so that we can savagely punish any country attempting an incursion, by defeating them with our greater force. How effective has this strategy been for the last four centuries? The result has been an almost constant succession of wars!

This list can go on and on, but if you pay attention, almost every evil in our society has to do with removing the spiritual component from our beliefs and policies. Almost every negative aspect of our dysfunctional culture can be instantly rectified by practicing Sacred Quantum Metaphysics.

You have a gained broader understanding of Applied Metaphysics; next, you need to understand how to change reality with your thoughts!

Choose Your World—Manifesting Miracles

"We are drowning in information while starving for wisdom. The world henceforth will be run by synthesizers, people able to put together the right information at the right time, think critically about it, and make important choices wisely"
—**E. O. Wilson**

If you are like me, you have just skipped ahead to this section because all of us want to learn how to create a better world. I caution you not to do this. It is essential for you to understand the connections between 5,000 years of metaphysical phenomenon and the recent scientific advances before attempting to transform reality. You might be able to accomplish a little bit without these insights, but "trial and error" is a very time-consuming and frustrating way to learn.

You now have in your hands a great resource of supporting information, which will be indispensable after deciding how to change your world. You may need to refer back to sections to understand how Masters have been able to accomplish something similar in the past, or to review the recent discoveries to understand the science behind similar events. This is why I listed all the different metaphysical principles first and then explained the important new scientific discoveries, so that you will know how they can be combined.

Choose Your World—Manifesting Miracles

In order to make permanent transformations, you need to understand what is possible, where those changes can be made, why there is such resistance to these innovations, and how to use all of this to your best advantage. The reality is, unless you have the full foundation and details of the overall integration of science and metaphysics, you won't know where to adapt your techniques when needed. It is almost impossible to summarize *Sacred Quantum Metaphysics*, so carefully build your foundation with all the information presented in the earlier chapters before you continue forward.

I will list the concrete steps that were promised in a handy outline. I will then take each one of the steps and explain the details. Next we will explore some of the fabulous possibilities that are available to you. Remember, this is only the beginning. When you are ready to take this magnificent journey, the next chapters will show how it is done.

Co-Creators of the Universe— Your Birthright

"Whether we like it or not, modern ways are going to alter and in part destroy traditional customs and values."
—**Werner Heisenberg, Nobel Prize winner for Quantum Mechanics**

The main reason for writing *Sacred Quantum Metaphysics* is so that all of us can realize our potential and learn how to create a better future. The more people using these techniques to transform our world, the easier it becomes for all of us. It is therefore imperative that we put our collective minds together to create an improved universe—one based on joy, cooperation, and love, instead of our current society based on fear, hatred, and envy.

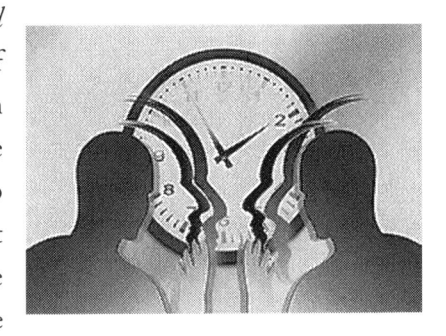

The metaphysical truism, "You create reality with your thoughts," has now been verified by modern science, especially through quantum theory. This truism is fundamentally correct, but there is so much more you need to know in order to make it happen consistently.

Since science has proven that mankind is able to alter the world, why don't all of us have the perfect home, car, or job? Mankind doesn't comprehend the real power we have at our fingertips, so we don't take the necessary steps to create what we need and want. When we lack a firm conviction that we can change the world, we never invest the time and energy needed to create a better future. Most of us just go day to day working, eating, sleeping—fulfilling our obligations as humans—without having a clue what is actually possible.

One of the main obstacles holding humanity back from our glorious future is because we are up against everyone else on this planet who is also creating their own reality. As you know, there are parts of the world where leaders want people to remain unsophisticated and uneducated, so they will be docile and easily manipulated. Those people are similarly creating their own reality, moment by moment, even when they have no idea this is what they're doing.

Author Gregg Braden[16] calculated it would only take 8,000 people combining their consciousness to alter mankind's collective future into a more positive direction. It is therefore imperative to get this information out to as many people as quickly as possible. Our world desperately needs many more metaphysicians, like yourself, who will be creating a much more positive society. This is why it is essential that all of us make a commitment to make at least one major change to the world, and then cooperate with others to accomplish it.

Metaphysicians tell us that it is our birthright to become the "Co-Creators of the Universe." Do you have a hard time believing this? If you do not believe you are capable of being a co-creator, you will certainly never practice the skills needed to become one—or you'll sabotage and discourage yourself before you can verify the possibilities. Just for the time being, keep an open mind to the possibility, because when Sacred Quantum Metaphysics is put into action, you will know this is true.

How Much Power Do You Have?

How much power do you have at your fingertips? In a previous chapter, I described how our universe makes an incredible amount of power available

---

[16] www.GreggBraden.com

to any of us,[17] but to positively remember how much power you really have, let's review a shortened version:

> Einstein showed us that matter is simply stored energy. So all the hundreds of billions of galaxies, each consisting of hundreds of billions of stars, each likely containing planets and moons, equal an incredible amount of matter. Multiply all this material times the speed of light squared—an absolutely unfathomably large number—and this tells you how much energy was available at the beginning of our visible universe.
>
> If this isn't mind-numbing enough, physicists think all this matter was just one billionth of the true amount of energy available at the moment of creation. They believe our entire existing universe is an insignificant statistical variation between all the matter and antimatter formed, before they mostly annihilated each other. Thus, the amount of energy existing at the moment of creation was one billion times more than what was needed to store energy in all those galaxies, stars, planets, etc.
>
> This is an enormous amount of energy . . . correct? But we now know this is only 4% of our known universe! Something also created the other 96% of the universe consisting of Dark Energy and Dark Matter.
>
> Where did all this energy come from? Quantum theory tells us that everything must have originated from some form of consciousness. Metaphysicians tell us that this is the same Observer consciousness or Essence

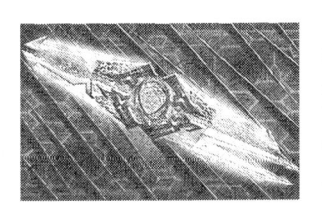

---

[17] See the "You Have It All—Inner-Power" chapter

Mind that you have. This means your consciousness also has all of this power available to it—when you will allow yourself to believe it.

Once you comprehend that your consciousness is an essential creating force, you can use it to alter your world. When you are creating a better world, why limit yourself? Why not give humanity a boost while improving your own life? When any of us start to use these principles to create a more perfect world, you improve it for everyone, including yourself. What you will soon ascertain is that your only constraint is the limitation of your mind, by not thinking grand enough.

Unlimited Possibilities

Are you prepared to create a new society? What type of world do you want to create now that you have the opportunity? Without the ability to envision an unlimited future, you will never implement the steps to put it into fruition. Decide what you would like to accomplish, and then make sure your inner thoughts support your intentions. Let's spend a few moments imagining what is possible:

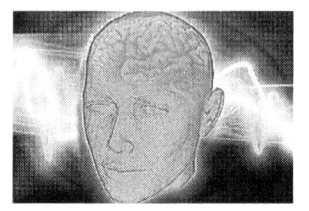

- Perhaps you believe we will never be able to elect a politician who has humanity's best interests at heart, and would not deceive the voters. If you think this way, guess what? You are right. There is no way you can create it, because you don't believe you can. When you believe in unlimited possibilities, anything is possible!

- Many of us would like to create a world where the selfish powerbrokers become insignificant and are replaced by loving, kind, and compassionate individuals. It has been prophesied, "The meek shall inherit the earth." Is our society finally ready to empower good and positive people to become our leaders, while marginalizing the negative and selfish people? When you want this, you can help make it happen!

- Would you like a world where we are all healthy and reasonably fit without disease? Conquering diseases is much easier when we allow consciousness to help, rather than to exclude its curative properties—like medicine does today with the placebo effect. Meditation has been scientifically proven to slow the aging process for those who practice it regularly. It should be possible to slow aging even more by the use of the science of mind-body healings.

- Suppose you are a true visionary who would like to remove poverty from our world. You have previously learned how to create Abundance out of nothing in our current economy. You can do this on a grander scale. Once you realize it is just a matter of scale, with more metaphysicians helping, everything becomes possible!

- Would you like to remove hunger from our planet? You were given examples of how enough food was created to feed 5,000 people out of very little, possibly simply from consciousness. How many people working in concert would it take to magnify this power sufficiently to feed everyone? Author Gregg Braden says 8,000 people. When we get 8,000 people together using Sacred *Quantum Metaphysics*, we will know for sure.

Choose Your World—Manifesting Miracles

Now is the time to learn the concrete steps needed to put the ancient metaphysics and the new scientific discoveries into a form where you can consistently co-create a better universe.

Applied Sacred Quantum Metaphysics

"The fanatical atheists . . . are like slaves who are still feeling the weight of their chains. . . . They are creatures who—in their grudge against the traditional 'opium of the people'—cannot bear the music of the spheres."
—Albert Einstein

Metaphysicians have told us for millennia that it is possible to alter our physical world by mindfully focusing consciousness. Mankind didn't make this type of metaphysical magic commonplace before today because we didn't have the benefit of the new scientific discoveries until just recently. You are no longer hindered by these limitations and these possibilities are now open to each and every one of us. What was once considered impossible, or even miraculous, has the likelihood of becoming routine.

Step-By-Step Instructions

These instructions bring together every aspect of what you have learned to make profound changes to your everyday world. You will be happy someone has put all this together, giving you the details, with concrete directions on how you can transform your heart's desire into reality.

Use these steps to allow you to create something beneficial for yourself and all mankind. As you implement the following step-by-step list, you will probably need to make some adjustments. Keep an open mind and allow yourself to be as flexible as possible, allowing innovation and adaptation to guide your efforts.

Choose Your World—Manifesting Miracles

Are you ready to create a far superior society than the one you have today?

1. Pick a few changes needed to make your life better, which will also improve the entire world.
2. Research everything you can about your potential subjects; use traditional and alternative sources.
3. After evaluating all the current research, select the one transformation that you would like to accomplish first.
4. Access any and all of the metaphysical principles pertaining to your intended desire.
5. Power up and utilize all scientific principles that`—Eden Phillpots

Let's go through each step specifically with a little bit more detail so that you can adapt them to any situation:

1. Your first step is to dream big about what you would like to enhance in your life and in the world. Pay attention to your inner hopes and desires. Remember, the whole point is to find things that you will be enthusiastic about. It might be helpful to re-experience your Precious Moment Example to create a mindset conducive to finding happiness.

This might take more thought and meditation than you think. Next, focus on a few of those desires—a maximum of five—which are most important to you.

2. Now gather all of the current research on your selected ideas. Access every bit of information, traditional and alternative, that pertains to each of your potential goals. It is important to spend some time researching each idea, because you may have initially had an inspiration. But when you do the research, you realize it might be too easy—or too complicated—for

now. Eventually, as you keep researching, you will narrow down your ideas to the one or two most feasible and interesting. Do not discard the rejected ideas entirely, just put them aside until you have more practice, skills, techniques, or science needed to make them more feasible.

3. One of your ideas will eventually emerge as the best one to accomplish first. Before initiating your project, meditate on whether you are willing to give this plan your intense effort, and to make sure your Higher Self is in agreement. When you get a resounding yes from both of these, you have made the best decision possible. Make this goal your stated intention with a succinct statement of one sentence describing what you would like to accomplish. Make it into an affirmation or a mantra when you practice these techniques.

Vow you will not give up until you have accomplished your objective! This is vital because nothing worthwhile is ever attained without some obstacles and challenges. Remembering your one sentence intention and your vow to continue until you succeed will prepare you for the inevitable doubts and difficulties you will encounter.

Setting a positive outcome is essential when you state your intention. Make sure your intention is supportive of the metaphysical principle of Free Will, whereby no one is harmed by your actions. When your intentions are negative, selfish, jealous, envious, resentful, fearful, angry, hurtful, or materialistic, you only create more negativity for yourself, and little change in the outside world. Beyond making yourself more miserable in the short-term, these intentions generate long-term negative karmic consequences.

4. Now is the time to tap into all the metaphysical principles you've learned about. Go back to any individual chapters that pertain to your goal and reread the basic principles. Just because you did not have to spend decades in a spiritual seclusion doesn't mean that you don't have to work at this.

Anything worthwhile takes effort, and certainly learning how to alter your physical world will take your dedication.

Next, access additional research into the metaphysics pertaining to your intended result. For example, you might be using meditation or other trance states to tap into your Inner Knowledge for insights needed to implement your changes. Certainly the Power of Love, as well as manifesting Abundance (not just wealth), can be beneficial here. Next, tap into the Akashic Records to find your best available resources. Be careful to only create a future that empowers positive outcomes.

5. Power up and utilize all the scientific resources that relate to your intended new reality. Some of these may include Einstein's Space-Time Continuum, $E=MC^2$, Quantum theory, altered states like hypnosis, Einstein's fourth dimension, or the Multidimensional universe.

Remember, the science of neuroplasticity has shown that you can literally rewire your brain every day of your life. It is proven science that when you change your thoughts consistently, you will hardwire your brain to think similar thoughts in the future. This can be incredibly effective for almost any intention you would like to accomplish.

6. Magnify your consciousness with appreciation for the budding enlightened master inside you. One of the easiest ways to get into this proper mindset is to spend some time in gratitude for the things that you already have. Choose *at least* five things making your life happy or are already working in your life. Don't just list them casually; spend some time really feeling how grateful you are for each one of these. This increases the vibrational frequency of your consciousness into a higher spiritual level and makes sure you are in touch with your birthright of being a co-creator of the universe.

SACRED QUANTUM METAPHYSICS

7. Next it is important to surround yourself with protection, which will keep your vibrations at a very high level through the rest of this procedure. Many spiritual sages have told us it is important to be surrounded with positive, loving, compassionate energy as we use our consciousness to make changes to the physical world. One way to do this is to surround yourself with the "White Light of Protection," which has been utilized for many millennia to keep spiritual seekers safe and highly focused. Other metaphysicians recommend creating a mental sphere around yourself, with mirrors on the outside to reflect away anything negative.

8. Enlist the help of your Higher Self, Guides, Guardian Angels, Divinity, Creator, or whatever is consistent with your belief systems. If you remember, the metaphysical principle of Free Will means you must specifically ask for help from any of these spiritual resources or they must stand by passively. Make sure that any help comes from a source of unconditional love, support, and compassion.

9. Connect to your Observer or put yourself in your preferred altered state of consciousness. Connecting with your Observer is how to dampen down the Ego. To reiterate a very important point: It is from the position of being in the moment, while connecting with your Observer, when power is accessed to make the changes you want. Spend a few moments allowing knowledge and insights from your Observer to manifest, and then magnify them.

Alternatively, any altered state will keep you from slipping back into your Ego state, and can be great tools for those who are not yet skilled in accessing the Observer. You know from previous chapters it is very difficult to create something from the position of our selfish egotistical human brain. This will keep you away from your limiting Ego.

The Benson meditation technique detailed in the "Quelling Monkey Mind—Meditation" chapter has been proven scientifically to alter your body—even your genetics! In this process you are combining your intention with the end result visualization for the duration of your meditation, creating scientifically verifiable cures.

There are many metaphysicians who tell us that it is vitally important to set a positive intent before using an alternative awareness to change the physical world. Always envision something positive that you want, and never try to get rid of things—or humans—that you don't want. With practice, you will be able to develop higher vibrational levels, with easier, more concrete spiritual connections, which will allow you to alter the world consistently.

10. Enlist others, when possible, to direct and reinforce your intention while you maintain an alternative awareness. Initially, like-minded practitioners can aid in your endeavors, conceivably with guided meditation. If this is something that is not readily available to you now, do not despair. Later everyone will be given an easy opportunity to connect with other metaphysicians, so each person will have the benefit of mutual support.

A two-party altered state of consciousness, like hypnosis, is always preferable when there is another spiritually minded person to assist you. Eventually connecting with the "Real You"—your Observer—will further enhance your alternative awareness, especially when a second person's assistance is available. Perhaps you can enlist the help of a friend or two, and you can make this even more powerful. Multiple people magnify the consciousness needed to alter reality. Here is how:

> One person maintains the Observer, while your helper directs his or her consciousness in the agreed direction to facilitate your intended results. The first person can just harness the internal energy he or she needs, while the second

person can consciously direct the energy toward whatever positive change in the world is desired.

It can be as simple as saying out loud, "You will create the perfect _____ (fill in the blank)" while the person is in meditation or another trance state. When you combine similar efforts with another person, it will be quicker and easier by using the helper's conscious mind to reinforce your desired end result.

You can create an affirmation or a mantra for each other. For instance, "You are happy, healthy, wealthy, wise and you have the perfect _____." Do this as often as possible until your intention manifests. Always remember to keep your meditations, mantras, visualizations, etc., as positive as possible.

When you are doing this alone, you can always connect with your Observer, or maintain your preferred alternative awareness, while combining your intention with your very detailed visualizations. Do it alone if you must, but your results will be magnified when you enlist the help of other enthusiasts. In the last chapter of this book, you will be given an opportunity to connect with an expanded spiritual community.

11. Draw up and magnify any and all energy available. Include the 96 % metaphysical unseen resources. Next draw up all your resources from your Inner Power, combine this with the 96% of the universe's Dark Energy and Dark Matter, plus all other energy sources. For example, since all the matter in our universe is simply stored energy, you can then use the very potent $E=MC^2$ with the quantum theory to your benefit. Transforming all this energy into a form that you and your Observer can utilize will give you the ability to change our physical reality.

12. Raise your vibrations to a very high level. Remember to review the Vibrational Universe and String Theory information for the metaphysical

and scientific connections needed here. You began with a high vibrational level by experiencing gratitude, so magnify those positive feelings of love, compassion, and joy in your thoughts. Metaphysicians who have unconditional love and empathy for all spiritual beings will have the highest vibrations available to transform the world.

13. Create a vivid mental picture of what you intend to change in our universe. Remember, the previous discussion on positive thinking demonstrated that the human subconscious mind can never visualize a negative. Make sure only positive actions are visualized. Envision the step-by-step progression toward your desired result. Depending on what was discovered in your initial research, insights will become evident about how to combine scientific principles with the metaphysics needed to create the transformations you desire. Examples are given later to provide illustrations of how this step can be adapted to any situation.

Using your consciousness to transform your reality from where it is today toward a much better future is how physical changes are manifested in our universe. There is no limit to what can be created here.

14. Now you are ready to co-create the universe. While connecting to the Observer or your favorite altered state, clearly visualize the end result of your perfect reality. Leave the details on how this will be accomplished up to Spirit, or the powers of the universe. You never want to limit Spirit, so always mentally include the phrase, "or something better" when visualizing. Spirit might have something even more fantastic in store for the world than what you can envision with your human perspective.

Make a serious commitment not to quit until you are successful in turning your intention into a reality. Everything worthwhile in life takes commitment and perseverance, including this. Remember the story of a future enlightened master who vowed not to get up until he had reached enlightenment? Make a similar vow to keep working on your intention until the efforts succeed.

15. Now picture your improved future as a completed reality. See this as an accomplished fact—something existing now and in perfect form. Some metaphysicians say at the end of this process, ". . . and so it is" or ". . . it is already done."

Do not get discouraged, because you never know when or how your intentions will manifest. Understanding the new scientific discoveries confirming Reincarnation means you have many lifetimes to have the results of your co-creating the universe manifest. In terms of eternity—since consciousness never dies—you will undoubtedly experience the results firsthand.

16. Now that you are certain your dream will become a reality, spend a few moments in gratitude for the new transformation just created. If spiritual resources were enlisted, show appreciation for the help received. The loving compassion in demonstrating gratefulness solidifies the successes, and also keeps the vibrations high, which keeps your creation manifesting.

17. Now spend some time in meditation and listen for direction to see if there are areas where you need to add, alter or adapt in the future. Determination and persistence are absolutely essential, but so is the ability to learn and adapt from experience with spiritual guidance. Since you have true Inner Knowledge, it is vital to access any additional information during meditation, which is specifically needed to adjust your procedures.

Remember to review the chapters detailing scientific principles and metaphysical insights as you refine your techniques. When implementing the step-by-step list, you will necessarily make more connections between Metaphysics and new sciences, but this doesn't mean they are the only ones possible. Keep an open mind and allow yourself to be as flexible as possible.

CHOOSE YOUR WORLD—MANIFESTING MIRACLES

Each time you are in an alternative awareness, practice steps 6 through 17, adding any new adaptations. Remember, anything worthwhile takes a lot of work and concerted effort. Certainly altering your physical and world will take a lot of perseverance. Few things are done perfectly the first time, and this is no exception. As with any skill, the more you practice this, the better you will become. This is one reason you made a commitment earlier not to quit. When you stick with these techniques, you will constantly improve, and be able to accomplish more each time. Practicing this consistently over and over, your intentions *will* become a reality. This is the beauty of Sacred Quantum Metaphysics.

18. It is critical that you document your successes at www.SacredQuantumMetaphysics.com to make sure other metaphysicians will have the benefit of your insights and improvements. You will also be able to benefit from other people's efforts by checking into this website. Mankind's science will progress so quickly once this process gets going, there will need to be a central information repository to magnify everybody's efforts together. I will not let you flounder once you have begun these steps. You will find ongoing support here for emerging metaphysicians who need it. Those who are interested in forming a spiritual community of like-minded practitioners will find a supportive environment here.

19. Once you have successfully created your goal and expressed the proper thankfulness, you are now ready to start this process over from the beginning—with the next idea you would like to see changed. Do not limit yourself by just thinking there is only one way to accomplish your goals. The "Creating Reality—Law of Attraction" chapter showed the spiritual universe already gives us everything you need to create whatever you want. The universe will have hundreds of different ways to accomplish your goal, when you will give it the flexibility to find the best one.

Sacred Quantum Metaphysics

When you stick with this, you will be astounded by the results. Now is a good time to give you some examples about how these steps can be put these into action.

Practical Applications—Creating Your Changes

"Atoms are not things; they are only tendencies . . . the atoms or elementary particles themselves are not real; they form a world of potentialities or possibilities rather than one of things or facts."
—**Werner Heisenberg**

When people are exposed to these 19 steps, they naturally comprehend how profound these insights are, but sometimes they need examples to begin formulating their own action plan. Let's take an easy example first, and work up to more complex changes, so you can envision what is possible:

Easiest Example

Suppose you would like to simply have more happiness and less suffering in your life. This is so easy that this is likely the most significant transformation that doesn't need the full 19 steps.

All it takes to make your own life joyful and more content is to understand the first few chapters of the "Metaphysical Principles" section. Simply resolve that you will end your own suffering by creating a happier life without worry, resentments, anger, expectations, fear, etc. Put the simple solutions given in these few chapters into practice, and it will be simple to end your own self-created misery.

Choose Your World—Manifesting Miracles

I recommend that everyone end their self-inflicted misery first, before attempting any of the more difficult transformations. This is such an easy process, which not only makes the rest of your life much happier, but will also remove your emotional "baggage" of resentment, anger, fear, etc. These also interfere with your ability to keep your vibrations high enough to manifest a better reality. The beauty of this is once you have removed the obsessive thoughts of the past or future, you have made a permanent connection with your Observer.

By enhancing and multiplying your current moments, plus empowering the metaphysical gifts of Love, Forgiveness, etc., you can easily create a blissful and tranquil life. Practicing the Precious Moment Example will keep you from wasting your time and energy by obsessing about the past or worrying about the future.

Impatience or Boredom

Some of us just want to use our time more efficiently. Do you get impatient waiting in lines at the grocery store, bank, government offices, etc.? How would you like to convert this time away from angry annoyance into an advantage in your life?

Metaphysically, this is often a time when Spirit is telling you that there is a reason you need to slow down. Is there a lesson you can gain by watching the people? Is there a thought you need to pay attention to, which you wouldn't be able to ponder when you speed through the line? Can you use this time to do a mini-meditation? Instead of becoming aggravated, find a way to enjoy the moment and make it a pleasant experience. You can always practice the Precious Moment Example any time you have a few moments.

The real benefit is, when you are creating a happier life for yourself, the ripple effects also enhance the rest of the world. As your life becomes more joyful, the people you interact with will benefit from your positive attitude. These individuals will subsequently improve the lives of others they contact. This is how the simple act of making your own life better can improve the lives for many thousands of people.

Mind-Body Example

Suppose you have already stopped obsessing about your past or worrying about the future, and are basically happy and content. Now you have the skills and confidence to tackle some more difficult transformations. Your next intentions don't have to be world changing; even small changes will have ripple effects, making the world a better place for all of us.

Most of us will eventually have the desire to transform our physical body in one way or another, so this is a great example.

> Justin (not his real name) is a good friend who, because he abused his body with poor food choices, self-medicating, rarely exercising, etc., was in danger of having a stroke or heart attack. His doctor told him if he didn't change his lifestyle to keep his blood pressure down he would need surgery to clean out his arteries.
>
> No matter how much he tried to be calm and serene, he was constantly fearful, anxious, and unable to get a good night's sleep. Due to his history of self-medicating, he was hesitant to use tranquilizers or other potentially addictive drugs. After learning about *Sacred Quantum Metaphysics*, he decided to try the 19 steps.

He first tapped into his Inner Power, making sure he had the right attitude to believe he could use these techniques. He worked through all the metaphysical steps to stop agonizing about the past or obsessing about the future, and he started enjoying the here and now. He decided to use the Benson meditation protocol as his favorite alternative awareness to improve his body. He clearly and repeatedly visualized his arteries being clear and unobstructed during these meditations.

Not only did he gain a much happier attitude, with added ecstasy and joy, but he was able to remove much of the stress that kept his heart under constant pressure. He made major improvements in his blood pressure after only six weeks of practice, and his doctor did not need to prescribe potentially harmful drugs. He spontaneously felt more energetic and began exercising!

Since he could do this when he previously closed his mind to spiritual solutions, most assuredly you will have no problems creating similar changes.

Life Changes

You can always use the 19 steps to change the more long-lasting transformations. For example:

"Mary" heard a lecture about *Sacred Quantum Metaphysics* and wanted to see if it would help her stop being frustrated with traffic as she commuted back and forth to work. She wanted to find some relief from her constant anger with other drivers, which she knew was detrimental to her health and serenity. Instead of trying to modify her behavior by "anger management," she decided she wanted to uncover the underlying cause of her anger.

After completing the 19 steps, Mary discovered much of her angst with traffic was misdirected. She realized what really bothered her was having to work a job she hated. She was unfairly taking her wrath out on the other drivers when she was actually angry with her inconsiderate employer. She was frustrated because she could not express her contempt without likely losing her income.

Mary spent some time spiritually connecting to her Observer and Inner Knowledge. She finally understood that she was creating her own misery by spending every workday at a job she hated. She realized it was fear of the future, and her needless worrying, that kept her with an employer who did not value her.

From the 19 steps, she realized that she can stop worrying, and quit being afraid of the future, by learning to experience being in the here and now. She also found some compassion through the Power of Love for her employer who was just another spirit doing the best he could. During meditations, she connected spiritually to her Akashic Records to get insights into what she agreed would be her true purpose in life. She discovered it was to become a strong, self-sufficient woman, after many lifetimes of being subservient to a man.

Mary understood that it is her metaphysical birthright to have an innate Inner Power, which gives her the ability to manifest changes she desires. She decided what she really needed is to allow the metaphysical principles of Abundance and the Law of Attraction to manifest in her life.

Mary made certain that her thoughts and internal chatter supported her newfound confidence and self-sufficiency. Then she listened for guidance in her quiet moments (during meditation) and trusted her abundance was not only possible, but also a spiritual promise, when her intentions are positive. It took a bit of a transition, but eventually she was able to quit her job and work for herself with little commuting, without suffering financially.

This is a great example because for many of us the biggest single time commitment we make during our lives is our employment.

So now you have been given some examples of what can be done with Sacred Quantum Metaphysics. As you practice these techniques on a few of the less difficult things, you will develop skills for some of the society-wide changes you learned about in the "Applied Metaphysics—Mysticism Explained" section.

Now is the time to look forward to what the future holds!

Personality Conflicts

Suppose you have a disagreeable coworker or neighbor in your life. Realistically, it is unlikely this person will change simply because you desire them to be different. Remember, spiritually you cannot transform a person who does not want to change. Even if this person magically agreed to be changed, it is very difficult for you to change another person's behavior.

The more likely solution is to find a way not to experience negativity being around this person. It is always easier to change yourself than it is to change others.

Certainly, when you first do the work to remove your self-created suffering from the past or future, you will become a much happier person in most situations, including this one. If this person still remains a problem, after you have removed your own suffering, then utilizing the full 19 steps will give you a complete spiritual solution.

Your Glorious Future

"I am not what happened to me, I am what I choose to become."
—Carl Jung

Now you have it:

- You were given an understanding of the ancient and current metaphysical principles.

- You have a wide-ranging understanding of new scientific advances made during the last century or so.

- You surveyed the history of scientific obstructionism, which will be needed to thoroughly comprehend what needs to be changed in our society.

- You examined how these two knowledge-based fields of science and metaphysics interrelate.

- You were exposed to the very powerful Applied Metaphysics, which explained supernatural marvels.

- You have been introduced to the 19 steps that explain how to create a much better world for you and your loved ones.

- Finally, you were given examples to make the process understandable.

You have all the essentials to co-create a much better world and culture. Mankind is on the precipice of a new era. I invite you to be a big part of this. In order to make the very important worldwide transformations permanent, it will take many people, just like you, to help in this endeavor.

Choose Your World—Manifesting Miracles

This is why *Sacred Quantum Metaphysics* is coming out now, because mankind is finally ready to cooperate to co-create our universe.

If you feel drawn—as part of your vision to create a better future for all of mankind—join us at the website www.SacredQuantumMetaphysics.com. Humanity needs your insights, spirituality, and your assistance! Please help this venture, even when it is only quietly during your meditations, as you create your own better future.

This next part is critically important! As you are successful in your endeavors, please document your results at this website. Scientific protocol demands that results be duplicated by independent researchers. Some people will not take notice until several of you demonstrate successful results for a particular transformation. We will accumulate your successes, so others can build upon your accomplishments. We also need to make sure the research and science are as up-to-date as possible.

Rest assured, I will not leave you to flounder alone once you have been introduced to these insights. For those of you who are on an intense spiritual path, the "Awaken the Enlightened Master Inside You" meditation is available for free download on the website. This is only the first step!

Some of you won't have a community of like-minded enthusiasts nearby who can assist you with your changes. For those of you who are not connected to a spiritual community, one of the purposes of the website is to provide a place where spiritually empowered individuals can come together to assist each other.

Sacred Quantum Metaphysics has given you the gift of a lifetime: the ability to co-create your universe. This is your birthright when you will allow yourself to claim it. What a glorious future you have ahead of you! I want to leave you with one last question: Is there anything in your life that makes you less than happy? I have five words of inspiration for you:

SACRED QUANTUM METAPHYSICS

GO OUT AND CHANGE IT!

Appendix A—What Is a "Dimension"?

"The universe is not hostile, nor yet is it friendly. It is simply indifferent."
—John H. Holmes

What exactly is a Dimension? A dimension is an area of space, which may include one or more directions of movement.

This is really much simpler than you might think. The easiest way to understand the differences between dimensions is to start from the simplest, and then move on to the more complex dimension.

Zero Dimension—A single point

Imagine for a moment a universe where there is only a single point. This world only exists as a single point in space, and can have absolutely no size, because if it did have any size at all it would require adding length, which would make it one-dimensional—or part of the next dimension.

If there were anything alive on this point in space, it could not move. Any movement in any direction would take it out of the zero-dimensional space and into the first-dimension.

1st Dimension—Line

Now when you take the above point in space, and put any direction at all to it, you create a line. This line creates a one-dimensional space.

Anything alive on this line can only traverse back and forth along this line. It can never deviate from the line because to do so would be to add another direction, which is only possible in the next dimension.

2nd Dimension—Flat Surfaces

If you take the one-dimensional line, and you move sideways from this line, you have just created a flat two-dimensional space. This is the world of "planes." Imagine a sheet of glass, which extends forever. If there are any objects in this world, they might be circles, triangles, squares, or anything that can be drawn on a flat surface.

In this 2-D world, a "being" would only go left, right, back and forth along this sheet of glass. It would have absolutely no awareness of up or down, because this 2-D world can only be flat.

3rd Dimension—Our Material World

When you now add an additional direction to a flat surface, you still have left, right, back, and forth, but now you add up and down. This is the everyday world of solids in which you and I live. Objects here have width, length and height—three dimensions.

A two-dimensional circle becomes a 3-D cylinder when you add height. A 2-D square becomes a 3-D cube when it goes "up." A triangle could become a pyramid.

You, like other beings in this 3-D world, can go left, right, back, forth, up and down—all three directions.

4th Dimension—Time

The fourth dimension still has the same movements as 3-D—right and left, back and forth, up and down—but now you add one other direction to these other three directions. Unfortunately, it is almost impossible for us to envision another direction from our length, width and height, because we can only see three dimensions with our eyes.

Metaphysicians say that unless we can journey into these higher dimensions, through altered states of consciousness or by allowing our consciousness to leave our physical body, we cannot comprehend the wonders of these deeper dimensions.

Once people return to our three-dimensional world, it is almost impossible for them to describe what they have just witnessed from our three-dimensional based language. They try to describe these deeper dimensions as best as they can by drawing on similarities to our 3-D world. It is exceedingly difficult to depict these experiences.

5th Dimension and Beyond

It is in the fifth dimension and higher where this gets even more difficult to comprehend. Remember, scientists now believe there are at least 11 dimensions to the known universe. There have been many details reported from these higher dimensions, but nothing can be verified except by personal experience.

If this sounds interesting to you, my hope is that you will also experience these deeper realms through Sacred Quantum Metaphysics techniques. With enough consistent reports from many individuals, we will begin to amass evidence of the true reality of our multidimensional universe!

Understanding Multidimensional Universes

What is a multidimensional universe? Mathematicians and String-theorists concluded there are 11 dimensions (see "The Brane New World—11 Dimensional Space" chapter). Allow yourself to envision this from the perspective of a lower dimensional being:

> Think about an everyday ream of copy paper. Here are 500 flat surfaces next to each other, which you might perceive as 500 two-dimensional planes. Each sheet of paper has another sheet of paper right next to it.
>
> Imagine each of these sheets is a separate 2-D universe. A 2-D being on any one of those sheets would only be aware of its single sheet "universe"—since there is no "up" for this being—and would have no knowledge that another 2-D world is right next to his world. He would be completely unaware of this "parallel" world right next to him—because it would be above or below him, which does not exist in his 2-D world.

Physicists speculate we have many "Parallel Universes" from the "Many Worlds Theory" of Quantum Theory. Similar to the 500 2-D universes existing in parallel in the ream of copy paper, our three-dimensional world might also have many three-dimensional universes existing in parallel, perhaps right next to us. We would not know that these are there, and we would have no ability to perceive them, unless our eyes could "see" into the higher dimensions.

This shows you the difficulty of being in one dimension, and trying to envision what's going on in the next deeper dimension without being able to directly observe it.

Sacred Quantum Metaphysics

Since it is easy for us three-dimensional beings to create two-dimensional spaces—floors, walls, ceilings, tables, roads, sidewalks, etc., (these are all 2-D spaces)—it should be just as simple for a 4th dimensional being to create multiple 3-D parallel spaces. Now you can begin to understand how multiple parallel universes are possible, and why they are so difficult for us to envision them.

Appendix B—Healing Modalities

"We are what our thoughts have made us; so take care about what you think. Thoughts live; they travel far."
—Vivekananda

For thousands of years, mankind has discovered incredible techniques used to cure diseases and heal injuries, long before pharmaceuticals and most surgeries. If you, as a budding metaphysician, will be using mind-body techniques to heal people, you will need to understand these traditional methods. This is what this Appendix B is intended to do. This is not meant to be an in-depth analysis of these techniques; it is just meant to give you an overall background so you can research something further when needed.

First, we must remember that science made a huge mistake by systematically excluding all historical mind-body cures. We don't want to make the same mistake today by systematically excluding all recent improvements, which might be effective. The important part is to examine each treatment to determine which is the most effective treatment possible, without prejudice in favor of one philosophy over another.

There will be practitioners from each of these disciplines who will complain about what is described, or what is left out, of each category. As with the rest of this book, there is a constant dilemma to decide how much information is essential to keep in, and how much is extraneous for the vast majority of readers, who can do their own research.

Appendix B—Healing Modalities

Today, the main argument against using these healing modalities is that they delay the start of treatments approved by the American Medical Association (AMA). Implicit in this argument is the assumption that AMA medicine is superior—which may or may not be true in various situations. This would make some sense if these AMA methods resulted in instantaneous cures. Many people go to a doctor and are told to call back in a day or two if the symptoms persist. Some patients are told to wait until a series of tests or lab procedures are performed. They don't seem to have any problem delaying treatment in these cases!

In the absence of a critical or urgent medical crisis, it is inconceivable why these healing modalities—cheaper, easier, and pain-free (usually dismissed by modern medicine as the placebo effect)—shouldn't be tried first. If ineffective, then the AMA procedures could be attempted next.

I believe there is a common energy source making each one of these healing modalities (including AMA techniques) viable. Someday mankind will understand the underlying mechanism, and be able to refine the various treatments to effectively target each particular disease or condition. Until then, the more people doing different techniques and documenting the results, the better off humanity will be.

To understand the following healing modalities in terms of Sacred Quantum Metaphysics, there are certain commonalities. The conscious mind of the therapist changes the material world just by focusing their consciousness on the desired result for the patient, who remains in a non-ego driven—some say altered—state of consciousness.

Reiki

Reiki is a gentle hands-on healing technique, whereby a Reiki Master or Practitioner heals the energy field of the recipient to create healing. Reiki means universal life force energy (*rei* = universal, *ki* = life-force energy). The basic principle is that there is an intelligent energy field surrounding each human, which acts as a conduit for the physical body, and controls the overall health of a person. It works on all levels: physical, emotional, spiritual, and mental—the body, mind, and soul.

According to this philosophy, when a person has a disease it starts with the disruption, or blocks, in the person's energy field. In order to manifest a cure, the energy field is soothed and then balanced; the energy field then heals the body. The healer does not heal the patient directly, but sets a mental intention of holding him or herself in the highest place possible, and offering themselves as a channel for the universal life force to flow from them to the receiver.

Reiki is painless, with little or no known negative side effects, and it is relatively inexpensive.

Healing Touch

Healing Touch is an energy-based, therapeutic approach to healing. The goal is to influence energy systems of the body, thus affecting physical, emotional, mental, and spiritual health and healing. Healing Touch, created by a Registered Nurse, initially helped patients with medical, surgical, psychiatric, hospice, pediatric, and geriatric conditions in Denver, Colorado. It has since spread all over the country and the world.

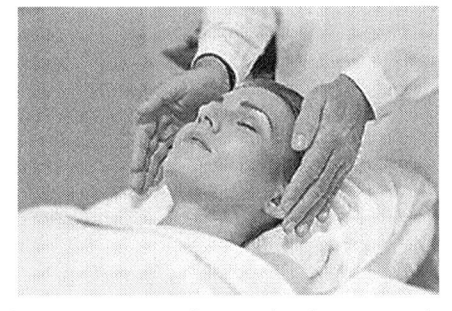

This technique treats the energy field of the person who needs the healing, and once the energy field is cleared and balanced, the body can be healed. The Healing Touch practitioner does not actually do the healing, but sets the intention for the highest and best good for the patient, then focuses energy from outside the body, which creates a healing environment. The practitioner is only the conduit of the energy.

APPENDIX B—HEALING MODALITIES

Reflexology

Reflexologists divide the body into ten equal vertical zones, five on the right and five on the left. Reflexology teaches that there are areas on the foot and hands that correspond to areas of the body, and by manipulating these, a person's health is improved. These can unblock energy (Chi or Qi) flowing through the entire human body.

The advantage to this effective treatment is that it is relatively pain-free, low-cost, and has no known side effects. An agreement needs to be made between the practitioner and the client that there is a dual responsibility for the healing process.

Acupuncture and Acupressure

Acupuncture and Acupressure are basically the same procedure. Both are used to stimulate various energetic points on a person's body. There are different energy centers going up and down the body (meridians). When the energy is blocked, it can result in a dysfunction of the body. Acupuncture uses a needle, and Acupressure uses pressure from the fingers to stimulate these energetic points, thereby releasing the energy.

Is this entirely a physical process? Some people think so, but more likely it is a combination of consciousness and physical stimulation that makes the healing possible.

Massage

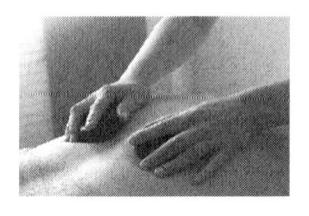

Manipulating the body to reduce tension and relax muscles is something that has been used for many millennia. Many massage therapists believe they are tapping into much more than just the physical body. Some therapists feel they are receiving spiritual information, which allows a deeper healing than a simple muscle manipulation.

Laying on of the Hands

"Laying on of the hands" was made popular in early Christianity but was in all probability adapted from ancient healing techniques. This technique has one or several people projecting healing through their hands to a person who needs physical or emotional healing.

Now you have been introduced to several mind-body healing modalities, which you can use in the future.

Appendix C—The Emperor's New Clothes

Historical Reincarnation

"Don't blindly believe what I say. Don't believe me because others convince you of my words."
—Buddha

This Appendix is not for everyone. It is mainly for people who were taught that reincarnation is a belief from Eastern religions, and thus often considered anti-Christian. What most people do not know is that reincarnation was very much a part of early Christianity. Reincarnation has been a central part of metaphysical thought for many thousands of years. For metaphysicians, reincarnation makes perfect sense for a variety of reasons.

Part of the resistance to reincarnation comes from people who want to deny any kind of spirituality exists, because we are only atoms, molecules, etc. Reincarnation requires that there be life after death, which is against the Materialist's dogma that nothing exists beyond the material realm. For these people, we can only hope they will open their minds to the recent scientific discoveries presented in "The New Sciences" section.

Some of the earlier traditions of mainstream Jewish thought (Kabbalah) also embraced the concept of reincarnation. It appeared to be part of the beliefs of whichever sect buried the Dead Sea Scrolls at

Appendix C—The Emperor's New Clothes

Qumran—probably the Essenes or Sadducees. When the Dead Sea Scrolls were translated, they showed that at least this one Jewish sect embraced a belief in reincarnation.

In today's New Testament, there are two different Gospels where Jesus reportedly said to his disciples, "Who do the people think I am?" They answered, depending on the version, "Elijah, Moses, or one of the Prophets[18]." Jesus can't be Elijah or Moses unless one of them incarnated into the body of Jesus. The fact that Jesus did not rebuke his disciples for their answer demonstrates that reincarnation was at least considered a possibility—conceivably Jesus was influenced by the philosophy at Qumran.

Early History

So what happened to make reincarnation such a forbidden part of Christian thought? When Constantine became emperor, he allowed Christianity to come out of the shadows and into the open. This allowed Christianity to be accepted as the official new religion in the Roman world, and Constantine to become the first religious leader of this newly established Christian church.

Since Constantine was emperor, he effectively mandated, with the agreement of other church leaders, what the Christian beliefs should be at the Council of Nicaea. He had a pivotal say in which Scriptures would be considered "holy" and which Gospels (like the Gospel of Thomas and the Gospel of Mary Magdalene) were excluded.

---

[18] Mark 8:27 NIV—See also Matthew 16:13Thanks for pointing out the confusion

The idea that the "soul" preexisted the body was a central part of early Christian beliefs. Part of this was based on the Psalms, when God reportedly said, "I knew you before you were born." The Origen of Alexandria, 186–255 AD, reaffirmed that "preexistence of souls" was a part of Christian doctrine at this time. Certainly your spirit existing prior to your incarnation is the foundational precondition for reincarnation.

Then the Emperor Justinian, in 543 CE, removed "preexistence of souls" from Christian thought by decree. He even made it punishable if someone disagreed with this new doctrine. Thus, a decree against the foundation of reincarnation came from a Roman emperor—not a Christian philosopher—which still influences Christian thought today!

Why would he do this? Metaphysicians think there is a lot of power for political or religious leaders, when you have only one chance to prove you are worthy of infinite reward (Heaven). When you have many lifetimes to decide for yourself what is right and what is wrong, these leaders lose their power.

According to this single chance philosophy, you must have an appointed religious leader to tell you what to think, because you are incapable of finding the truth yourself. This gave them the power to tell you what behavior is "right" and what actions are "wrong"—they decided what was "sinful" and what was not. This gave the emperors a huge amount of control over people for many centuries.

Gnosticism

In early Christianity, there was a competing philosophy to the Roman emperors often called Gnosticism. The word Gnosis referred to the belief that we all have a "knowing" of our divine connection. The Gnostics believed God was not something separate from us, but a part of us. Many believed each of us is a spark off the divine energy of God. It is our purpose

Appendix C—The Emperor's New Clothes

to perfect our character in order to return to the loving presence of God. Some people express this as "consciousness experiencing itself."

Gnostics believed you do not need an emperor, Pope, or any other intermediary to give you the answers you need. You have direct access to wisdom and a direct relationship to Spirit. Most Gnostics believed in reincarnation.

It is interesting to imagine what our world would be like if the Gnostics prevailed, and the Roman emperors failed, in their attempt to control Christianity.

Appendix D—What This Book Is and Is Not

"It is always how to write truly and having found what is true, to protect it in such a way that it becomes a part of the experience of the person who reads it."
—Ernest Hemingway

There's been a tremendous amount of pressure to make this book into a scholarly treatise. I had to spend a great amount of thought on what is essential information for the vast majority of the readers, and how much is TMI (too much information). I had to decide what is essential for you, the reader, to get the most out of this in the least amount of time.

Obviously, I think your time is valuable, and I will do everything possible to give you just the essence of what you need. I think it is best to keep each chapter as short as possible, just giving you the essential common language details so that anyone can pick up this book and put the techniques into practice.

I could write an in-depth tome-size analysis on each and every one of the preceding chapters, if it were necessary. But this is not the purpose of this book—and it really isn't needed. You can find many volumes treating each and every topic discussed here in a studious manner—except perhaps the Sacred Quantum

Appendix D—What This Book Is and Is Not

Metaphysics techniques—presented earlier. Just look at how many scholarly books have been written on the subject of Quantum Mechanics alone, and you will understand why this book cannot become a research thesis. This is simply a skeleton overview of some of the discoveries, which have been made over 5,000 years, including recent scientific advances, which reveal the true reality.

Realistically, there is not enough space in a hundred books of this size to summarize 5,000 years of metaphysical secrets of nature. The real goal is to give you a broad overview of the principles, and show you how you can put them into use in your everyday life. You can then access more information on any one of these topics if you absolutely need it.

For example, when I had experts reviewing these chapters, each expert had suggestions for adding technical terms and definitions as well as volumes of information to clarify those terms and definitions. Then, of course, you would need a glossary, footnotes, etc., to keep all those terms and definitions straight.

Would most of you need this amount of detail to understand how to use these techniques to create a better life for yourself? No, and it would just bog down most people with boring minutia. Some editors even suggested I should put in the exact origin of whoever invented a particular concept or term. I had to conclude that most people would not only need this information, but they would also be completely uninterested in it!

I decided to dispense with most footnotes and the endless references to other publications, except to provide suggestions for further reading. Besides, how could anyone footnote a technique or principal that may have been discovered and subsequently taught even before writing was invented? Would most of you need this amount of detail to understand how *Sacred Quantum Metaphysics* works and then use these techniques to create a better life for yourself? Some of you might, but most of you would just need to understand the essentials. When any of you desire more details, you are welcome to conduct further research in the future.

It is not productive to quote other researchers and then "footnote" each source. You know knowledge progresses too fast in our world today to care about where a reference from the past came from. You are much better off searching new concepts and ideas, so that you get the most up-to-date information. It really is not important which sources were believed to be important years ago, but which ideas are important for you to understand today.

I'm going to make the terminology in this book as reader friendly as possible, so you won't need a dictionary or glossary. This is meant to be easy to understand by everyone. I will give you a term here and there that you can use to research when you want more information. But it would just bog down most of you to list technical terms, and then require you to look up the definitions. Earlier I said that this book is not for people who are unable to Google something to get more information if needed.

I do not mean this in any way as a criticism of what other people have done with their books or information. I am just explaining the logic behind the overall structure of this book and illuminating why I did not want this book to become a research paper. At current count, this book is already hundreds of pages long, and I already had to make very tough decisions on how to keep it as concise as possible. Adding a few hundred pages, just to avoid the inevitable current criticism that I will get for not having them, is really pointless.

What criticism? People who want to pretend there is no spirituality in our universe will pick apart this information and find something to criticize, no matter what I do. To make this information boring and impossible to comprehend is exactly what these people would like to see. I am going to do whatever is best for you, and not worry about trying to appease those who are not interested in finding truth, but who are mainly invested in maintaining their own predetermined beliefs.

Appendix E—Vital Further Reading

Journey of Souls and ***Destiny of Souls*** by Dr. Michael Newton. Life-Between-Life research.

Afterlife Experiments*: Breakthrough Scientific Evidence of Life After Death* by Gary E. Schwartz, Ph.D.

The Relaxation Response and ***Relaxation Revolution*** by Dr. Herbert Benson. Meditation research.

Buddha's Brain by Rick Hanson, PH.D. Neurobiology.

Life After Life by Dr. Raymond Moody. Near-Death Research.

Proof of Heaven by Eban Alexander, M.D. Near-Death.

Reincarnation, and Immortality by Amit Goswami, Ph.D. Quantum theory of Consciousness.

The Hidden Messages in Water by Dr. Masaru Emoto.

Past-life Study - The Division of Perceptual Studies—U. of Virginia by Dr. Ian Stevenson. Reincarnation research.

Appendix E—Vital Further Reading

Many Lives, Many Masters by Dr. Brian Weiss. Past-life study.

See also:

- **Nag Hammadi Scrolls** and the **Dead Sea Scrolls**
- **String Theory**
- **11th Dimensional Membrane Theory**
- **Quantum Theory and Quantum Mechanics**
- **Einstein's Space-time Continuum**
- **Matthew 16:13 and Mark 8:27**
- **www.RichHaas.com**—Details of the above material.

About the Author

Writer, Metaphysician, and entrepreneur, Rich Haas, B.A., CHT, CHt, CHI, CLBLT, father of four children (and a Golden Retriever), operated a successful science-based hypnotherapy practice and school for many decades near Morrison, Colorado. Rich lectures on a myriad of scientific, metaphysical, and spiritual topics to diverse educational and social associations, teaches meditation to various gatherings, and is excited to share his knowledge with you to help create your better life.

Rich attained a psychology degree from San Jose State University, California in 1975. He is a Dual-Certified Hypnotherapist (National Association of Transpersonal Hypnotherapists (NATH) and the National Guild of Hypnotists), Certified Hypnotherapy Instructor (NATH), Past-Life Regressionist, and a Certified Life-Between-Life Therapist (NATH). Find the complete history and other information at www.RichHaas.com. See the Sacred Quantum Metaphysics Facebook page and www.SacredQuantumMetaphysics.com. Rich welcomes your thoughtful questions, curiosity, and skepticism at #SacredQuantum on Twitter.

Printed by Amazon Italia Logistica S.r.l.
Torrazza Piemonte (TO), Italy